*eighth edition*

# CALIFORNIA GOVERNMENT
*in National Perspective*

YUAN TING ★ SHELLY ARSNEAULT ★ STEPHEN STAMBOUGH

CALIFORNIA STATE UNIVERSITY FULLERTON

D0384330

# Kendall Hunt
publishing company

# Contents

## CHAPTER 1

# California's Constitution

*Yuan Ting*[1]

Constitutions are the most fundamental political documents in American society. Constitutions establish governments. In a basic sense, constitutions govern governments. In this chapter, we examine how California's political process is governed by its constitution, with emphasis on three topics: broad similarities among all the American states with respect to their constitutions; a brief look at California's own constitutional history; and finally, our most important topic, the special features of the California's constitution that help give the state its distinctive political character.

## State Constitutions in the Federal System

Constitutions establish the basic institutions of government and allocate power among those institutions in two ways: by granting certain powers to one or more institutions and also by denying certain powers to one or more institutions. Frequently, constitutions also deny specific powers to any governmental institution by granting (or "reserving") them solely to the people. Constitutions also provide for their own change through their mechanisms for amendment.

Since constitutions are the final word governmentally, they are always superior in legal and moral force to laws passed by the governments they create. But while state constitutions are superior to state laws, the federal (the United States) Constitution is superior to state constitutions. The U.S. Constitution directly refers to state constitutions but once, and does so to assert the supremacy of the federal Constitution and its laws and treaties. Article VI of the U.S. Constitution states:

> This Constitution, and the Laws of the United States which shall be made in Pursuance thereof; and all Treaties made, or which shall be made, under the Authority of the United States, shall be the supreme Law of the Land; and the Judges in every State shall be bound thereby, any Thing in the Constitution or Laws of any State to the Contrary notwithstanding.

---

[1]Previous versions of this chapter were coauthored with Keith O. Boyum and Phillip L. Gianos, to whom I extend my thanks.

**1**

## Boundaries and Limits in the U.S. Constitution

The U.S. Constitution draws various other boundaries between what the national government may do and what the state governments may do. For example, in Article I, Section 10, the states are forbidden to make treaties with other nations; only the national government of the United States may do that. Likewise, the same section of the U.S. Constitution forbids states from impairing the obligation of contracts, thereby protecting a key feature of American capitalism.

## Constitutional Flexibility

Since the federal Constitution is one of delegated or granted powers, the national government may not exercise any power not given to it by the U.S. Constitution. But this is not as simple as it seems. This is mainly due to the general and sometimes imprecise language used in assigning powers to the national government. Here is the essential genius of the architects of the U.S. Constitution, for the way in which 225-year-old language pertains to the specifics of contemporary circumstance allows flexibility to the Constitution through its interpretation, a matter that stimulates continuing debate. Pending the outcomes of these debates, the specifics of what powers the national government may exercise can change.

State governments, by contrast, are assumed to have powers unless they are denied them by either the U.S. Constitution or the states' own constitution. This creates considerable latitude within which state governments may operate. In practice, however, there are several important similarities among virtually all state constitutions, to which we now turn.

## Similarities in State Constitutions

All state constitutions have preambles—an opening statement of purpose and intent. Each state constitution has a bill of rights, closely modeled on the federal Bill of Rights (Amendments 1 through 10 of the U.S. Constitution). In California, however, these rights are stated at the very beginning of the document in Article I Declaration of Rights. The California Constitution provides for freedom of the press, freedom of speech, freedom to assemble and petition, freedom of religion, and due process of law and in general parallels the U.S. Constitution as to rights specifically secured to the people. Although state constitutions are essentially autonomous documents that do not have to rely on the federal Constitution for granting civil rights to the states' citizens, there have been some attempts to limit judicial independence in interpreting the language of state constitutions (see Chapter 9).

All state constitutions reflect the U.S. Constitution's provisions for checks and balances and separation of powers by establishing separate legislative, executive, and judicial branches, and by sharing powers among them. California is no exception to this, though specific applications of this general rule in the state's constitution are an important feature of California politics and will be discussed in detail below. Within this broad setting of similarities to other states, there are specific provisions of California's constitution that make the document, and the political system it creates, distinctive.

# California's Constitutional History

One of the more interesting features of California's political history is that the state has had two constitutions (Louisiana leads the states in this respect with eleven). The first was adopted in 1849, just before California became a state in 1850. Hastily drafted, much of the language was taken from other state constitutions without necessarily taking into account the essentially frontier nature of the territory that became California. While the document served reasonably well for 30 years, by 1879 its deficiencies became so severe that a constitutional convention was called to draft a new document.

Delegates to the convention fashioned an extremely long and detailed document, with particular emphasis on expanding and strengthening the bill of rights and placing severe limits on the power of the state legislature. This period was also the dawn of the Progressive movement in California, a movement whose profound effects we still see in the present-day state constitution.

Progressivism was essentially a middle-class movement created in response to the political consequences of great economic power. Progressive political ideas profoundly affected the politics of many states especially those in the West, including California (see Chapter 2 for further discussion of this movement and its impact on political culture in California). At the time, the greatest evil in the world of California Progressives was the Southern Pacific Railroad, whose power and reach made it the most powerful force in the state, dwarfing, in the views of its critics, the ability of the state government to control it. During this period legislators could be rented, if not necessarily purchased outright, by the Southern Pacific. The architects of the constitution of 1879, by limiting the power of the legislature, were indirectly trying to limit the power of the railroad.

A further set of Progressive reforms, added to the 1879 constitution via amendment, occurred between 1900 and 1913. Foremost among these were the direct democracy institutions of the initiative, referendum, and recall. These are discussed below and also in Chapter 3. These direct democracy mechanisms are central to California's politics and to this day give the state much of its distinctive political character. It was also in this period that distinctive and politically important regional differences began to appear in California, a topic discussed more fully in Chapter 2.

Between 1879 and 1962, the state constitution, responding to the enormous growth and increasing diversity of the state and driven by the use of the direct democracy reforms, grew rapidly and unevenly. The California Constitution had become a large and unwieldy document, and while periodic attempts were made to simplify the constitution, none really succeeded. In 1962, the voters approved, and the legislature appointed, a commission to revise the state constitution. Its goal was to examine the 1879 document completely, including its many amendments, and to recommend changes and a complete reorganization.

The process took years of study, and many more years of proposing amendments for voter approval in many successive elections. During this period the constitution continued to grow. By 1966, when the first "clean-up" amendments were offered to the voters, the document had been amended 344 times, and its length had grown from 16,000 words to 70,000, making it the fourth longest constitution of any government in the *world*, after those of Louisiana, Alabama, and India. By the 1974 elections, most of the proposed amendments had been submitted and voted upon, and the revision was essentially complete.

The Progressive legacy and the reform period of 1962–1974 largely created the document that governs California today. As this brief history suggests, California's formal written constitution is largely a creature of the state's social, economic, and political setting. Formal constitutional provisions define the rules of the political game, but these provisions also affect the informal setting of California's politics. In a sense, California has two constitutions, one formal and one informal, each of which affects the other. The root word of "constitution" is "constitute," and California politics is constituted of both formal and informal rules. In the section that follows, we briefly describe some of the special features—formal and informal—that shape present-day political life in California.

# California's Formal and Informal Constitutional Features

## The California Constitution Is Long and Complex

The length of California's constitution is remarkable. On identically sized pages, the U.S. Constitution, including amendments, occupies 27 pages. The California constitution takes up more than 150 pages. To compile an index for the U.S. Constitution requires seven pages. To do the same for the California Constitution one needs more than 70 pages (Table 1.1).

One reason for this length is that all state governments create county and city governments. Accordingly, the California Constitution devotes considerable attention to these topics. But that does not fully explain the great length, or the bewildering variety

Table 1.1   Comparison between the California and United States Constitutions

|  | California | United States |
|---|---|---|
| **Designation** | The Constitution of the State of California | The Constitution of the United States of America |
| **Shape/Design**<br>• Length<br>• Variety of Provisions | • Extremely lengthy<br>• Ranges from broad, essential topics to extremely specific and limited ones | • Very short<br>• Deals only with broad essentials |
| **Special Features** | • "Direct democracy" provisions (initiative, referendum, and recall) make amendment more frequent and open to ordinary citizens | • The Supremacy Clause provides that the U.S. Constitution prevails in instances of conflict with state constitutions |
| **Importance** | • Restrictions on actions by government, especially regarding taxing and spending | • Rights secured by the first 8 and the 14th Amendments are enforced by all courts, federal and state |

of specific and rather narrow topics addressed by the state's constitution. For example, the California Constitution speaks to such things as the sale of alcoholic beverages on airplanes, the alumni association of the University of California, the use of bingo games by charitable organizations, the cafeteria budgets of state agencies, the right of citizens to fish, property tax exemptions for grape vines less than three years old, and the use of water and water rights in California (see Chapter 14 for further discussion about how the state's constitution protects water and other natural resources for all Californians).

One looks in vain for comparable topics in the U.S. Constitution. Why all the detail in the California Constitution? One answer is the ease with which the California Constitution may be amended via direct democracy procedures. Initiative measures present an avenue for amending the constitution apart from actions that may be taken by a governor and legislature. Another part of the answer has to do with the weak political party system of the state, a topic that we will discuss in more detail below and later in Chapter 4. Weak political parties tend to go hand-in-hand with a strong interest group system because groups tend to fill the vacuum created when parties are weak.

Across the United States, states with strong interest groups and weak parties tend to have longer and more complex constitutions. Interest groups, as Chapter 4 describes, can be very effective in achieving their political goals through amending constitutions in addition to their usual activity of lobbying legislators and governors. This last point is significant, for it is important to remember that provisions in the California state constitution that deal with, for example, exempting grape vines less than three years of age from property taxes are part of the constitution itself, not simply ordinary laws (called statutes). Constitutional provisions are much more difficult to change or remove than are statutes.

## The California Constitution Provides for "Direct Democracy"

At the heart of the Progressives' reforms was the belief that an effective way to circumvent the power of economic interests over state government, especially the legislature, was to permit the citizens to vote directly on major issues and to recall public officials from office. California's constitution provides for just that in the form of the initiative, the referendum, and the recall. The initiative permits citizens to propose, and then vote on, either statutes or constitutional amendments. The referendum permits citizens to halt enforcement of laws already passed by the legislature and signed by the governor, and then to vote on whether those laws should be continued or repealed. The recall permits citizens to remove public officials from office. This provision lay largely unused for many years until 2003, when the combination of an unpopular governor—Democrat Gray Davis, who was re-elected in 2002—combined with a well-financed recall campaign led to Davis's replacement in 2003 by Republican Arnold Schwarzenegger, an election that received worldwide attention. More recently in 2011 a recall election was held for the council members in the City of Bell for misappropriation of public funds.

These direct democracy provisions of California's constitution give extraordinary power to citizens, but also to interest groups, who have been their most frequent users. The initiative, referendum, and recall are among the most important and interesting features of California government, and they raise significant questions about democratic politics and the nature of representation.

## The California Constitution Provides for Weak Political Parties

Political parties link citizens with government; they also link those inside government with each other through a system of party loyalty and mutual aid. To the extent that parties are weak these linkages are weak, and government and politics thereby change in character. To some, relatively weak parties are desirable since they encourage citizens to evaluate issues and candidates free of party constraints. To others, including many political scientists, weak parties encourage irresponsibility in governing and make it difficult for citizens to get a thoughtful grasp on complex issues and to assign credit or blame for government actions.

California's parties are weak by virtue of political tradition and constitutional design. Local political contests—those for county and city government—are officially nonpartisan. State laws that govern the activities and organization of political parties also contribute to party weakness. The most important recent example of this is the 2010 passage of Proposition 14 which created what is known as a "top two" system in which candidates for state office from all major and minor parties compete in a first round of balloting with the top two vote recipients, regardless of their political party affiliation, advancing to the general election.

Such provisions mean that other institutions, primarily interest groups and professional campaign management firms that use the media heavily, fill the vacuum left in the absence of strong political parties. Chapter 4 treats these important topics in detail. The weak party system also significantly affects the manner in which the state's voters behave, and this topic is addressed in Chapter 3.

## The California Constitution Provides for a Strong "Plural" Executive

The governor of California—the state's chief executive—is given some powers beyond those given to the President of the United States. Chief among these is the item veto, which enables the governor to void specific items in the state's budget. Thus California governors have greater power over the state budget and greater bargaining power with the legislature than a president has with respect to these matters in the national arena.

Unlike U.S. presidents, however, a governor may find his or her own executive branch fragmented. California's constitution provides for what is called a plural executive branch in which the executive branch offices of governor, lieutenant governor, secretary of state, attorney general, treasurer, insurance commissioner, and controller are elected in individual races. Divided party control of the executive, with some elected Democrats and some Republicans, is always possible and often happens. In fact, the nominally nonpartisan superintendent of public instruction may be a member of the political party opposed to the governor's party. In the Deukmejian administration (1983–1991), all the other partisan executive branch offices were held by Democrats although the governor was a Republican. From 2007 to 2009, Republican Governor

Schwarzenegger's lieutenant governor was Democrat John Garamendi. In contrast, U.S. presidents and vice presidents are elected together, and the other comparable national officers are nominated by presidents and serve in the president's cabinet.

California's governorship is thus an office with some significant differences compared to the position of U.S. presidents. Chapter 7 explores the role of the governor in comparison with the American presidency.

## California's Constitution Provides for a Nonpartisan Judiciary

In accord with the political tradition of the state, the California Constitution establishes an extensive and nonpartisan judicial system. All levels of the California judiciary—municipal courts, superior courts, courts of appeal, and the state supreme court—must be filled by members of the state bar—that is, licensed attorneys. As in many other states, California's judges are subject to election. Unlike some states, however, such elections in California are officially nonpartisan. In practice, most judges in California are initially appointed by the governor to fill a vacancy. All are subject to periodic election. For the higher, appellate judicial offices, incumbents are subject to what is called retention elections, in which voters determine whether an appellate court judge shall be retained in office for another term (normally 12 years). In these elections, voters do not choose between two candidates but instead vote whether to retain a single judge. Chapter 9 addresses these and other aspects of California's judiciary.

## California's Constitution Established, then Abandoned, a Professional, Full-Time Legislature

One of the most celebrated aspects of California government between 1966 and 1990 was its state legislature. Unlike those in many other states at the time, California's legislators are full-time, well-paid, professional lawmakers. Also unlike the practice of many other states, California used to provide considerable staff support for its legislators. In the 1970s, in fact, the state legislature was a model for other states for what a competent, informed legislature should be. A 1990 constitutional change adopted by initiative (Proposition 140), however, dramatically and fundamentally changed the legislature by reducing its staff and imposing term limits on its members. In the 21st century, California has an institutionally weakened legislature populated by short-timers. Chapter 8 analyzes the legislature in greater depth, with conclusions about the nature and future role of the institution.

## California's Constitution Establishes an Extensive System of Local Government

A major responsibility of any state constitution is to create local government, chiefly counties and cities. In California some of these jurisdictions are immensely large and powerful, even when considered on a national scale. The city and the county of Los Angeles, for example, dwarf many state governments in the range of their responsibilities, the size of their budgets, and the power wielded by their officials. Focusing as we frequently do on national and state government, it is easy to forget that many of the things most important to citizens—the quality of their children's schools, how good the local parks are, and the level of public safety—are the responsibility of city and county officials.

California provides for an extensive system of local governmental institutions that emphasize nonpartisanship and the efficient delivery of services. Underlying these apparently politically neutral ideas, however, is a complex system of political activity, as described in Chapter 10.

## California's Constitution Faces Increasing Criticism and Pressures for Revision

At the heart of the California Constitution lies something of a paradox: while the basic structure of the document has not recently been changed, it has been nonetheless frequently—usually through the initiative process—amended in ways that have substantially altered state politics and policy (see Chapters 12–14 for further discussion of state policy in education, criminal justice, and environmental protection). Fiscally, the state operates under a number of initiative-established constraints: Proposition 13 (passed in 1978), which capped property tax increases and shifted some traditional county responsibilities—especially education—to the state; Proposition 4 (1979), which established government spending limits; and more recently Proposition 98 (1988), which guaranteed a fixed proportion of state revenues to K-12 public schools; Proposition 99 (1988) and Proposition 10 (1998), which increased taxes on tobacco products and earmarked those revenues for antismoking and early childhood health programs; and Proposition 39 (2000), which made it easier to pass school bond measures. More recently, in response to severe budget problems, voters in California have passed Proposition 22 (2010) which prohibits the state from borrowing or taking funds used for transportation, redevelopment, or local government projects and services; Proposition 25 (2010), which changes legislative vote requirement to pass budget and budget-related legislation from two-thirds to a simple majority, but retains two-thirds vote requirement for taxes; and Proposition 26 (2010), which requires approval of two-thirds vote for certain state and local fees. These measures dictate where revenues come from and where they may be spent, and they do so in ways that are hard to change. Chapter 11 analyzes how these measures and other reforms have shaped the process and outcome of California state budget.

At the same time, initiatives have also been used to substantially modify California's political processes by providing for an elected insurance commissioner in 1988 and both term limits for state officials and reductions in state legislative expenditures in 1990. All this added up to fundamental changes in the fiscal and political environment of the state and to increasing criticism that the state had become ungovernable, a belief that Arnold Schwarzenegger used to his advantage in the 2003 gubernatorial recall election.

In the mid-1990s an effort to address constitutional reform arose in the form of a state Constitutional Revision Commission. A wide variety of proposals for changing the state's basic charter was brought to the commission, including reform of the budgetary process, modifications of the initiative process (the initiative was the prime suspect in the minds of many critics), and the creation of a unicameral (one-house) legislature. Other observers were more pessimistic. Their forecast was for more piecemeal, sometimes thoughtless, constitutional change promoted via the initiative process whenever an interest group could raise enough money to mount a campaign. No action was taken on these proposals, however. In late 2004, in another move to restructure state government and address the state's huge budget shortfall, a commission established by Governor Schwarzenegger forwarded a complex and controversial set of more than 1,200 recommendations for change. With a succession of what became yearly crises, a dismal pattern was established: a budget crisis followed by a messy resolution followed by calls for reform followed by another budget crisis. Even as the budget crisis of 2009 was temporarily resolved in late February, there were new calls for a California Constitutional convention to attempt, yet again, to make the state more governable. And these calls have led to the passage of Proposition 20 (2010), which redistrict congressional districts in the state and Proposition 25 (2010) with majority vote for the state legislature to pass the budget (see Chapter 11 for further discussion of the state budget). These constitutional amendments represent some of the latest attempt by voters to change the political and budgeting processes to address the increasingly severe budget problems in California.

## Conclusion: California Government in National Perspective

A discussion of California's formal and informal constitutional features inevitably involves references to how those features affect the state's politics, and how in turn California's politics affects its constitution. Constitutions, including informal constitutions, are neither pure symbol nor only a matter of historical interest. Constitutions are enormously important in understanding why California government is the way it is—sometimes rational and efficient, sometimes inefficient and frustrating, always a matter about which groups and individuals contest, normally out of the sight of the casual citizen observer, but occasionally in colorful, public, and bewildering ways.

If there is a moral of this story, it may be this: State constitutions set the tone, define the structure, and outline the limits within which laws and administrative decisions govern the lives of us all, no matter in what state we live. Our lives as citizens in a federal system are a complex and changing mix of local, state, and federal laws and rules. As a starting place for understanding California government in national perspective, a review of the California Constitution is the best place to begin. But there is more to be said. The rest of the story follows in the next 13 chapters.

# CHAPTER 2

# California: Political Culture in the Migrant State

*Matthew G. Jarvis and Paul Peretz*[1]

Republican ex-talk show host Bob Dornan represented two different congressional districts from 1985 to 1996. The first was in West Los Angeles, a seat Dornan lost when district boundaries were redrawn. Dornan moved to Orange County, where he ran successfully in a district centered on Garden Grove. For most of this period, his ultraconservative positions resonated with his conservative white Orange County constituents. Dornan adapted successfully to an influx of right-wing Vietnamese immigrants. But over the years, increasing numbers of left-leaning Hispanics came to live in his constituency, and Bob Dornan adapted less successfully to them. Democratic political unknown Loretta Sanchez looked at the changing nature of the constituency and thought that there had been enough shift in the population that a moderate Hispanic candidate would be able to mobilize sufficient support to defeat Dornan. In a hard-fought election in 1996, she won with 51% of the vote, becoming the first Democratic congressperson from Orange County. In 2010, while Republicans were winning in most of the nation, she won with 57% of the vote, and she won with nearly 64% of the vote in 2012. The moral of the story is that in politics, demographics matter.

## Introduction

In a democratic society, political outcomes are largely determined by the political beliefs of its citizens. *Political culture* is the term used by political scientists to describe the networks of beliefs about politics and policy that undergird political action in that community.

These beliefs are in part dictated by the self-interest of individuals. In most societies, poor people and rich people, minority and majority groups, and rural and urban residents have somewhat different beliefs, and typically these follow the self-interest of the people in that group.

But self-interest does not explain everything about citizens' beliefs. People are heavily influenced by those around them. Most influential are the beliefs of one's family members, with children often voting in very similar ways to their parents. But the views of their friends, their church, their union, their teachers, those in their ethnic group, and the media all have an effect on people's political beliefs. This can lead people to vote to

---

[1]Earlier versions of this chapter were authored by Phillip L. Gianos.

support candidates they see as representing the group they identify with or sympathize with, rather than their own personal interests. Examples are Oprah Winfrey, one of the richest people in America, campaigning for the Democrats, or rich Jewish people on the West Side of Los Angeles giving more support to programs for the poor than those living in San Bernardino, a much poorer area.

In general, the political beliefs of Californians are similar to those of people in the rest of the United States. They believe in democracy, freedom, justice, a system of laws, and political (but not economic) equality. There is general support for our federal system of government and for the federal and California constitutions. But Californians' beliefs are not identical to those in the rest of the United States and within California those in different regions of the state have somewhat differing beliefs. Finally, the groups that live in California have changed over time, leading to considerable change California's political actions.

## Migration and California

California is a migrant state. In 1848, when America won the Mexican–American war, there were thought to be 50–150,000 Native Americans and another 15,000 Spanish and Americans in California. In 2013, California was home to over 38 million people. The nature of these migrants is what has shaped California.

Figure 2.1 shows the growth in California's population, and Figure 2.2 shows the rate of change of the population in each decade. The discovery of gold in 1848 in Northern California led to a huge increase in the white American population, with the number of non-Native American Californians rising to 380,000 by 1860. What the newcomers found was a land with a temperate climate and abundant fertile land and water in the northern half of the state, but little water in the semi-desert south and central valley. Most early migration was therefore to the north, and it was only after the development of extensive irrigation projects in the 20th century that growth in the southern half of the state began to outpace that of the northern half and the central valley became the agricultural center it is today.

The 1920s saw the rise of Southern California, based on an oil boom (in 1923 a quarter of the world's oil came from California), new movie, aerospace and garment

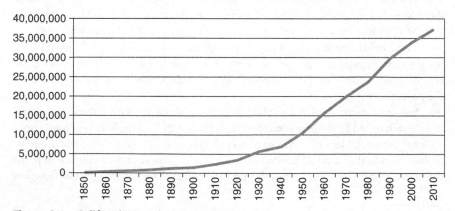

**Figure 2.1**    California Population 1850–2010

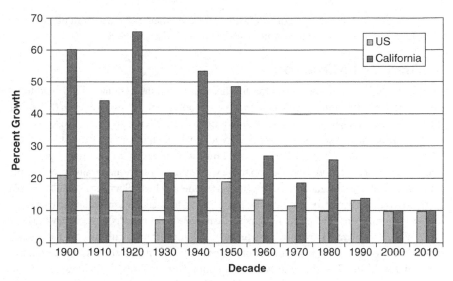

**Figure 2.2**   Percent Growth in Population

industries, and port jobs. In 1920, both San Francisco and Los Angeles had around 500,000 people. By 1930, the population of San Francisco had risen to over 600,000 but that of Los Angeles had risen to over 1,200,000.

As we can see in Figure 2.2, California's population grew much more rapidly than that in other states. While many Californians are taught in school that the key influx was of emigrants from the Dust Bowl states in the 1930s, this is largely myth. In fact migration was low in the 1930s, and it was the 1920s, the 1940s, and the 1950s which saw the bulk of migration to California from other states. Internal migration slowed after 1965, and after 1990, there were more people leaving for other states than arriving from other states. But this loss was more than made up by increased immigration from Mexico, Latin America, and Asia and by relatively high birth rates. By 2014, California had a population of over 38 million, about one-eighth the population of the United States.

Immigration from 1850 to 1960 was primarily from the eastern half of the United States and to a lesser degree from Europe. Most migration followed the east-west roads and rail lines, with Northerners and Midwesterners settling disproportionately in northern California, and those from the South and the border states moving to southern and inland California. After 1920, many more migrated to Southern California, drawn by its warm winters, its cheap housing, and the jobs in the shipping, oil, garment, aerospace, automobile assembly, tire, and armaments industries. By the mid-1960s, as housing prices rose and some of its industries faded, migration from other parts of the United States slowed, and after 1990, California lost more people than it gained from the other states, as young moderately educated whites moved to nearby states drawn by more employment opportunities, a lower cost of living, and lower housing prices (Kolko, 2013; Gray and Scardamalia, 2012). But, despite this, California's population continued to grow, as a relatively high birth rate was accompanied by extensive immigration from Asia and Latin America, leading to yet another adjustment in the political culture of the state.

Increasingly, California has become a "gateway" state where migrants from other countries first settle, but where more Americans move *from* than move *to*.

## A Theory of Migration

People usually move to make life better for themselves and their families. They tend to be more educated than similar people in the areas they come from and less tied down than other people. As examples, people without children move more often than people with children, renters move more than homeowners, and young people move more than older people (Molloy, Smith, and Wozniak, 2011. Because migration is costly, if they move a great distance, they tend to be more affluent than those where they come from. Because most people migrate to better their standard of living, they are generally less affluent than similar people in the areas they migrate to. They are also more willing to change, more willing to take risks, and display more drive and entrepreneurship than those in the country or state they move to.

Where immigrants are moving from places with different cultures than the place they are moving to, they do a number of things to reduce the isolation attendant on migration. Successful first immigrants often encourage others from their family or area to join them. This second wave of migrants typically settle next to one another and recreate much of the culture of the place they come from, creating new areas that feel a lot like the places the migrants came from.

These new communities can threaten the existing inhabitants who generally feel that those coming to their community should behave as much like them as possible and should accept their guidance. When economic times are bad, the old inhabitants can come to resent these readily identifiable newcomers who may be prepared to work harder than they do for less money and thereby threaten their livelihood.

The newcomers typically steer away from politics initially, concentrating their energies on making money and building up assets that will enable their children to be even more successful than they themselves have been. In some immigrant communities parallel governing structures can grow up with the community, settling many of its problems internally through quasi-governmental mechanisms.

In democratic societies, existing political parties eventually come to see them as potential supporters and seek to bring those votes to their party. This partly integrates them into the existing political structures. Over time as they become more integrated, and a new generation arises that grew up in the new country, there is increasing dispersal into the wider community, the old informal quasi-governmental structures erode, and the group begins to seek a more active part in the political process.

In the areas where they have come to be a majority, the new groups will eventually run for office and take part in governing. But by the time this happens they will have become much more integrated into the preexisting culture, with their leaders being more integrated than their followers. As a result the ascent of new political leadership will cause less change than one might initially expect.

## Effects of Heavy Immigration in California

As we have seen, there are few states in the Union that has been more formed by migration than California. Many think that this continual influx of entrepreneurial migrants has led California to be a leader in seeking new solutions to old problems and in creating new industries and processes. As a result, California has often led the rest of the United States into new areas in fashion, media, industry, and government. Movies, television, theme parks, airplanes, and information technology are California's signature industries and many of its cultural innovations have heavily influenced other areas of the United States. California has also been innovative in politics, leading the way on direct democracy, diversity, and tolerance of homosexuals.

This willingness to experiment was shown in California's reaction to the political domination of the Southern Pacific Railroad in the late 19th and early 20th centuries. Instead of simply retaking control of the legislature, Californians instead instituted the complex experiment with direct democracy described in Chapter 4, in an attempt to prevent any future firm from using money and influence to overturn the will of the people. And when Californians thought the local political parties had become corrupt, instead of simply reforming the parties they instead banned local candidates from mentioning their political party affiliation and instituted a more professional council-manager system.

But heavy immigration often leads to fear among existing inhabitants that their culture, their morality, their religion, their jobs, and their political power will be eroded by the new immigrants. This too has been a recurrent feature of the California scene, with many pushing to slow down change. Such a reaction is likely to be larger when the incoming group is more different from the existing groups and when economic hard times increase the competition for jobs.

California has seen much anti-immigrant activity. The anti-Chinese Los Angeles Massacre of 1871 led to gradually increasing anti-Chinese policy and culminated in the complete banning nationally of Chinese immigration until the 1940s. In the 1930s, there was considerable resentment against Mexican Americans who were seen as taking American jobs, and by the end of the decade, one-third of the Mexican American population of Los Angeles, including many citizens, had been forcibly repatriated to Mexico.

During the Second World War there was much popular support in California for the forced internment of Japanese Americans, and in more recent years every economic downturn has led to agitation aimed at illegal immigrants. This fear has sometimes gone beyond reaction to immigration itself, to a more general political movement toward more stability and law and order, especially in Southern California.

If these two things seem contradictory it is because they are. Many observers see California as shifting periodically from one of these poles to the other, with periods of reaction often following periods of innovation.

# Regionalism and Political Culture in California

One basic political cultural fact is simple: the relatively small area of Southern California—traditionally defined as the seven counties south of the Tehachapi Mountains—contains roughly 57% of the state's population, with the bulk of that population living in the Los Angeles metropolitan area. The immediate political effect is that a small geographical portion of the state has the majority of the state's population, wealth, and voters. Most of the rest of California's population is split between the San Francisco Bay Area and the inland areas of California in and around the San Joaquin Valley.

Historically, many issues in California politics have been sharply and enduringly defined in terms of region: state legislative apportionment, water rights, gasoline tax revenue allocation, the location of public university campuses—indeed, any issue that involves allocating resources within the state. Candidates for statewide office are regularly described in terms of their home region, and Southern California candidates often have an advantage over northerners because of the population concentration in the south. In recent years, governors have been exclusively southerners: Arnold Schwarzenegger, Gray Davis, Pete Wilson, George Deukmejian, Jerry Brown, and Ronald Reagan were all from Southern California. However, as is true in other states, the dominance is less strong than one might expect due to the overarching forces of partisanship and ideology.

The political consequences of these differences are clear. Historically Southern California and the San Joaquin valley had a more conservative voting history than northern California. The results of statewide races, including those for governor, U.S. senator, president of the United States, and statewide ballot propositions, often depended on the ratio of more liberal and Democratic northern votes to more conservative and Republican southern and central votes.

In 1964, the Republican presidential primary, for example, Barry Goldwater took all the state's southern counties by a sufficient margin to overcome the support for the more liberal Nelson Rockefeller in the rest of the state. The primary win in California was critical in Goldwater's eventual nomination for president. In 1994, Proposition 187, which dealt with illegal immigration, won in every part of the state *except* the Bay Area and was especially popular in the Riverside–San Bernardino area, where it won by 40%, and in Orange and San Diego counties, where it won by 34%. And in Orange County, the headquarters of California Republicanism, Republican presidential candidates until recently had been able to count on two-to-one or even three-to-one advantages over their Democratic opponents, offsetting the rest of the state and assuring the Republicans winning all of California's electoral votes, an increasingly valuable prize as California has grown into the most populous state.

One of the most dramatic acknowledgments of regionalism in California has been the regular revival of proposals to split California into two or more separate states, including several nonbinding pro-breakup advisory measures placed on the primary ballot in some rural northern counties in 1992, where, preaching to the choir, they won considerable support. In 1993, for the first time in 130 years, the state Assembly briefly considered a proposal to split the state into three parts: north, central, and south. In 2014, venture capitalist Tim Draper submitted a ballot initiative for the 2016 ballot to split the state into six states, though the attempt failed to get the required number of valid signatures; like all such efforts, this would have required the approval of not only the state but also Congress, which would be unlikely.

But in recent years, while the San Joaquin Valley has remained steadfastly conservative, Southern California has been trending steadily to the left, narrowing the difference between the southern and northern regions. Democrats have been sent to Congress from Orange County—long considered a bastion of conservatism—and the state that gave the United States Richard Nixon and Ronald Reagan has been conceded in advance

**Table 2.1**    Regional Differences in Political Conservatism

|  | Opposition to Gay Marriage (2008) (%) | Vote for Romney (2012) (%) |
|---|---|---|
| **North** | 44 | 31 |
| **South** | 54 | 39 |
| **Central Valley** | 69 | 50 |
| **California (total)** | 52 | 37 |

to the Democrats by more recent Republican presidential candidates such as George W. Bush and John McCain.

Table 2.1 shows the current division between the three main regions in terms of two recent votes. Proposition 8, which banned gay marriage in California, is a good indicator of cultural conservatism. The support for Republican Mitt Romney in 2012 shows the degree to which the regions support the more liberal Democratic Party or the more conservative Republican Party. As can be seen the north remains more liberal than the south, but the voters in the south are now much less conservative than those in the San Joaquin Valley.

## California's Regions: Some Explanations

How did these differences come about? The reader will not be surprised to find that we think that both the difference between the north and south and the recent leftward trend in the south can primarily be explained by patterns of migration.

The bulk of post-Depression immigrants to Southern California came from the Midwest and the states bordering the South, following the east west roads and railway lines. Few came from Europe. A total of 6.5% of the 1940 population of the Los Angeles area came from Italy, Ireland, Sweden, England, Germany, France, or Russia. The comparable proportion of Bay Area residents was double that for Southern California.

Besides the differences in region of birth and in the sheer numbers of immigrants that differentiated northern from southern California, cultural and religious differences existed as well. Los Angeles emerged, relative to the Bay Area, as a predominantly Protestant area with a strong fundamentalist flavor. Catholics were not only more numerous in San Francisco but what Catholics there were in the south were disproportionately of Latino descent compared to Bay Area Catholics, and were relatively powerless.

Religion also appears to have been a more central part of life in the south than in the north: during the 1920–1940 period, per capita church membership in Los Angeles was the highest in the nation. Southern California was thus settled by people whose regional and religious characteristics predisposed them toward a more moralistic and conservative social, economic, and political orientation.

Two important consequences followed from this immigration pattern. First, these relatively conservative new arrivals in the south shaped the Southern California political culture in their own image. Second, the affinity ties discussed earlier led people to move to areas where they felt more comfortable, strengthening the regional difference.

But the conservative character of the south gradually eroded as new migration patterns led to a gradual change in the character of the voters. Some of this new migration dates back to the Second World War when the extensive war production in the south (Los Angeles contributed 17% of all war production) and its status as an embarkation center for the Pacific theater brought African Americans and Hispanics to the Southland. The number of African Americans quadrupled between 1940 and 1950, and the Bracero program, devised to stop illegal immigration is now thought to have instead encouraged it (Gratton and Merchant, 2013).

But the key event was a major change in American immigration laws. Prior to the 1960s overseas immigration had come primarily from Europe, tied to immigration quotas for European countries, and the impact was primarily on the East Coast of the United States. But in 1965, an amendment to the 1951 Immigration Act made a crucial alteration. The amendment made family reunification rather than skills or national origin the primary basis for immigration into the United States. This was intended to put a kinder face on continued European immigration into the United States, by allowing in family members of previous European immigrants.

However, it turned out that the families of European immigrants were enjoying the new prosperity in Europe and were disinclined to migrate. But the large impoverished families of previous Latino and Asian migrants were only too eager to migrate. This tendency was further increased by the admission of refugees from Asia and the legalization of illegal immigrants from Mexico. This opened the floodgates to migrants from Asia, Mexico, and Latin America who gained much more from migrating than those in prosperous Europe. Asian immigration rose from about 150,000 to 1.7 million and Mexican and Latin American immigration tripled. A disproportionate number of these new immigrants settled in California, leading to a slow transformation of the political culture of the state (DeLaet, 2000, 79–83).

At first, as theory would predict, the new migrants were relatively apolitical with much lower voting rates than the rest of the population. But as the migrants became more settled and had children educated in the United States, they began to take more interest in politics. A key event was Proposition 187, Governor Wilson's attempt in 1994 to deny benefits to illegal aliens, which was perceived by Mexican immigrants as being discriminatory. This led to increased voting and increased political mobilization.

The impact of these new immigrants was increased by the departure of less affluent whites from Southern California after 1990. Gray and Scardamalia (2012) estimated that a net 3.4 million people have left California since 1990, and that they are disproportionately made up of less affluent younger white families (Kolko, 2013.) These would normally be more likely to vote Republican and their departure reduces the Republican vote. The increase in black and Hispanic voters and the departure of white voters changes have resulted in more minorities being elected and more success for the Democratic Party in California.

African Americans were the first minority group to gain political power in California, and their political achievements remain the most notable, though Latinos have recently increased their representation. The first African American was elected to the state legislature in 1918; in 1948, his successor was joined by a second African American in Sacramento. In the 2013–2014 session, there were seven African American assembly persons and two state senators. The first African American member of Congress from California was elected in 1962; there have been four African American seats in Congress for much of the time since the 1970s, and there are currently three. Willie Brown, generally considered the most powerful Assembly speaker in the last 40 years is African American, as is a more recent Speaker, Karen Bass. However, the political power of African Americans in California has peaked, and we expect that many of the positions that they currently hold will be taken by Hispanics as Hispanics become the majority in formerly African American areas such as Watts and Compton.

Latinos have only recently begun to flex their political muscle in California. Starting with the election of Ed Roybal to the Los Angeles City Council in 1949 there were a gradually increasing number of elected local government officials. By 1973, there were 231 elected officials and by 1989 this had increased to 580. In 1962, the first Hispanics were elected to the California Assembly and Ed Roybal was elected to Congress. By 1990, there were four Hispanic assemblypersons and three Hispanic state senators. Redistricting and the rapid increase in Latino voter participation during the 1990s have yielded as many as 29 members of the state legislature and 10 seats in Congress. Latinos have also recently been elected to important political positions such as Mayor of Los Angeles and Lieutenant Governor. Four of the last eight Speakers of the Assembly (generally seen as California's second most powerful post) have been Hispanic.

The increasing political power of Hispanics has shifted the balance of power between the two parties in California. The California Assembly has had a Democratic majority for all but two of the last 43 years. In 2010, when there was a big national surge toward the Republicans, California Democrats maintained control of both the state Assembly and the state Senate won the governorship, and all the other statewide races, won the U.S. Senate race and won 34 of the 53 House seats. In 2012, the Democratic Party won two-thirds of the seats in both the Senate and the Assembly, together with all the statewide offices, and 38 of the 55 seats in the House of Representatives. The voting in the Governor's race shows why. Exit polls showed Republican Meg Whitman as receiving 50% of white votes to 45% for Democrat Jerry Brown. But 64% of Hispanics and 77% of African Americans voted for Jerry Brown, giving him a solid majority in the race.

## The Future Political Culture of California

What does the future hold? Part of that future is already here: the 2010 census confirmed that California is a "majority-minority" state, meaning that whites are not a majority in California, though whites were still the largest single racial group in California. Estimates (for only the decennial census counts everyone) are that Latinos, as of March 2014, are now the largest single racial group. Projections also now hold that it is likely that no single racial group will ever be the majority of Californians. Figure 2.3 shows the current and projected balance of ethnic groups in California. The elephant in the room is the increasing percentage of Californians of Hispanic origin. This is largely driven not by continued immigration from Mexico (though that plays a part) but by the relatively high birthrates of the Hispanic population. In the last 25 years we have also seen periods of white out-migration, often driven by the desire to find cheaper housing.

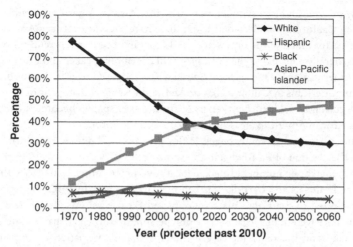

**Figure 2.3**   Racial Breakdown of Californians 1970–2060 (projected)

What this means for the political culture of California remains to be seen. One likely result is the continued dominance of the Democratic Party in California politics, as lower income Hispanics become a steadily larger part of the electorate.

As we can see in Figure 2.4, for most of the period Californians were only a little more likely than other Americans to vote for Democrats and could be induced with an attractive candidate, such as ex-California Governor Ronald Reagan in 1980, to vote Republican. But since 1984 California has always voted for the Democratic presidential candidate and as more Hispanics voted, the margin of victory has steadily widened.

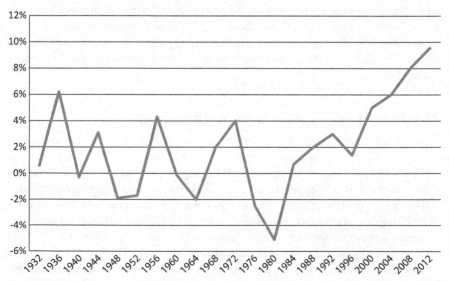

**Figure 2.4**   Difference between California's Democratic Presidential Vote and the Vote by All Americans

By 2012, Californians were 9% more likely to vote for President Obama over Mitt Romney than the rest of the nation. But over time Hispanics, like Italian Americans, should become more integrated into the general culture and their income and status may well improve, making them somewhat more receptive to the Republican Party.

Finally, it seems worth pointing out that the future political culture of California is hard to predict. Lower house prices could bring whites back to California, or at least stem their outflow. Lower Hispanic birthrates would slow down the rise in the number of Hispanics (in fact, small reductions in birthrates have already led to future projections no longer including Hispanics attaining majority status). Future wars might lead to new floods of refugees. But absent these shocks it seems likely that current trends toward a more diverse and inclusive political culture will continue.

# References

DeLaet, D. 2000. *U.S. Immigration Policy in an Age of Rights*. Westport, Conn.: Praeger.

Kolko, J. 2013, February 12. Why Do People Leave California?—Trulia Trends. Retrieved September 2, 2014, from http://www.trulia.com/trends/2013/02/why-do-people-leave-california/.

Gratton, B. and Merchant, E. 2013. Immigration, Repatriation, and Deportation: The Mexican-Origin Population in the United States, 1920–1950. *International Migration Review*, 47(4), pp. 944–75, December.

Gray, T. and Scardamalia, R. 2012. The Great California Exodus: A Closer Look. *Civic Report*, No. 7, September 2012. Manhattan Institute. Retrieved September 2, 2014, from http://www.manhattan-institute.org/pdf/cr_71.pdf.

Molloy, R., Smith, C. L., and Wozniak, A. 2011. Internal Migration in the United States. *Journal of Economic Perspectives, American Economic Association*, 25(3), pp. 173–196, Summer.

# CHAPTER 3

# California's Voters

*Stephen J. Stambough*

A voter in Fullerton, Orange County, California, was able to cast dozens of separate votes in the 2012 general election: one for a presidential and vice-presidential ticket; one for the U.S. Senate; one for the U.S. House; one each for State Senate and Assembly; several for important but lower profile local offices such as high school district board, local school district board, city council, county commissioners, and multiple statewide and local ballot propositions.

That's a lot of voting. In fact much is asked of California voters every election. Much, also, is asked of U.S. voters in general. By putting so many things up for a vote—including, in California, everything from amending the state constitution via initiative to electing city clerks—Americans cast votes in numbers that lead the world (Dalton, 1996, p. 46).

In this chapter, we look at California voters and voting. California voters are asked to participate in both indirect and direct democracy through the voting process. Indirect democracy is when voters select representatives who act on issues of public policy such as when we elect city council members, state legislators, and governors. Direct democracy refers to the process in which voters direct pass or reject public policy proposals. We begin with a discussion of California voters in a national context.

## Comparing the California and National Electorates: Some History

To look at the electorate is to look primarily at its two main elements: Republicans and Democrats. The present structure of the California Republican and Democratic parties was established during the New Deal era. The benchmark election for the New Deal was the defeat in 1932 of Republican Herbert Hoover by Democrat Franklin Roosevelt. In its response to the New Deal, the California electorate demonstrated both its responsiveness to and independence from national trends.

In 1930, California voters sent only one Democrat to the U.S. House of Representatives; in the national Roosevelt sweep of 1932, 10 California Democrats went to Washington. From 1932 to 1948, Democratic presidential candidates won California's large crop of electoral votes; and from 1932 to 1946, the Democrats controlled the state's Congressional delegation. In these respects, California was typical of the nation.

But there was a big exception to this pattern of Democratic ascendancy: while in many states the national Democratic sweep helped establish the Democratic Party as the dominant party in *state* as well as national politics, California voters remained steadfastly Republican when voting for statewide offices. In 1932, the year of Roosevelt's huge win over Hoover, the Democratic Party was unable even to field candidates in 17 of 80 contests, and it was not until 1938 that the Democrats were able to elect a governor.

Why this pattern? The Democrats, even by California standards, were a weak and poorly organized party and were not able effectively to capitalize on the national Democratic trend. The state's press, led by the *Los Angeles Times*, was intensely Republican. Finally, the Democrats ran a number of candidates who attempted to capitalize on the Depression by supporting radical economic programs that frightened more voters than they attracted.

The election to the governorship in 1942 of Earl Warren continued Republican domination at the state level, even while Democratic candidates did well in elections for Congress and the presidency. In 1953, Warren resigned the governorship to become Chief Justice of the United States. In the aftermath of Warren's departure, the state Republican Party suffered a series of internal struggles for control, as the Democrats had during the Depression era. With the end of the Eisenhower era in national politics (1953–1961) came the end of Republican dominance of state offices. Since that time, the broad contours of the California electorate have been similar to those of the nation, due in part to a simple fact: over the years, with population growth, California has constituted an increasing fraction of the national population. California is often on the leading edge of demographic changes in the country; therefore, some of the impacts are seen earlier and more intensely in California such as the recent and growing importance of the Latino population in the California electorate.

## Comparing the California and National Electorates: Partisanship

The most basic political orientation most of us have is partisanship—the sense that we are Republicans, Democrats, or identify with a third party, such the Libertarians or the Greens. While this sense of partisanship is weaker than it was several generations ago (Wattenberg, 1996), it is still the single most important fact of political life for most people. Partisanship is the primary, and for many people the sole, way they relate themselves to the political world.

When we compare survey responses from both California and the entire United States on partisanship, three things are especially noteworthy. First, the advantage Democrats had in the 1950s and 1960s both nationally and in California was reduced by the end of the 20th century, though not enough to reduce the Democrats to second place. Second, partisanship in California closely follows partisanship in the United States. In 1972, for example, the California and national electorates were essentially identical in their partisan preferences, and since then differences are slight. Third, the electorate overall has become less committed to either the Republicans or the Democrats; the fastest growing part of the electorate in California is comprised of those who decline to state an affiliation with any political party, large or small.

At present neither major party can claim a majority of voters in California, and third parties, though small, command a greater total share of the electorate than they did a generation ago. According to the California Secretary of State's Office, over the past decade party registration has been stable among Democrats in California. In 2003, 44.4% of registered voters identified as Democrats. By 2011 that number was nearly identical at 44.0%. The story is different among Republicans in California. Over the past decade, Republican identification declined from 35.2% of the registered voters in California to 30.9%. The Republican decline was accompanied by a subsequent increase in voters who declined to declare any partisan affiliation.

# Voters, NonVoters, and Turnout

Turnout is critical in elections; since both major parties have the potential to win statewide contests, mobilizing supporters to reach that potential is vital. Mobilization means two things: getting people registered and then getting them to turn out on election day.

Comparing voters and nonvoters in the United States and California reveals some similarities and some differences. While sex and regional differences between voters and nonvoters are insignificant, the young and the less well educated are heavily *under*represented in the electorate and the older, better educated, and more well-off are substantially *over*represented. Republicans and conservatives are slightly more likely to turn out to vote than Democrats and liberals. In these respects the California voter is like his or her national counterpart. Voters live in different social and economic circumstances than nonvoters, and they carry these characteristics with them into the voting booth. The result is that voters are slightly more conservative, more Republican, older, and better educated, and have higher incomes, than those who do not vote.

Examining turnout shows some additional similarities between California and the United States, but some differences as well. Between the arrival of the New Deal in 1932 and 1972, Californians turned out at higher rates in presidential election years— sometimes substantially higher rates—than the United States as a whole. Since 1976, turnout in California kept up with or occasionally lagged behind that for the country as a whole, at a time when the national turnout rate in presidential elections was declining to around 50%.

Part of this turnout decline in the United States and in California is due to the expansion of the electorate, via the 26th amendment to the federal Constitution in 1971, to include those 18 to 20 years of age. This age group, then and now, is noteworthy for its low turnout rate. But the even steeper decline in California's turnout relative to the rest of the country has also to do with another demographic change: a greater proportion of California's population is now comprised of just those groups who have tended to historically vote at lower rates, most especially Latinos.

The big story of California politics over the last 20 years is this growing Latino electorate. Ten percent of the state's registered voters in 1990 were Latino; by the turn of the 21st century that proportion had nearly doubled. These newly registered Latino voters generally were younger, less well educated, had lower incomes than their predecessors, and were much more likely to be Democrats. Despite their Democratic registration, however, these new Latino registered voters were very similar ideologically to the rest of

California's voters. This means there are many young Latino voters whom both parties are working to attract and retain.

Two more aspects of turnout deserve attention. The first is the advent in 1994 of federal motor voter legislation designed to increase registration and turnout by making it more convenient to register at such places as state motor vehicle offices. Approximately 800,000 Californians registered to vote under motor voter, and while it is difficult accurately to assess its effects, the statewide turnout rate since motor voter suggests that while registration may have increased registration it did not increase turnout, primarily because motor voter was designed to encourage people to register who are also the least likely to vote.

A second aspect of turnout is the significant increase in recent decades in Californians' voting via absentee ballot. Originally designed as a convenience for people who were going to be away from home on election day, absentee ballots have now become a regular part of campaigns' get-out-the-vote (GOTV) efforts. Absentee ballots allow campaigns to target their strongest supporters and virtually assure that they will vote.

Both parties now use absentee ballots vigorously, which explains the significant upsurge in their use. In 1966, just 3.3% of all votes cast in California were via absentee ballots; by 1986, the percentage had almost tripled to 9%; by 1990, it was 14.1%. In the elections of 2000 and 2004, roughly 30% of all votes cast were absentee—a figure matched in the United States as a whole, as increased absentee voting became a national phenomenon. In the days when absentee ballots were rarely used, a large majority of absentee voters favored Republican candidates and issues. This is much less the case now that absentee ballot campaigns are employed by both major parties and the number of Democrats and Republicans voting absentee is quite similar.

The tendency for the California electorate to be Democratic might appear to predict a state electorate consistently though not overwhelmingly Democratic in its voting, but turnout tends to equalize the parties' chances. In recent decades the state has elected four Republican governors (Reagan, Deukmejian, Wilson, and Schwarzenegger) and four Democrats (Edmund G. "Pat" Brown, his son Jerry Brown, Gray Davis, and Jerry Brown again for nonconsecutive terms), supported Nixon, Reagan, and Bush for president with its electoral votes, elected Republican Wilson to the U.S. Senate, and passed conservative initiatives supported by Republicans and opposed by Democrats.

But California has also elected Democrats to the U.S. Senate (Cranston, and currently Feinstein and Boxer), voted twice for Bill Clinton, divided its state legislature between a Democratic Senate and a Republican Assembly, divided its 52 seats in the U.S. House down the middle in 1994–1996 with each major party holding 26 seats, and elected a Democratic governor and legislature in 1998. California Democrats have enjoyed more consistent success in the last few cycles, however. In 2014, Governor Jerry Brown was reelected to an unprecedented fourth term as governor. In addition, Democrats once again won every election for statewide office including a hotly contested State Comptroller election. The fact that the Democrats have swept all statewide elections in 2010 and 2014 is even more impressive given the fact that those were both election years in which the Republican Party swept to large victories in most of the rest of the country.

The pattern of divided control has weakened, however. In the 2000 elections, California voted for the Democratic candidate Al Gore, re-elected Democratic U.S. Senator Dianne Feinstein to rejoin another Democratic U.S. Senator, Barbara Boxer, and sent to the House of Representatives a delegation that was nearly two-thirds Democratic. The voters in 2000 also sent to Sacramento a State Assembly that was nearly two-thirds Democratic and a State Senate that was also nearly two-thirds Democratic. The shift toward the Democratic Party in California reached a new high with the elections of 2010. Even though Republicans nationwide were the big winners of the 2010 elections, California went the other direction, every statewide elected office in California was won by the Democrats. By 2012, this pattern held and grew stronger as Democrats secured supermajorities in each legislative chamber permitting them to govern with no ability of the Republican minority to stop them even on tax policy that generally requires more than 60% of the legislative vote to pass. The national Republican wave of 2014 did impact the California Democrats by reducing their majorities below the supermajority threshold but they still have sizable majority and stable control of the legislature.

# California Voters and Presidential Elections

How California votes is important for another reason: the state's 54 electoral votes comprise 20% of the minimum 270 electoral votes needed to elect presidents. Under the Electoral College, winning the California popular vote by a single individual's vote delivers to the winner one-fifth of what is needed for victory. In any presidential election in which the winner's national popular vote margin is narrow but includes winning California, the state becomes particularly important. In the 14 presidential elections since 1948, Californians have been on the presidential ticket eight times as nominee for president or vice president. Remarkably, all these California national candidates were Republicans. In fact, no Republican had won the presidency without carrying California since 1880, when James Garfield was elected, until the election of 2000.

Over time California's share of all electoral votes has increased as the state's population and therefore its electoral vote has grown while the total number of electoral votes has remained constant at 538. In two cases in recent decades—Kennedy in 1960 and Carter in 1976—the national winner lost California. In all other cases, California voted for the winner. In the election of 2000, California supported the popular vote winner Al Gore, but not the electoral vote winner, George W. Bush.

In several presidential elections California's electoral votes were an especially important fraction of the winner's electoral vote total. For Harry Truman in 1948, for Richard Nixon in 1968 (but not in Nixon's 1972 landslide reelection), and for Bill Clinton in 1992 and 1996, California's electoral votes were especially important. In Clinton's, case, this was made clear by the record number of trips he made to California in his first term (more even than Ronald Reagan, who had a home in the state) as well as during the 1996 campaign. As far as the popular vote percentage is concerned, Californians have voted in presidential elections in much the same way as the rest of the country but has been trending solidly Democratic since Clinton's victory in 1992.

# Party Coalitions in California: Social Composition and Ideology

American political parties are loose coalitions of many groups rather than well-organized, integrated institutions. California party coalitions differ along social, economic, and ideological lines in ways similar to those of national parties.

The Republican coalition is evenly divided between males and females; the Democratic coalition, however, is skewed in the direction of female identifiers. Republican partisans are overwhelmingly white, the Democrats much less so. This is especially true with respect to blacks, who comprised in recent years 16% of Democratic identifiers but less than 1% of the Republicans. Asians are roughly divided between the two parties, and Latinos are Democratic in tendency.

Simply put, the Democratic coalition in California is more diverse and representative of the state's population than its Republican counterpart. This is also true among Republicans and Democrats nationally, and helps partially to explain why the Democrats, while they have historically held an edge in identification over Republicans, have also had a turnout problem. The more diverse Democratic coalition includes proportionately more individuals whose social characteristics—especially lower levels of education—are associated with lower levels of political activity.

Policy preferences between each of the major parties' identifiers differ in predictable ways. For example, while both Republicans and Democrats support abortion rights in the first three months of a woman's pregnancy, Democrats' support is considerably greater. On this and many other issues, California's Democrats differ from its Republicans in predictable ways, and both parties' identifiers in California are similar to their national counterparts.

# The Three Electorates

One final aspect of the California voter deserves attention because it focuses on some distinctive aspects of voting in California: the three different settings in which the California voter may act.

## The California Voter in General Elections

In a *general election* the most visible races are usually for control of political office: the winner in the race for governor or U.S. senator in a general election wins the office outright. This is a crucial distinction between general elections and primary elections, for the winner of a primary (held in March) wins only the right to run in the general election (held in November) as the official candidate of his or her party for the office. General elections also, however, almost always involve on initiative measures as well.

In the general election, races are contested between highly visible candidates of the major parties. The candidates are usually well known, they get substantial media attention, and the voter is more likely to use partisanship as a cue in guiding the voting choice. Such elections are termed *high stimulus* elections, and because this, turnout tends to be relatively high as well.

This means that marginal voters—those who are unlikely to vote when the stimulus value is low—are more likely to vote in a general election than in other types of elections, especially primaries. Marginal voters add an element of volatility to the electorate because they are more easily swayed by considerations other than partisanship. Media campaigns, candidate personality, and a strong concern with a single issue—of the kind that can be generated by an initiative campaign, for example—may be more important for such voters than they are for the committed partisan voter. These tendencies hold for California as well as for the nation.

## The California Voter in Primary Elections

The second electoral setting is the *primary election*, and here there is no direct national comparison. A primary is essentially several parallel elections, one for each party, in which party nominations for office are at stake, though primary ballots also include initiative measures. Primaries are elections *within* parties, not between them—or they were until voters approved a blanket primary via initiative in 1996, discussed at the end of this section.

Since primaries involve several candidates from the same party—that is, Democrats versus other Democrats, Republicans versus other Republicans—several important consequences follow. First, because partisan lines are not drawn, and because the candidates are often philosophically closer to each other, turnout tends to be lower in primary races than in the general election. The electorate shrinks, but it also changes in composition, not just size. The Democratic primary election electorate is not only smaller but also more liberal than the Democratic general election electorate. Likewise, the Republican primary electorate is not only smaller than its general election counterpart but also more conservative. The primary electorate for both major parties is therefore smaller, more ideologically aware, and less centrist.

Candidates facing such an electorate face a different strategic problem than general election candidates. Candidates must appeal to people who are more politically involved, more politically informed, and more intensely ideological in their beliefs. This means that primary electorates are more likely to nominate extreme candidates who appeal to the party faithful but who may not be as palatable to the larger, more diverse, and more moderate general electorate. Even if the more moderate candidate wins the primary the primary race itself may be divisive for the party in the general election.

California primary elections were changed radically, however, with the March 1996 passage of Proposition 198, which created a blanket primary—one in which voters are not limited to voting only for the candidates of the party with which they are registered. Under Prop 198, any registered voter could vote for any candidate in primary elections regardless of the candidate's party affiliation. The March 2000 primary was the first to be held under these rules, with a single primary ballot on which the names of all candidates for a given office appeared. This procedure, similar to those in several other states including Alaska, Louisiana and Washington, permitted crossover voting—that is, a Republican could cast a vote for a Democratic primary candidate, and a Democrat could likewise cast a vote for a Republican candidate for a given office, and then vote for a candidate of his or her own party for another office on the same ballot.

This raised the possibility that parties would be even further weakened and that one party could raid the other's ranks in primary elections, hoping to damage the party by nominating a weak opposition candidate who would be easier to defeat in the general election. Supporters of the blanket primary argued the precise opposite, claiming it would promote more moderate nominees in both parties by encouraging candidates with bipartisan support.

There was indeed crossover voting in the March 2000 primary: seven and one-half percent of Republicans voted in the Democratic primary, three-quarters of them for Al Gore. Twenty-two and one-half percent of Democrats voted in the Republican primary, with just under two-thirds of them supporting Arizona Sen. John McCain. There was little evidence that either Republicans or Democrats made any effort to do mischief to the other party but instead voted sincerely, not strategically. Still, there were a few close state races in which one could argue, as the losing candidates did, that mischievous crossovers might have made affected the outcome.

Both major parties, joined by the Libertarian and Peace and Freedom parties, challenged Proposition 198 in the courts and in June 2000, the U.S. Supreme Court held on a 7–2 decision that the measure was an unconstitutional violation of the first amendment, saying it "forces political parties to associate with—to have their nominees, and hence their positions, determined by—those who, at best, have refused to affiliate with the party and, worst, have expressly affiliated with a rival."

In response this decision, two competing measures were placed on the November 2004 state ballot. Proposition 62 required primary elections in which voters could vote for any state or national candidates (with the exception of the presidency) regardless of the candidate's or the voter's party affiliation, with the two highest vote-getters being listed on the general election ballot, even if both candidates were members of the same party. The measure was designed to revive the open primary in a way that would survive review by the courts. Propositions 60 was intended specifically to counter Proposition 62 by requiring that the general election ballot include the candidate who received the most votes from among the candidates running in each party's primary election the previous March. In the November election, voters reaffirmed the closed party primary by supporting Proposition 60 and defeating Proposition 62. Reformers kept trying and were successful with the passage of Proposition 14 in 2010 (see Chapter 4 for more detail). This proposition altered the primary process for future elections. It will be interesting to see how parties and voters respond to the new structures.

## The California Voter and Direct Democracy

The third electoral setting brings us to our second type of democracy, direct democracy. Direct democracy is often understood to include three main types: *initiative, referendum, and recall*. Initiatives are ballot propositions in which the voters are asked a direct policy question that is proposed by citizen groups who collected enough signatures to qualify for the ballot. If the initiative passes, the policy directly becomes law while circumventing the need for state legislative and gubernatorial approval. Successful initiatives are still subject to judicial review by the courts however. *Referendums* are ballot questions that are a direct reaction to legislative activity by our elected branches of government. If a law is passed, opponents can try to qualify a referendum for the ballot, which would ask voters if the law should be implemented or repealed. The final version is *recall*. In recall elections, voters can remove an officeholder from office before the normal term has expired. The highest profile example of this was the recall of Governor Davis is 2003 and the replacement election of Governor Schwarzenegger.

California has a long history of an active system of direct democracy. The entire movement in the United States for this system grew from the Populist and Progressive era movements and is still found primarily in the western part of the United States. Direct democracy in California has often involved highly controversial issues, involve extensive and costly media campaigns, and arouse intense emotions. Examples in California include Proposition 13 about taxes, Proposition 187 about undocumented immigrants, and Proposition 8 about gay marriage. In fact, California has one of the most active systems of direct democracy in the country. According to the Initiative and Referendum Institute, California has consistently been among the top states in the number of ballot measures in a given year. While Proposition 13 in 1978 is often viewed as a watershed moment in California direct democracy, it is 1988 that marks a breakthrough moment in our usage. In 1988, California voters were asked to vote on 15 separate statewide ballot measures including four separate ones that dealt with auto insurance regulation.

The frequent use of direct democracy in California entered a new era after the 1978 passage of Proposition 13. It was at that time that California began a sustained era of activity. One explanation is the growth of what scholars refer to as the initiative industry (McCuan and Stambough, 2005). The rise of professional campaign firms that specialize in signature gathering, polling, campaign strategy, and advertising makes it easy for groups to access the resources needed to mount a serious direct democracy campaign. Being able to overcome the barrier of mounting a campaign, with enough money, greatly accelerated the frequency of measures being proposed and qualifying for the ballot.

There are several unique aspects to how voters react to direct democracy elections compared with voting behavior in elections that include actual candidates for office. Fundamentally, the question is how do voters make their decisions about ballot measures when there is no candidate information or partisan affiliation. When voters must choose between candidates, the voters know at least basic information about the candidate based upon the information on the ballot. The candidates name, partisan affiliation, and occupation are listed on the ballot. Voters who want to vote for female candidates might be able to vote based upon the first name. Ethnic surnames might provide information to voters as well depending upon their preferences. A candidate's occupation might provide some information if a voter wishes to vote for someone listed as a small businessperson, an educator, or other familiar occupations. The most often used piece of information on the ballot in candidate elections is party affiliation. The vast majority of Republicans and Democrats will vote for a candidate of their own party. Therefore, all the information that the voter needs to use to make a decision is the party affiliation of the candidate.

Direct democracy elections offer no such information. A ballot measure is not a person so it does not have a gender or an ethnicity. Measures may deal with policy issues often associated with gender or ethnic issues but the measure itself does not. Measures also do not have occupations. Measures may be supported or opposed by political parties but they are still distinct. Absent a public campaign, voters may not know the positions of the political parties on the different measures. All of this does not mean that similar information short cuts are not available to voters. If a voter is either happy with the status quo or risk averse when it comes to change, the default position is to vote no. In addition, voters also are sent an explanation of the ballot, which includes the official ballot explanation from the Secretary of State's office accompanied by arguments for and against the measure, by recognized supporters and opponents. If a voter is pro-union or anti-union, that voter can use the union endorsement to help guide the voting decision.

# After Florida: A Note on Voting Procedures in California

Much of the drama and complexity involving Florida's role in the 2000 presidential election occurred because most election procedures in the United States are creatures of state, not federal, law. Most elections in the United States are conducted under a combination of state and county rules. Since states create counties, the amount of latitude counties have in running elections depends on how much latitude they are given by the states.

Florida provides relatively little guidance in these areas, and this latitude complicated matters in Florida considerably when different county-based canvassing boards debated over such matters as whether to count hanging chad ballots in which tiny rectangles of cardboard on voting cards were not completely removed, or dimpled chad ballots in which only an indentation was present on a ballot. Individual Florida counties also varied considerably in how they secured the integrity of ballots, especially absentee ballots, before they were counted. There was also concern about important decisions in Florida being made by local and state officials who were active, partisan participants in the campaign, most prominently Florida's Secretary of State, who was co-chair of George Bush's Florida's campaign and who was also the chief election officer of the state.

California law provides more guidance on these matters than does Florida law. While the Secretary of State of California is, as in Florida, an elected official who runs as a member of a political party and is also the chief election officer of the state, most county election officials in California (and unlike Florida) are not themselves elected but are rather appointed, on an officially nonpartisan basis, by county boards of supervisors. Some other comparisons with the Florida case: the confusing butterfly ballots, of the kind used in Florida's Palm Beach County, are not used in California. There is a statewide standard for counting chads: if they dangle from two corners, they count. Any other pattern, including dimpled chads, does not. In Florida, overseas absentee ballots were allowed additional time, under Florida law, to arrive for counting. In California, such ballots must arrive by election day. And under California law, officials have 28 days in which to count ballots and certify the results; Florida law provides for a period of 7 days. After that 28-day period, *any* candidate in California can ask for and get a recount, provided the candidate pays for its costs.

## Conclusion

The California voter is a closely watched political animal. In many respects—partisanship, presidential voting, turnout, and issue positions—voters in California look a lot like U.S. voters in general. But there are differences. Operating in a huge and diverse state with weak parties, and able to vote regularly on everything from obscure local offices to amending the state constitution, voters in California have enormous latitude and great power.

California's reputation as a political bellwether derives not from some magical quality granted its citizens but from the realities of the state's demography and its politics. Size and diversity mean that any interest or issue will likely be found in California; weak parties mean voters have considerable latitude; and the tradition of direct democracy via initiative means voters' wishes on virtually everything are often decisive. All this means that California's voters make a difference, not just within the state, but in the nation as well.

## Reference

Dalton, Russell J. (1996). *Citizen Politics: Public Opinion and Political Parties in Advanced Industrial Democracies.* New York: Chatham House.

# CHAPTER 4

# Political Parties and Interest Groups in California

*Stephen J. Stambough[1]*

Organizing politically is one of the most fundamental actions for a functioning democracy. At their core, both political parties and interest groups serve this purpose. Both are groups of citizens united to pursue political agendas and causes. Of course, political parties are visible distinct from interest groups in that they tend to be a broader coalition of various interest groups brought together by the desire to recruit, train, and run candidates for public office.

In this chapter, we begin by exploring California political parties in several ways. First, we discuss the Progressive legacy in California that still impacts (and weakens) California's political parties. Second, we look at the state of the two-party system in California by exploring levels of party competition in California and trends in partisan support. Third, we examine the cohesiveness of California's political parties from the perspective of the voters and legislators. We then turn our attention to interest groups in California. Finally, we comment upon changes in party structure and tactics in contemporary California.

## The Progressive Legacy of Party Restrictions

California's parties have been structurally weak throughout much of the last hundred years because of laws passed by the state legislature and the voters in initiative measures, laws that provide for direct primaries, civil service reforms, legal prohibitions on endorsements and financing, non-partisan elections, and a shortage of party conventions and offices. Most of these laws were passed during the Progressive Era, a time shortly after the turn of the century when middle-class reformers in America rallied against corrupt political machines and business monopolies.

The progressive leader in California was Governor (later U.S. Senator) Hiram Johnson. He rode to office on a campaign against the power of the Southern Pacific railroad and "political bosses" in both parties. Like most progressive leaders, Johnson found the "political machine" a more vulnerable target than the railroads and other corporations. Therefore, the main thrust of progressivism in California was not effective regulation of

---

[1]This chapter is a revision of previous chapters built upon contributions by Keith Boyum, Bert Buzan, Phil Gianos, and Sandra Sutphen. We thank them for their contributions and friendship.

business, but the destruction of the traditional party organization (McConnell, 1970, 30–50). The direct primary, civil service, the initiative, referendum and recall, non-partisan local elections, the detailed restrictions on the ability of party leaders to endorse or fund candidates, and the weak, formal party structure survive in contemporary California politics as a legacy of progressive power in the state.

One of the enduring legacies of the Progressive Era reforms on the impact of political parties in California elections is with the nomination process. When citizens register to vote in California there is a choice of party registration. Voters can identify with one of the major political parties, one of the recognized minor political parties, or even choose to *Decline to State*. This last category is what people casually refer to as Independent voters. Since political parties are groups united to pursue a political agenda, parties often want some assurance that their nominees will pursue the party's policy goals. Therefore, parties are often suspicious of opening up the nomination rules to include participation by *Decline to State* voters or even cross-over voters from another party.

Basically, Democrats don't want Republicans choosing the Democratic nominee and vice-versa. It is also believed that if *Decline to State* voters participate in the nomination process, the party's nominee will likely have to compromise on the party agenda to attract these voters who are generally less ideologically extreme.

The values of the Progressive Era in California are at the core of the struggle between a more open and a more closed nomination process. Over the last 20 years, California voters used the initiative process multiple times to reduce the influence of partisans on the nomination process and be inclusive of those with no party preference and those who may wish to cross party lines in the primary. Indeed, in 1996, the voters of the state endorsed Proposition 198, which instituted a blanket primary. In a blanket primary, voters of either party can vote for a candidate seeking the Republican **or** Democratic nomination (but not for both) for any office on the ballot. This system, opposed by the leaders of both parties, destroyed the entire notion of a primary election as gathering, however impersonally, the party faithful. This system was used in the 1998 election but was later invalidated by the courts after objections by both major and minor political parties who did not want to expand the nomination process beyond their own membership.

Supporters of the Progressive Era inspired efforts to weaken political parties came back with another attempt in the form of Proposition 14 passed in 2010 that created what is known as a "top two" system. In this system, parties do not nominate candidates through the traditional primary system for offices other than president and a few party organizational offices such as Party Central Committee members. For all other offices including for governor, Congress, the state legislature, and many other offices, all potential candidates from all major and minor parties compete in the first round of balloting. The top two vote recipients—regardless of party—advance to the general election. Reformers hope that this will create situations for more moderate officeholders. Supporters hope that candidates will need to appeal to the middle of the ideological spectrum in order to make it to the general election. It is too early to know the long-term impact of these reforms; however, it has created some situations in which two candidates from the same party faced each other in the general election.

Likewise, state law for many years, expressly forbade state party leaders and organizations from endorsing candidates in primaries or contributing money to their campaigns. These strictures deprived California political parties of several of their major functions: the recruitment of new candidates, the management of campaigns, and the balancing of a party ticket along class, ethnic, factional, and regional lines. In 1988, the U.S. Supreme Court struck down California's prohibition against party endorsements (*Eu v. SF Demo. Comm.*). The Democratic Party has exercised its option to endorse candidates. But the Republican leadership, as a study of Orange County Republican officials many years ago had predicted (Berg, 1980), preferred to continue operating as small, informal cliques of influential private individuals. The classic progressive tradition dies hard in contemporary California.

Other legal restrictions deny party leaders in California access to political patronage, those government jobs, and other perquisites that often are necessary to the maintenance of strong political organizations. Civil service is extensive, and the vast bulk of state employees have little personal financial stake in the outcome of elections. A 1990 U.S. Supreme Court decision (*Rutan v. Republican Party of Illinois*) apparently has nationalized California's progressive outlook on patronage, a practice that appeared already to have been headed for extinction (Katz, 1991).

Indeed, large numbers of elected offices stand completely outside the partisan arena. All local elected officials in California are chosen on a non-partisan basis. A mere handful of states go as far as California in carrying out the traditional American ideal of "taking party politics (or, at least, party labels) out of government." The U.S. 9th Circuit Court of Appeals struck down California's prohibition against partisan endorsements of local candidates in *Renne v. Geary*, but the U.S. Supreme Court reversed that decision on procedural grounds (*Los Angeles Times*, June 18, 1991).

# Political Party Cohesion in California

## Voters

The Progressive Era inspired reforms consistently attempted to weaken the structure of political parties. The remaining question is whether political parties behave in a way that reflects these attempts or do the members of the party act as if the parties are strong. Political scientist Leon Epstein (1986) defined political parties as "*Any group, however, loosely organized, seeking to elect governmental officeholders under a given label.*" There are several dimensions to this definition. First, there must be an identifiable group that generally must have some common goals for public policy. Second, this group can be viewed as a group of citizens voting for office, a group of candidates seeking office, or even a group of successful candidates making policy and preparing for their reelection. Third, there is reference to at least some basic level of organizational structure with the purpose of contesting and winning public offices.

In this section, we examine the first two of these components by looking at the cohesiveness of California voters and legislators within the major political parties. Does knowing an individual's partisan affiliation tell us something substantive about the political positions of the individual? Individual people may be Democrats, Republicans,

Greens, or a member of any number of even smaller parties for a variety of reasons. Few individuals agree with every policy any one political party promotes and instead base their party affiliation on whatever issue they believe is most important or even non-issue–related concerns such as family tradition (to some degree partisanship is inherited), influence of peers, or even the appeal of charismatic leaders.

Even with some variation of beliefs within the political parties, in California Republican and Democratic identifiers are comprised of groups that differ demographically, geographically, and ideologically. Demographically, California Republicans and Democrats follow similar patterns to the composition of the national party coalitions. According to the research by the Public Policy Institute of California, Californians follow the same pattern as the national parties in that women are more likely to identify as Democrats while men are more likely to identify as Republicans (Baldassare, 2007). Furthermore, ethnic minorities make up a larger percentage of Democratic Party identifiers then are found among Republican Party identifiers.

These demographic differences are reflected in policy preferences. The same report found that Democrats were much more likely to be in favor of more taxes versus cuts in social programs, in favor of gay marriage, and to believe that immigration is a net benefit instead of a net burden for Californians. Fundamental differences on social and economic policy issues by Democrats and Republicans create a difficult hurdle for those who advocate a post-partisan California.

Recent elections suggest a different reality for parties in California than for much of the country. In 2010, while most of the country turned to the Republican Party following two consecutive wave elections that favored the Democrats, in California Democrats swept the elections. The Democratic nominee won every statewide Constitutional office and Democrats maintained their sizable majorities in the State Legislature and with the U.S. House delegation. In 2012, the Democrats followed the 2010 results by winning supermajorities in each state legislative branch permitting the Democrats to act without any input by the legislative Republicans. These supermajorities were lost by the next election in 2014 but the Democrats still maintain sizable majorities in each chamber. While it is true that the voters who do not identify with either political party can sway elections one way or another it has become very difficult for Republicans to win major elections in California. In addition, the partisan identifiers themselves reflect a highly polarized electorate (Baldassare, 2007) and, thus, demonstrate a high amount of partisan cohesion among both Democrats and Republicans.

## Legislators

In our understanding of political parties, however, the goal of a political party is to elect officeholders who will enact policy. Therefore, a more comprehensive examination of the cohesiveness of contemporary parties should include what political scientist V.O. Key called *party in government*. In other words, how cohesive are the political parties in their legislative voting patterns on the issues faced by these officeholders. Political scientist Keith Poole collected data that allow us to examine this question by computing a score for members of Congress based upon their voting records for every two-year period. These scores range from $-1$ (most liberal) to $+1$ (most conservative).

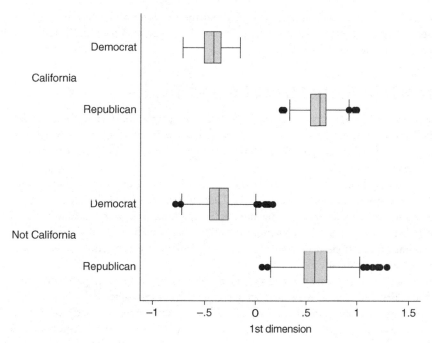

**Figure 4.1**

Using these scores we show partisan cohesion from 2001 to 2013 in Figure 4.1. This figure shows the distribution of ideological placement for every member of each party during that period. The top part of the figure shows this distribution for only the California congressional delegations during that time. The bottom figure shows the distribution for the other 49 states combined.

A quick examination of the figure suggests that although both parties are fairly cohesive with the Democrats staking out positions to the left of the Republicans, there are some differences between the California delegations and the rest of the country. California's delegations are a little more distinct with no overlap by the parties. Throughout the decade there is not a single Democrat from California who is further to right than any Republican. That is not true at the national level where there is some overlap among the conservative Democrats and liberal Republicans although greater polarization has been developing at the national level as well. It also appears that the California Democrats are slightly more liberal than those of the rest of the country and California Republicans are slightly more conservative than those of the rest of the country. A difference-in-means test for both parties suggests that these differences are statistically significant.

What this indicates is that the California congressional delegation is more polarized than the rest of the country as a whole. This level of party cohesiveness is advantageous in that the parties do offer the voters distinct, consistent alternatives in public policy. However, it can be disadvantageous since the Congressional delegation does not seem to have anyone representing the ideologically moderate positions favored by many voters. This type of polarization is what the reformers in favor of the new nominations system hope to change. It will take some time for the potential impacts of the reform to be realized if they materialize at all.

# Trends in Party Structure and Tactics

As mentioned earlier in the chapter, California's political parties developed in a decidedly anti-party political environment. Dating back to the Progressive Era, many reforms have been passed to try to weaken the power of political parties in California. As seen in the previous section, the end result for California's congressional delegation is still a polarized and cohesive party. Therefore, somewhere along the process parties must have some strength to forward an agenda. That strength cannot be found, however, in the classic understanding of organization. In fact, party organization in California is so weak that one of the classic distinctions in political party analysis, the division between temporary institutions (e.g., conventions) and permanent organizations (e.g., central committees) is insignificant.

By state law, the state party conventions are the only "temporary" party structures in the entire state. There are no precinct or county conventions to form the classic "pyramid of participation" in which local activists gather at their voting precincts, pass resolutions, and elect delegates to the county convention who, in turn, pass resolutions and select delegates to the state convention. No one votes for the California parties' state convention "delegates" as such all party nominees for state executive offices, state legislature, and Congress (plus a few other party officials at the Republican convention) constitute the state convention.

These *ex officio* delegates, delegates by virtue of holding some other office, write a meaningless party platform in August of every gubernatorial election year. In presidential election years the state convention also has the duty of selecting the party's nominees for presidential electors. The method of selecting the state convention and its duties are so routine as to doom it to insignificance and isolation.

The County Central Committee is the only party organ that the party voters elect. Americans from the East and South are astounded by the absence of *any* precinct level party organization in California. Even here, interest among all but a handful of activists is minimal.

The State Election Code places fewer restrictions on the campaign activities of the County Central Committee than on other party organs. The committee may financially assist local candidates and may exercise considerable discretion in deciding where to allocate it money. But the committees cannot determine the outcomes of the party primary elections, and, therefore, often cannot hope to compete with the personal campaign organizations of the candidates. Only the death of a party nominee gives the county committee a limited sort of control over candidate recruitment. In that event, the committee bears the legal responsibility for choosing a new party standard bearer.

The State Central Committee consists of an ex officio membership prescribed by each party's by-laws. The state committees are so disorganized and underfinanced that they play little campaign role outside a few closely contested legislative races.

# Substitutes for Parties

## Organizational Substitutes: Extra-party Groups

Political activists in California have circumvented the weak and overly regulated formal party structure with extra-party groups that can operate outside the law and at least attempt to perform traditional party functions like recruiting candidates, financing campaigns, and formulating policy programs.

The oldest of these extra-party groups is the California Republican Assembly (CRA). Progressive Republicans organized the CRA in the 1930s, and the group can claim much of the credit for the survival of California progressive Republicanism into the 1950s. Not bound by the state regulations on party organizations, the CRA's local and statewide committees provided funding, expertise, and a prestigious endorsement for Republican moderates facing primary opposition.

The Democratic Party has never experienced a strong extra-party group to compare with the Republicans' CRA. The closest the Democrats have come is the California Democratic Council (CDC). Liberal Democrats, inspired by the presidential campaign of Adlai Stevenson, organized CDC in 1953. CDC was a more mass-based organization than its Republican counterparts, working through large conventions rather than selection committees. The CDC was undoubtedly important to the Democrats' revival in the late 1950s. But, in the 1960s, the CDC fell victim to the social and political divisions of the Vietnam era. Speaker of the Assembly Jesse Unruh tried to form a more moderate group, the Democratic Volunteers Committee (DVC). This newer extra-party group failed to establish itself, while the CDC's importance has waned (Stone, 1991).

> All the extra-party groups display a middle-class ideological fervor that isolates them from mainstream political power. Given this perspective, they are much more inclined to debate issues and to support the hopeless candidacies of "true believers" than to "pick winners" in the primaries. This tendency does not render the groups meaningless, but it does serve to limit their effectiveness as organizational substitutes for the political party.

## Electoral Substitutes: Campaign Management Firms

California, with its weak parties and proximity to Hollywood, pioneered the use of public relations firms in the management of campaigns. The oldest campaign management firm in the nation, Whitaker and Baxter, got its start in California in 1933. Other famous California public relations firms involved in political campaigns include Baus and Ross, Spencer-Roberts, Cerrell and Associates, and Butcher-Forde, the Orange County experts in the last-minute campaign mail blitz.

Until the early 1960s, public relations firms were the "secret weapons" of a few sophisticated and well-heeled candidates. Today, nearly everyone employs them. Campaign management firms, as they are more commonly called today, may produce media advertisements, provide dramatic coaching for the candidate, poll voters, fabricate "issue positions" likely to resonate the popular attitudes the polls uncover, and schedule campaign stops.

## Electronic Substitutes: Internet-Based Grassroots

The newest trend in political parties in California is something that swept the country after people realized the political advantage to using something created right here in California. The information and electronic era brought forward—in part—by the success and creativity of Silicon Valley, slowly worked its way into the political scene.

At first, parties and campaigns used the Internet as an electronic version of the brochures they would produce and hang on people's doors. Now, throughout the country and in California, political parties are finding ways to organize through building a small group dynamic for large groups of Californians. Political scientist Mancur Olson argued that one of the problems with effective group formation was that it was easy for individual members to avoid participating within large groups (Olson, 1971). One way to overcome this *free-rider* problem was to form small groups within the larger organization. People had a stronger sense of identity to the small group and experiences direct peer pressure to maintain activity with the organization.

For groups as large as the California Republican and Democratic parties, using the Internet to coordinate and promote small, specialized groups within the parties is an effective way to mobilize supporters and avoid losing the contributions of talent, money, and time that these people could give to the party. If you go to either party's website (www.cagop.org and www.cadem.org), you can easily find links to either county or local clubs for each party. Some of these clubs are identified by geography such as the Laguna Beach Democratic Club or the Irvine Republican Council. Other clubs identify particular constituent groups or interests within an organization such as the Rush Limbaugh Club of Southern Orange County or the Vietnamese American Democratic Club of Orange County. By being able to bring together a collection of small, niche groups throughout the state, the Internet has helped the parties build stronger resource bases. The next step is to see if this technological approach to creating an effective small group dynamic can be applied to state political parties as well. As with many political trends and technological trends, California is often on the leading edge of this innovation and will be worth observing over the next few years for clues to its use.

# The Nature and Importance of Interest Groups in California

## Why Study Interest Groups?

Interest groups gather together persons who share at least one need or goal, and who seek to influence policy-makers to act favorably. In this, interest groups may be similar to political parties, which also gather like-minded people together in order to achieve public policy goals. Political parties, however, seek to win and hold government offices. Interest groups do not, and this is a critical difference between them. As a result, interest groups need have no sense of accountability to the public at large. Groups press their points of view to make new policy and also to prevent the making of new policy. In doing so, interest groups are so central to political processes that one cannot understand politics without understanding something about interest groups.

## Interest Groups in the California Environment

Concern about special interests being contrary to the public good is as old as America itself. Writing in *The Federalist*, Number 10 (1787), James Madison warned of the dangers of "factions."

> The regulation of these various and interfering interests forms the principal task of modern legislation, and involves the spirit of party and faction in the necessary and ordinary operations of the government.

In the control of interest groups, as in so many other areas of life, California's greatest asset has always been its diversity. California is not exclusively dependent on either agriculture or industry. It is not as desperate to attract business as are formerly impoverished Southern states, nor has organized labor dominated as in many areas of the East, nor does any extractive industry dominate, like oil in Louisiana or coal in West Virginia. If the power vacuum created by the Progressives' destruction of the parties resulted in strong California interest groups, at least no single interest group has ever dominated the Golden State in modern times.

## Progressivism in California

The California "solution" to the problem of factions and parties is also a result of the "Progressive" movements that occurred in many Western states around the turn of the 20th century. A coalition of middle-class reformers, known as the *Progressives*, sought to eliminate what they saw as the corrupting influence of special interests on California politics. The Progressives were not radicals. They believed that corporations and other private interests had a right to prosper and to petition the legislature. Thus, a direct attack on the interests was out of the question.

The Progressives contented themselves with measures designed to weaken the strong political party organizations that the interests allegedly controlled with their money, contacts, and favors (McConnell, 1966). They regulated political party activities, and denied party organizations control over government jobs. Loose coalitions of middle class reform groups superseded party campaign organizations. Direct citizen participation in party primary elections replaced conventions as the means of nominating party candidates. Civil servants replaced party "hacks" on the government payroll. Local officials were elected on a non-partisan ballot, and even the California legislature came under the control of bipartisan cliques.

The Progressives hoped to replace the hated party "machines" with a purer and more direct form of democracy, leading to the adoption of such direct democracy techniques as the initiative, the referendum, and the recall. The Progressives could not predict that these tools—designed to permit more control by middle class voters—would instead become a mechanism for "special interest" electoral dominance in the later part of the century.

Through much of the state's history, California's weak parties invited a strong interest group influence over the state's policymaking process. Indeed, California during the 1930s and 1940s even had a lobbyist, a person hired to represent interest groups in Sacramento, as a "secret boss." His name was Arthur Samish, and even the governor of the state, Earl Warren, admitted that Samish had more influence in the legislature than he, at least on issues affecting Samish's clients (Samish and Thomas, 1959,13–14).

Arthur Samish performed many of the functions of a political party. He collected funds for a great number of otherwise unrelated clients. He used the funds to help elect state legislators, often Republicans of the progressive stripe. When Samish's corporate clients urgently needed a bill passed, Samish cashed in his electoral chips. Otherwise, the befriended legislator was free to vote his personal or constituency interests. Samish shunned the spotlight and did not meddle in affairs that did not concern his clients. But his influence eventually made him a media celebrity. When Samish's antics became a national scandal, he could not account for the millions of dollars he had dispensed, and he retired to the federal penitentiary (Velie, 1949a, 1949b). With that, California began its first serious effort to control lobbying by requiring spending reports from those seeking to influence public policy.

## The Most Effective Groups in California Politics

The effectiveness of a group attempting to lobby policy-makers is dependent upon a number of factors. These include a narrow focus and available resources that include money, grass-roots membership, the skill and expertise of trained legislative advocates (another term for lobbyists), timing, and of course, the nature of the issue itself.

Moreover, lobbyists have always been most effective when they wish to block a proposed action. Lobbyists who engage in negative action—preventing a proposed policy—rather than positive goals—attempting to initiate change—are in a better position to influence cautious decision makers.

California lobbyists are highly professionalized, often with advanced educational degrees, competent staffs, and well-run offices (Briscoe and Bell, 1986). The most successful lobbyists in California are those representing real estate interests (The California Association of Realtors), the alcoholic beverage industry, horse-racing interests, the health industry (including both organizations of medical personnel and hospital associations), insurance industry, and governmental agencies, including associations representing cities, counties, and governmental employees, particularly public school teachers (the California Teachers Association). Many of these groups are affiliates of national organizations (the AFL-CIO, manufacturers associations, and financial institutions).

After major political reforms were instituted in California (see below), a number of public interest groups have also emerged to counter the more narrow, economic interests of special areas such as insurance and real estate. Some of these groups devote themselves to governmental reform—the League of Women Voters, Common Cause—and others specialize in changing economic regulation—Consumer's Union, Taxpayers' Association. More narrowly focused groups, concentrating on specific issues such as the environment (Friends of the River, Sierra Club), or insurance (Proposition 103 Enforcement Project) are as likely to battle governmental agencies as they are to attempt influence on the legislature.

# Reforms in California

Interest groups pursue all the available political processes to influence the outcome of public policy in their favor. They draft model legislation that they hope will be introduced by legislators and become law. They bring cases before the courts to obtain judicial relief and influence precedent. They work with governmental agencies to affect the regulatory process and ease administrative control over their enterprises. All these are considered the legitimate exercise of First Amendment protections of the "right to petition for redress of grievances."

The most controversial aspect of interest group participation in politics, however, has long been their involvement in the campaign and electoral processes. Political action committees are, for many prospective and current legislators, the largest source of campaign contributions. As campaign costs have escalated with increasing dependence on expensive media—particularly television—exposure, the ability to attract substantial contributions becomes an overwhelming concern for potential office holders. Attempts to regulate interest group involvement, at both the national and state levels, have resulted in the unintended consequence of actually shifting more power into the hands (and pocketbooks) of interest groups.

Public ambivalence and a pervasive sense of futility about political reform in California are clearly reflected in the initiative and legislative history. Voters passed major reforms in 1974, 1990, and 1996, and in 2000, repealed much of what they had established in 1996. The major initiatives that have been passed by California voters include Proposition 9 (1974), Proposition 73 (1988), Proposition 140 (1990), Proposition 208 (1996), and Proposition 34 (2000). In between elections, voters have watched the courts overturn several reforms.

**Proposition 9** established the Fair Political Practices Commission to enforce a broad array of political and campaign reforms. In the 1988 primary, two campaign reform proposals were passed by the voters, **Proposition 68**, sponsored by Common Cause and **Proposition 73** sponsored by elected officials of both parties. Since Proposition 73 outpolled Proposition 68, its provisions prevailed where the two were in conflict. Proposition 73 would have implemented much stricter campaign limitations from PACs (limited to $2,500 per candidate per year) and individuals ($1,000 per candidate per year), banned transfers between candidates, and limited expenditures on the part of political parties as well. Additionally, it expressly prohibited public financing of campaigns. In 1990, the California Supreme Court overturned most of Proposition 73.

The 1996 election again found dueling propositions on the ballot. **Proposition 208**, which gathered more votes than **Proposition 212**, promised some serious reform, including stringent limits on contributions ($500 for statewide candidates; $250 for legislative races) and limited spending by political parties. Sponsored by Common Cause, it out-polled Proposition 212 that was backed by the California Public Interest Research Group (a Ralph Nader off-shoot). California legislators, faced with the possibility that the strict limits imposed by Proposition 208 might be upheld by the courts, placed **Proposition 34** on the November, 2000 ballot.

Proposition 34 repeals much of Proposition 208. Voters may want reform and may have thought they were voting for reform, but they undid the strict limitations on campaign spending they had authorized just four years before. Proposition 34 replaces Proposition 208's strict limits with much more generous amounts. It repeals the limits on political party contributions (so-called "soft money"), a major provision of 208.

## Money, Campaigns, and Interest Groups

As a result of Propositions 9 and 140, public information about campaign contributions is now available (http://cal-access.ss.ca.gov). Likewise, there has been an enormous increase in registered lobbyists and PACs in the years following the passage of Proposition 9. More importantly, campaign contributions are now easily available from the Secretary of State's office. As mandated by the Legislature in 1997, all contributions are now reported electronically and made available over the Internet by the Secretary of State. The interested citizen will find PACs categorized by industry or interest affiliation and can track their campaign contributions and other expenditures.

Despite these reform efforts, contributions to political campaigns still constitute a major activity for California interest groups. If nothing else, interest groups contribute to campaigns because they believe it buys them access to legislators. A legislator may or may not vote on an issue the way a group wants, but few legislators will not listen to the plea of a significant campaign contributor.

## Interest Group Politics in California

Much of what we know about interest group politics in California is borrowed from what we know about interest group politics in general. The types of groups are generally the same; the core functions are generally the same, and even reason why people join groups are generally the same. There are a few characteristics of the California political system which impact the way interest group politics operate within the state and differentiate it from other parts of the country. In this section, we explore the impact of two of the most important on California's interest groups: legislative term limits and direct democracy.

### Legislative Term Limits

During the early 1990s, California joined most western states in adopting some form of legislative term limits. In 1990 California voters approved **Proposition 140** to limit members to no more than 6 years in the State Assembly and 8 years in the Senate. At the time, no one really knew what effect legislative term limits would have because no state had experienced the effects of legislative term limits. Since term limits were designed to alter the composition of the legislature, it was reasonable to believe that this alteration would have an effect on the use and balance of political power in Sacramento.

Since interest groups are rational actors, it is reasonable to expect that the interest group community would react to the new political environment with strategic changes suited toward the pursuit of their goals but reflective of the new institutional rules. Two political scientists (Gordon and Unmack, 2003) examined interest group behavior in California in a post-legislative term limits environment. Their study suggested that interest group behavior did change as a result of legislative term limits. They found that interest groups altered their patterns of campaign contributions.

While interest groups still based their donation decisions upon targeting their contributions toward positions of power, they acted as if the positions of power changed. In the pre-term limits era, money flowed to ranking members of important committees particularly committees overseeing the issues. In the post-term limits era, committee chair positions rotate quickly as membership rotates quickly. Therefore, a group is unable to establish a long-term political relationship with long tenured individuals who may serve on a committee for decades. Instead, it appears that the groups have changed their strategy and instead are basing their contributions upon political party affiliation and are using the party organization as a structure to guide their donations. These findings are consistent with findings in another study (Moncrief and Thompson, 2001) which suggest that lobbyists believe power in post-term limits California shifted away from individual members and to permanent organizations like party, professional staff, and even the governor. Such activity may reinforce the trend toward greater party cohesion in the legislature.

## Direct Democracy and Interest Groups

Like most of the western United States, California has a system of direct democracy (see Chapter 3). The progressive reformers believed, among other things, that direct democracy would provide a way for the citizens to thwart monopolistic control of governing by the entrenched special interests. Some recent commentators suggest that this progressive dream has been replaced with an initiative industry of high priced campaign firms hired by entrenched interest groups (Broder, 2002).

However, an analysis of interest group use of the initiative process in California suggests a different conclusion (Donovan et al., 1998). In their analysis of California general election initiatives from 1986 to 1996, the researchers found a substantial difference between the success rates of broad, diffuse interests, and narrow special interests. The success rate for the initiatives pushed by broad and diffuse groups was much higher than the success rate for those measures sponsored by narrow, special interest groups. Only 14% of the measures supported by narrow groups passed while approximately 52% of those measures supported by broad, diffuse groups passed. These findings were preliminary but suggest that perhaps a certain type of interest group (narrow special interests) is disadvantaged while using the direct democracy system in California. Therefore, it is not surprising that these interest groups focus their energy on traditional lobbying and use of campaign contributions within the legislature itself.

These findings do not, however, suggest that interest groups—even narrow ones— avoid our system of direct democracy. As Californians we know this is not true. In fact, some scholars have argued that California is in an era that can be described as *"Initiative-Centered Politcs"* (McCuan and Stambough, 2005). This new politics is in many western states but with California as the centerpiece. One part of initiative-centered politics is that there is an advantage to interest groups using the initiative process even if they are fairly certain they will lose on Election Day. Since politics is a repeated game, losing on Election Day is not viewed as the end of the process. Narrow groups also use the initiative process for many purposes other than passing a law. Some use it to help promote an agenda for long-term adjustments in public opinion. Some use it to demonstrate regional strength even in a statewide defeat in order to pressure regional legislators to support their agenda in the legislative process. Others employ a countermeasure strategy that designed to confuse voters into not passing other, similar legislation. These strategies do not always work, but they provide an answer to why narrow interest groups continue to use the initiative process even with knowledge of the low success rate of such groups actually passing legislation directly by the voters.

## Conclusion

In California, political parties and interest groups act within a unique environment of historic attempts to weaken their influence and an open system, especially direct democracy that can actually increase their influence. Knowing their goals, resources, and impact on voters and policy are key to understanding their activities within our state.

# CHAPTER 5

# Race and Ethnicity in California Politics

*Scott J. Spitzer*

## Introduction: Curing the Mischiefs of Faction

It is a common misnomer that our founding fathers created a Constitution that would above all else empower the public through democracy. In fact, the framers of the Constitution were wary of democracy, while recognizing that only a government consented to by the people could be legitimate.[1] James Madison, who is often referred to as the father of the Constitution, was deeply concerned that democracy without limits would result in a "tyranny of the majority." His solution, beyond the checks and balances of the Constitutional order, was to promote the greatest possible diversity of "factions" so that none could ever claim a ready and near-permanent majority to the detriment of others.[2] In considering California's tremendous multicultural and multi-ethnic diversity, this Madisonian vision of factional diversity has arrived. The incentives and opportunities for cross-racial and ethnic cooperation are strong in California politics, but there are long-term historical legacies and strong differences in the social, economic, and political experiences of each group that impose obstacles to such coalition building. Moreover, the largest groups can achieve many of their goals without establishing political partnerships across racial/ethnic differences. This chapter offers an overview of the state's racial and ethnic diversity, the political experiences of the largest of these groups, and the opportunities and challenges that are presented in seeking to overcome a divisive politics: what Madison called "the mischief of factions."

In particular, the analysis focuses on the degree to which the major racial and ethnic groups in the state have achieved **political incorporation**. The latter is defined as "the extent to which self-identified group interests are articulated, represented, and met in public policymaking."[3] The degree to which a group is successfully politically incorporated can be assessed by investigating (1) the level of their political participation,

---

[1]For an excellent articulation of this perspective, see Robert Dahl, 2003. *How Democratic is the U.S. Constitution? Second Edition.* New Haven, CT: Yale University Press.

[2]Issac Kramnick, ed., 1987. James Madison, Alexander Hamilton and John Jay, *The Federalist Papers.* New York: Penguin Books. Paper number X, pp. 122–128.

[3]The term political incorporation is drawn from Rufus P. Browning, Dale Rogers Marshall, and David H. Tabb, *Racial Politics in American Cities, 3/E.* Upper Saddle River, NJ: Pearson. See esp. Chapter 1. This description is drawn from a discussion of their work in: Ricardo Ramirez and Luis Fraga, 2008. "Continuity and Change: Latino Political Incorporation in California since 1990." Chapter 4 in Sandra Bass and Bruce E. Cain, eds., *Racial and Ethnic Politics in California: Continuity and Change.* Berkeley, CA: Berkeley Public Policy Press, Institute of Governmental Studies, pp. 64–67.

(2) the number of their group that are elected as political officials, and (3) the achievement of policies that address important needs in their communities.[4] In addition, given the multicultural and multi-ethnic diversity of the state, it is also important to assess how these groups can both achieve political incorporation for themselves while simultaneously creating larger state-wide majorities in coalition with other groups. These are the central questions briefly addressed in this chapter, and they are essential for a more in-depth study of California's racial and ethnic politics.

## Diversity in the Golden State

California is not only the most populous state in the nation it is the most diverse as well. In 2000, California became a **minority-majority** state, with the combined population of racial and ethnic minorities exceeding 50%.[5] With a population including sizeable groups of immigrants from over 60 nations, and with no group claiming a majority of the state's population, in 2014 Latinos surpassed whites as the largest racial/ethnic group in the state (see Table 5.1). This diversity has been a part of California's development from the state's beginnings, as waves of migration and immigration have added population and new groups to the state. In the years since the passage of the 1965 Immigration and Nationality Act, which liberalized national immigration policy and allowed for increased flows of immigrants from Latin America, Asia, Eastern Europe and other regions of the world, the state's population grew tremendously. Beginning in the 1970s, California experienced the largest wave of immigration in its history, with millions of new Americans coming into the state from Mexico, China, Vietnam, and scores of other nations.

**Table 5.1**   California's Diverse Population, 2014[6]

|  | Population | % |
| --- | --- | --- |
| Total | 38,451,604 | 100.00 |
| Hispanic | 14,996,759 | 39.00 |
| White only | 14,900,962 | 38.80 |
| Asian | 5,014,573 | 13.00 |
| American Indian | 167,128 | 0.40 |
| African American | 2,216,250 | 5.80 |
| 2 or more races | 1,017,655 | 2.60 |

[4]The term political incorporation is drawn from Rufus P. Browning, Dale Rogers Marshall, and David H. Tabb, *Racial Politics in American Cities, Third Edition.* Upper Saddle River, NJ: Pearson. See esp. Chapter 1.

[5]I use the term minority here with some reservations. In California, no racial or ethnic group is a majority of the population. However, historically, African-Americans, Latinos, and Asian-Americans have been identified as racial/ethnic minorities and treated as such by the U.S. census. I adopt this common use of the term here, despite the fact that no group is a majority anymore in California.

[6]Author's calculations based on projections from California Department of Finance, 2013. *Report P-3: State and County Total Population Projections by Race/Ethnicity and Detailed Age, 2010–2060.* Accessed on September 16, 2014 at: http://www.dof.ca.gov/research/demographic/reports/projections/p-3

The current diversity emerged rapidly throughout the 1980s and 1990s. In 1970, nearly 80% of the state's population was white, but by the end of the 1990s whites were a slim majority—52%—of the state's population.[7] As noted above, currently whites are no longer the largest racial group in the state, and demographers project that they will become an increasingly smaller proportion of the state's population as birth rates among whites are far outstripped by birthrates among Latinos and Asian Americans.

California has therefore emerged in the early 21st century as the new "Ellis Island" for the United States.[8] It now has the largest proportions of the nation's Latinos, Asian Americans, American Indians and Alaska Natives, and the third largest population of African Americans (see Table 5.2). The much smaller proportion of African Americans, compared to these other groups, is of particular interest in understanding California's racial/ethnic politics, and will be taken up in greater detail below.

**Table 5.2**   California's Share of National Racial & Ethnic Minorities, 2013[9]

|  | Hispanics (%) | Asian (%) | American Indian (%) | African American (%) |
|---|---|---|---|---|
| California's share | 27.8 | 33 | 17 | 6 |
| Next largest state share of group's population | TX: 18.7 | NY: 10 | OK: 9 | FI & NY: 8 each |

These changes in the state's population offer powerful cultural and political implications for California and for the nation as a whole. Indeed, this advanced state of racial and ethnic diversity in California is likely to be replicated in a number of other states throughout the nation in the near future. Already Hawaii, New Mexico, and Texas are minority-majority states, and based on U.S. census figures, we can safely assume that Nevada, Maryland, Georgia, and Florida will reach that status in the next decade.[10] By 2043, moreover, the census projects that the United States as a whole will be minority-majority, led by population growth in western and southern states, as well as in a select number of east-coast, highly urbanized states.[11]

As California leads the nation with rapidly expanding racial and ethnic diversity, what can we learn from the resulting political opportunities and challenges? In some

---

[7]Belinda I. Reyes, ed., 2001. *A Portrait of Race and Ethnicity in California: An Assessment of Social and Economic Well-Being.* San Francisco, CA: Public Policy Institute of California, p. 6.

[8]Ellis Island was the entry point for millions of new immigrants to the United States in the years before and after World War I. For an excellent overview of the history and politics of American Immigration policy, see Daniel J. Tichenor, 2002. *Dividing Lines: The Politics of Immigration Control in America.* Princeton, NJ: Princeton University Press.

[9]Author's calculations based on U.S. Census Bureau data. Hispanic population figures are calculated from U.S. Census Bureau, 2010 Census, Summary File 1. All other figures are calculated from U.S. Census Bureau, 2014. *Annual Estimates of the Resident Population by Sex, Race, and Hispanic Origin for the United States, States, and Counties: April 1, 2010—July 1, 2013.*

[10]*Statistical Abstract of the United States,* ProQuest online edition. 2014. Table 19: Resident Population by Hispanic Origin and State, 2012. Accessed on September 19, 2014.

[11]U.S. Census Bureau, 2012. "U.S. Census Bureau Projections Show a Slower Growing, Older, More Diverse Nation a Half Century from Now." Accessed on September 23, 2014, at https://www.census.gov/newsroom/releases/archives/population/cb12-243.html.

ways the California's experience with diversity is instructive: cities and states with increasingly racially and ethnically diverse populations, and the nation as a whole, can learn from California's efforts to successfully represent their changing population in government and policymaking. On the other hand, California is in many ways a unique political system, a hybrid of republican government and direct democracy, with an unusually large number of local governments and special districts. As the state has no single racial or ethnic majority, groups must partner with each other to achieve the state-wide majorities needed to elect the Governor and other executives (see Chapter 7), and to pass or block initiatives or referenda (see Chapter 3).

At the same time, however, as immigrants have tended to settle in relatively homogenous communities with others who share their national, racial, and ethnic background—**ethnic enclaves**—they may achieve a majority or large plurality of voters for elections in smaller, local electoral districts. This makes it possible for the largest groups—especially Latinos—to achieve substantial representation in the state legislature, as these representatives are elected in smaller jurisdictions.

One result is that in the most recent Congress, 13 of California's 53 elected members of the U.S. House of Representatives were Latinos: 25% of the state's House delegation.[12] For the most recent state legislature, 9 state senators (22%) and 17 members of the state assembly (21%) were Latinos, and the last three Speakers of the Assembly—the most powerful leader in the state legislature (see Chapter 8)—have been Latinos.[13] These trends are even more pronounced in elections for local government: In 2014, Latinos were 407 of the state's county or municipal leaders, 717 of the state's elected education and school board officials, and 84 of the state's elected judicial and law enforcement officials.[14] Latinos have also been elected Mayor in some of the state's largest cities, such as Los Angeles's Antonio Villaraigosa and most recently Robert Garcia in Long Beach. However, the state has yet to elect a Latino Governor and currently there are no Latino state-wide elected executives, although in 2014 Alex Padilla was elected as Secretary of State.[15] Moreover, in the 1990s, a series of state initiatives aimed at imposing restrictions on new immigrants passed by wide margins, despite being opposed by the majority of Latinos. The most notable was proposition 187 which passed in 1994, denying unauthorized immigrants public services, including education. Proposition 187 was overturned by

---

[12]Author's calculations based on Latino Decisions, 2013. "Latino Representation in the 113th Congress." Accessed on September 23, 2014 at http://www.latinodecisions.com/blog/2013/01/25/latino-representation-in-the-113th-congress/.

[13]David G. Lawrence and Jeffrey Cummings, 2013. *California: The Politics of Diversity.* Stamford CT: Cengage Learning. Table 7.1, p. 124.

[14]National Association of Latino Elected Officials (NALEO), 2014. *Hispanic Public Elected Officials, by Office and State.* Accessed on September 19, 2014, at www.naleo.org.

[15]California Secretary of State, 2014. *California Roster, 2014.* Accessed on September 5, 2014 at http://www.sos.ca.gov/admin/ca-roster.htm. In 2014, Padilla was elected in the statewide race for Secretary of State, with 53.6% of the vote. "California General Election: Semi-Official Election Results," December 5, 2014. Accessed on December 7 at http://www.vote.sos.ca.gov. There has been one Latino Governor, but he was not elected and served for less than one year. Romualdo Pacheco became Governor in 1875 when Governor Newton Booth was elected to the U.S. Senate. Pacheco served until the next Governor was elected. See U.S. Library of Congress, *Hispanic Americans in Congress, 1822–1995.* N.D. accessed on September 23, 2014, at http://www.loc.gov/rr/hispanic/congress/pacheco.html.

a federal court in 1997, and it galvanized Latino political activity to oppose the measure (see more discussion below).[16]

The other sizeable racial/ethnic groups—Asian Americans and African Americans in particular—have also been relatively successful in locally based elections, and less so in statewide contests. However, their respective political experiences in achieving political incorporation have been quite different. It should be noted that the historical political experience of these groups in California, and in the United States more broadly, are very different. These historical differences have led to different experiences and different timing in the achievement of political incorporation. As the relative political incorporation of each group is assessed in terms of participation, election to government, and achievement of policies benefiting their group, these different historical experiences will also be considered.

## Political Participation of California's Racial/Ethnic Minorities

The first measure of political incorporation is the participation of a group in politics. The most visible and arguably most important facet of this participation is voting. Voter registration rates for Californians have increased significantly over the last decade, with 17.7 million people registered—nearly three-fourths of eligible voters. The demographics of registered voters, however, differ considerably from the population as a whole: whites are a clear majority of the state's registered voters—56%—while Latinos are only 22% of registered voters.[17] While whites are no longer the majority population of the state, they are the majority among the participating electorate. The gap between white and non-white voting turnout is more pronounced the less visible the elections. In the 2008 election, when Barack Obama was elected president, voting turnout in California was historically high, and the differences between whites and other racial/ethnic groups were narrow. For that historic election, 57% of Hispanic citizens voted, 11.5 percentage points fewer than whites. However, in 2010, when there was no presidential election, 35.4% of Hispanic citizens voted, more than 20 percentage points lower than the 56% of whites voting in that election (see Table 5.3). This gap is all the more remarkable considering that in 2010 there was a gubernatorial election in the state where immigration policy was a centrally important issue. Given the importance of immigration to Latino voters, one might have expected more Latinos to participate than these data reveal (see Chapter 7 herein). In 2014, this trend was repeated: Despite being 39% of of the state's population, whites were 59% of the voting electorate in that election, while Latinos, who slightly outnumber whites in the overall population, were only 18% of the state's electorate. Asian Americans, who are 13% of the state's popula-

---

[16]Terry Christensen and Larry N. Gerston. 2008. "Initiatives as Catalysts for Racial Politics," Chapter 6 in Bass and Cain, eds., *Racial and Ethnic Politics in California*. Berkeley, CA: Berkeley Public Policy Press, Institute of Governmental Studies.

[17]Dean Bonner and Eric McGhee, March 2014. "Party Registration in California." *Just the Facts*. San Francisco, CA: Public Policy Institute of California. Accessed on September 5, 2014, at http://www.ppic.org/main/publication_show.asp?i=1090.

tion were only 11% of the electorate, but African Americans, who are 5.8% of the state's population were 8% of the state's electorate.[18]

While Latinos are more numerous than African Americans, the latter vote at significantly higher rates. For example, in the 2012 presidential election, 61.1% of African Americans voted, while only 48.5% of Hispanics voted. Asian Americans tend to vote at even lower rates than Latinos: in 2008 52.4% of Asians voted compared to 57% of Latinos (although in 2012 Asians and Latinos voted at virtually the same rate).

**Table 5.3**   Registration and Voting Turnout Rates Among California's Racial/Ethnic Groups 2000–2012[19]

| | Percent (18+) | Percent Registered Citizen 18+ | Percent Voted (18+) | Percent Voted |
|---|---|---|---|---|
| **Year 2008** | | | | |
| Total Population | 55.1 | 68.2 | 51.2 | **63.4** |
| White non-Hispanic alone | 69.8 | 72.9 | 65.6 | **68.5** |
| Black alone | 65.7 | 67.2 | 63.8 | **65.2** |
| Asian alone | 43.8 | 59.4 | 38.7 | **52.4** |
| Hispanic (of any race) | 36.8 | 62.8 | 33.4 | **57.0** |
| **Year 2010** | | | | |
| Total Population | 50.6 | 60.9 | 39.2 | **47.1** |
| White non-Hispanic alone | 66.0 | 68.4 | 54.1 | **56.0** |
| Black alone | 54.0 | 56.1 | 41.0 | **42.6** |
| Asian alone | 38.1 | 50.1 | 26.1 | **34.3** |
| Hispanic (of any race) | 33.6 | 52.0 | 22.9 | **35.4** |
| **Year 2012** | | | | |
| Total Population | 54.2 | 65.6 | 47.5 | **57.5** |
| White non-Hispanic alone | 69.4 | 72.0 | 61.9 | **64.3** |
| Black alone | 65.8 | 68.5 | 58.7 | **61.1** |
| Asian alone | 42.0 | 57.9 | 35.2 | **48.6** |
| Hispanic (of any race) | 37.1 | 56.6 | 31.8 | **48.5** |

[18]Figures are from CNN's exit polls, at http://www.cnn.com/election/2014/results/state/CA/Governor#exit-polls. November 20, 2014. Accessed on December 7, 2014. See table 5.1 for state population figures by race and ethnicity.

[19]Author's calculations based on figures from the U.S. Census Bureau, *Current Population Survey, 2008, 2010 and 2012, Table 4b: "Reported Voting and Registration of the Total Voting Age Population, by sex, Race and Hispanic Origin for States."* Accessed at http://www.census.gov/hhes/www/socdemo/voting/publications, on September 5, 2014.

The impact of these lower turnout rates among the traditional racial and ethnic minority groups is muted in California, for several reasons. First, the Democratic Party has a huge advantage over the state's Republican Party: 43.4% of the state's voters are registered as Democrats versus 28.4% as Republicans (those with no party preference are 21.2% of registered voters).[20] Since more than three-fourths of Republican likely voters are white, the large numbers of Latino, Asian American, and African American voters for Democrats can still elect Democrats despite lower turnout among these constituencies.[21] As a result, Democrats won huge victories in the state's 2010 elections, despite the fact that whites were 71% of likely voters, according to a field poll taken just before that election. In fact, in 2010 Latinos were only 16%, Asian Americans 8%, and African Americans 5% of likely voters (the lower percentage of African Americans is primarily a function of their far smaller share of the overall population).[22] Governor Brown easily won the election, defeating Republican Meg Whitman with 53.8% of the vote to Whitman's 40.9%. Moreover, Democrats widened their advantage in the state legislature to a two-thirds majority.[23] This is particularly noteworthy, as Republicans swept to a new majority in the House of Representatives, and won major victories in state elections across the nation—except in California. In 2014, these patterns were repeated. Whites were overrepresented in the electorate as noted above, but this didn't alter the outcome of the election. While 54% of whites voted for Governor Brown, 89% of African Americans and 73% of Latinos did as well.[24] Democrats won every statewide elected executive election, and continue to dominate the state's congressional delegation, with 37 Democrats and 14 Republicans in the House of Representatives and 2 Democrats in the U.S. Senate. In other words, despite winning a smaller majority of white votes compared to racial and minority votes, Democrats still dominated the state's elections.

Besides the dominance of the state's Democratic Party, and the strong favoring of that party by racial minorities, a second reason that the lower turnout among these groups is muted is the growing size of their combined population. As racial minorities continue to account for an increasing share of the state's population, despite lower turnout rates their portion of the state's active electorate is also increasing. In 2012, Latinos, Asian Americans, and African Americans combined were nearly 40% of the state's voters, which was about the same as their share of the population. In that election, Obama's large victory over Republican nominee Mitt Romney in California was nearly entirely accounted for by continuing support from the state's racial and ethnic minority groups.[25]

---

[20]Mark Baldassare, Dean Bonner, and Jui Shrestha, August 2014. "California's Likely Voters," *Just the Facts*. San Francisco, CA: Public Policy Institute of California. Accessed on September 5, 2014, at http://www.ppic.org/main/publication_show.asp?i=526.

[21]Ibid. About half of Democratic likely voters are white, while 23% are Latino, 12% are Asian, and 11% are African-American.

[22]Mark DiCamillo and Mervin Field, November 2, 2010. "About 9.5 Million Californians Expected to Participate in Today's Election." *The Field Poll, release #2366*, Table 3, p. 5.

[23]California Secretary of State, November 2, 2010. *Statement of Vote. Revised January 6, 2011*. Accessed on August 21, 2014 at http://www.sos.ca.gov/elections/sov/2010-general/complete- sov.pdf.

[24]CNN exit polls, at http://www.cnn.com/election/2014/results/state/CA/Governor#exit-polls, November 20, 2014. Accessed on December 7, 2014.

[25]Mark DiCamillo, November 19, 2012. "The Growing Political Might of Ethnic Voters in the 2012 California Elections." *The Field Poll, release #2435*, p. 1.

Therefore, while their turnout may be low, these groups' overall numbers are so large that they still provide a winning margin for candidates in statewide elections.

Third, all three of these groups—Latinos, African Americans, and Asian Americans—have favored the Democratic Party's candidates in recent years. This creates a majority coalition that is a formidable opponent for the state's Republican Party. This coalition has been successful in recent elections, as they joined together in voting for Governor Brown, U.S. Senator Boxer, President Obama, and for initiatives such as Proposition 30 in 2010, which raised taxes on the state's wealthiest individuals in order to close the state's debt and increase funding for public education. In 2014, as noted above, both African Americans and Latinos continued with these trends, voting for Governor Brown in large majorities However, according to Karthick Ramakrishnan, Asian Americans may be moving slightly in the direction of the Republican Party. In 2014, two Asian candidates won election to the state legislature as Republicans: Janet Nguyen is a newly elected Vietnamese state Senator from the 39th district, and Young Kim is a newly elected Korean Assemblywoman from the 65th district.[26]

Still, the continued gap between the voting turnout of whites and traditional racial and ethnic minorities in California may explain some of the challenges that these groups have faced in the two other areas of political incorporation: representation through elective office and policymaking addressing their community's priorities. In particular, if each group votes independently of the other groups, and coalition partnerships are weak, then political incorporation at these two levels will be incomplete.

# Representation of California's Racial/ Ethnic Minorities in Government

Groups must be able to achieve representation in government to be able to realize their collective political and policymaking goals. Members of a given racial/ethnic minority may be well served by elected officials who are not from their group, who can provide **substantive representation**—representation of their group interests in policymaking. However, a level of **ascriptive representation** is an important indicator of political incorporation, whereby the proportion of state and local government leaders from a particular racial/ethnic group approximates their proportion in the population.

Table 5.4 indicates that whites and Democrats have a greater representation in California's legislature and congressional delegation than their general population, while women, Latinos, and Asian Americans are underrepresented. African Americans are slightly underrepresented in the state's congressional delegation and state Senate, but are overrepresented in the Assembly. These figures suggest two things. First, participation gaps between whites and non-whites have an impact on election outcomes. Second, the longer a group has been actively engaged in politics, the more likely they are to achieve elected office.

---

[26]Taeku Lee, November 10, 2014. "Did Asian Americans Switch Parties Overnight? No." *The Monkey Cage. Washington Post.* At www.washington post.com/blogs/monkey-cage/wp/2014/11/10/did-asian-americans-switch-parties-overnight.

**Table 5.4**   California State Legislature Ascriptive Representation, 2013–2014[27]

|  | Senate (40 total) % (Number) | Assembly (80 total) % (Number) | % of State's Congressional Delegation (53 House & 2 Senators) | % of the State Population |
|---|---|---|---|---|
| Democrats | 73 (29) | 69 (55) | 73 (40) | 43.6 |
| Republicans | 28 (11) | 31 (25) | 28 (15) | 28.7 |
| Women | 14 (11) | 26 (21) | 36 (20) | 50.3 |
| White | 60 (24) | 45 (56) | 63 (35) | 38.8 |
| Latinos | 23 (9) | 21 (17) | 16 (9) | 39 |
| African Americans | 5 (2) | 9 (7) | 5 (3) | 5.8 |
| Asian Americans | 8 (3) | 10 (8) | 4 (2) | 13 |

African Americans were able to gain political incorporation over the long-term, having arrived in California in large numbers during the early post-World War II years. Following the Civil Rights movement of the 1960s, African American voter participation climbed in California. Blacks were elected to leadership positions in the state legislature—the Speaker of the Assembly was led by San Francisco's Willie Brown for more than a decade in the 1980s and early 1990s, and Karen Bass of Los Angeles recently held the position as well. Los Angeles Mayor Tom Bradley was the first black mayor of a major American city, and served five terms in that position.[28] While their political influence in the state may be waning, as they are overshadowed by the rapid growth and large size of Latinos, African Americans have developed strong local political organizations and voter loyalties in Assembly, Senate, and House of Representatives districts.

As a consequence, although African Americans are only about 6% of the state's population, California recently elected (2010) its first African American Attorney General, and African Americans are overrepresented (compared to their population) in the Assembly, and historically among the leadership positions in the state legislature. However, while Governor Brown won his election in 2010 by over 1 million votes, Attorney

---

[27]Data on racial breakdown of legislators drawn from David G. Lawrence and Jeffrey Cummings, 2013. *California: The Politics of Diversity.* Stamford CT: Cengage Learning. Table 7.1, p. 124. Data on white members of state legislature compiled by author.

   Data on party registration in California are from California Secretary of State, December 31, 2013. "154-Day Report of Registration." http://www.sos.ca.gov/elections/ror/ror-pages/154day-primary-2014/historical-reg-stats.pdf, accessed on September 24, 2014.

   Data on percent female from U.S. Census Bureau, 2013. *State and County Quick Facts: California.* Accessed on June 17, 2014 at http://quickfacts.census.gov/qfd/states/06000.html.

   Data on California's Congressional delegation from: National Association of Latino Elected Officials (NALEO), Education Fund, *2014 Latino Primary Profile: California,* p. 5; Ava Alexandar, 2010. *Citizen Legislators or Political Musical Chairs: Term Limits in California.* Center for Governmental Studies: Los Angeles, pp. 20–21.

   See Table 1 for data on California's racial/ethnic minority populations. Numbers do not total 40 Senators or 80 assembly members due to: vacancies; 2 members of the Assembly with Middle Eastern ethnicity; and minor parties.

[28]On the Bradley Mayoralty and racial/ethnic politics in Los Angeles, see Raphael J. Sonnenshein, 1993. *Politics in Black and White: Race and Power in Los Angeles.* Princeton, NJ: Princeton University Press.

General Kamala Harris won her statewide election by fewer than 100,000 votes, garnering 46.1% of the vote versus. Steve Cooley's 45.3%.[29] While these were different elections, both occurred among the same voters. With one Democrat winning by a wide margin, and the other by a narrow one, this suggests that race may have been a factor in limiting the size of Harris's victory. It also points to the challenge that racial minorities have in reaching the statewide majorities required to win executive office.[30]

Asian Americans have not achieved the same measure of political incorporation as Latinos or African Americans. Although they account for approximately 13% of the state's population, they are only 8% of the state's Senators, 10% of the state's Assembly members, and 4% of the state's elected members of the U.S. Congress (see Table 5.4). Asian Americans have two statewide elected executives after the 2014 elections: John Chiang, the state Treasurer, and Betty Yee, the state Controller—and three members of the Board of Equalization is also Asian American. In contrast to African Americans, who have long been actively engaged politically, and who have higher voter turnout rates than any other racial/ethnic minority in the state, Asian Americans have tended to shy away from political engagement historically. There are two reasons that scholars advance as explanation for this lack of political engagement in the Asian American community. First, Asian Americans have tended to focus their efforts on economic and educational advancement rather than political advancement. First and second generation Chinese, Vietnamese, and Filipino immigrants have settled in ethnic enclaves and sought to create successful small businesses and put their children through universities and graduate school. While this does not preclude political engagement, in many Asian American communities running for office or issue advocacy has been less of a focus than these other priorities. Second, the Asian American community is far less unified politically than African Americans or Latinos in California. While 43% of Asian Americans in California supported Barack Obama in the 2012 election, 21% supported Mitt Romney.[31] This is in contrast to the overall vote for Obama in California, who received 60.2% of the vote versus 37.1% for Romney.[32] Moreover, there were considerable differences among ethnic groups, with Japanese Californians supporting Obama the strongest (56%), and Filipinos supporting Romney the strongest (33%).[33] In terms of party identification, a large proportion of Asian Americans are non-partisan: 52%. This reflects, at least in part, an overall reluctance about passionate engagement in political activity, and a lack of long-standing ties with established political organizations.

---

[29]California Secretary of State, November 2, 2010. *Statement of Vote. Revised January 6, 2011.* Accessed on August 21, 2014 at http://www.sos.ca.gov/elections/sov/2010-general/complete-sov.pdf.

[30]Harris won her 2014 election by a much larger margin, winning 57.5% of the vote. This suggests being an incumbent trumped Harris's racial identity in helping her win reelection. California Secretary of State, 2014. "California General Election: Semi-Official Election Results." December 5, 2014. At http://www.vote.sos. ca.gov. Accessed December 7, 2014,

[31]Karthick Ramakrishnan and Taeku Lee, 2012. *The 2012 General Election: Public Opinion of Asian Americans in California.* National Asian American Survey (NAAS), p. 4.

[32]California Secretary of State, November 6, 2012. *Statement of Vote. General Election.* Accessed on August 21, 2014 at http://www.sos.ca.gov/elections/sov/2012-general/sov- complete.pdf.

[33]Ramakrishnan and Lee, 2012. p. 4.

Based on this cursory examination of the data, the political incorporation of California's racial and ethnic minorities remains incomplete. Whites continue to dominate the state executive positions, and are disproportionately represented in the state legislature and U.S. congressional delegation. While Latinos, African Americans, and Asian Americans have achieved a measure of success in the state legislature, and in many local governments across the state, making the leap to a statewide office requires successful partnerships with other groups.

In some ways, the fact that large majorities of Latinos and African American, and a smaller majority of Asian Americans, identify as Democrats, helps to explain why the party has a disproportionate level of representation in the state legislature and congressional delegation. With 44% of the state's registered voters identifying as Democrats, the party has three-fourths of the seats in the state legislature and in the state's congressional delegation. Matt Barreto and his co-authors have argued that Latinos help California stay a "safe democratic state" and that this has been critical both locally and nationally. California sends the largest delegation of any state to Congress, and therefore is central to the Democrats' effort to close their gap with the Republicans in the House of Representatives.[34] The combined support of the state's racial/ethnic minorities for Obama in 2008 and 2012, and for Governor Brown in 2010, have made California a strong Democratic state over the past decade. This suggests that when groups are allied with each other, the majority-minority status of the state can produce outcomes that majorities of each group desires.

## Policy Representation

While a full review of racial/ethnic minority engagement in public policymaking in California is beyond the scope of this chapter, it is worthwhile to briefly examine this last level of political incorporation. Participation and electoral representation are valuable intrinsically. Increased levels of civic engagement through voting and other forms of political activity demonstrate to other Californians that Latinos, African Americans, and Asian Americans have a critical role to play in the governing of the state. Moreover, increased participation is often contagious: as other members of the group witness the interest and activity of confirmation of the group's importance in civic affairs, they are also important in and of themselves. But the end goal of participation and electoral power is to redirect government policies and resources toward the collective priorities of one's community.

In many ways, the policy concerns of Latinos, African Americans, and Asian Americans are no different than those of whites: good jobs, quality public education, safe and secure communities, a clean environment, and reasonably low taxes. For example, Asian Americans' issue priorities in the 2012 election were similar to the rest of the nation: the

[34]Matt Barreto, Ricardo Ramirez, Luis R. Fraga, and Fernando Guerra, 2009. "Why California Matters: How California Latinos Influence the Presidential Election." Chapter 7 in Rodolfo de la Garza, Louis DeSipio and David Leal, eds., *Beyond the Barrio: Latinos in the 2004 Elections*. South Bend, IN: University of Notre Dame Press.

economy and jobs were their foremost concerns.[35] At the same time, there are distinctive concerns that have long been central to racial minorities in particular: economic inequality and poverty, access to quality education, and immigration. While there are other issues—civil rights and voting rights for example—these three are particularly important for Latinos, African Americans, and Asian Americans in contemporary California.

## Economic Inequality and Poverty

Poverty rates in California are higher than in most of the nation: nearly 17% of the population is below the federal poverty line, which is the 16th highest percentage of all the states in the nation.[36] At the same time, California has some of the wealthiest people nationally, and therefore has a very large gap between the "haves" and "have-nots." Latinos and African Americans have higher poverty rates than other groups in the state, with about 24% of each group below the poverty line. In contrast, Asian Americans and whites have far lower poverty rates, at 12.6% and 9.8%, respectively.[37] In addition, in 2013 while 36% of African-American children and 32% of Latino children in California lived below the poverty line, only 12% of Asian American and 11% of white children were poor.[38]

These data suggest that California's Latino and African American populations, who are better represented in state and local government than Asian Americans, have yet to translate their political power into economic policies that have effectively diminished economic inequality and poverty among a sizeable proportion of their community. Moreover, it also suggests that these two groups have a strong incentive to form a coalition and advocate for policies that could address these issues, but that Asian Americans will likely not share an interest in this agenda.

## Access to Education

While California has one of the most expansive public education systems in the nation, ranging from publicly funded preschool through some of the best universities in the nation (UCLA, Berkeley), it also suffers from increasingly intense racial/ethnic segregation.[39] In 2008, Latino students were nearly half of the students in Southern California, heavily concentrated in Los Angeles, Riverside and San Bernardino. Meanwhile 17% of students in Orange County were Asian, nearly twice the share for the entire re-

---

[35]Ramakrishnan and Lee, 2012. p. 5.

[36]Alexander Hess, Alexander Kent, Thomas Frohlich, and Robert Serenbetz, September 18, 2014. "America's Richest (and Poorest) States." Accessed on September 24, 2014 at http://247wallst.com/special-report/2014/09/18americas-richest-and-poorest-states.html.

[37]Sarah Bohn and Matt Levin, August 2013. "Poverty in California," *Just the Facts.* San Francisco, CA: Public Policy Institute of California. Accessed at http://www.ppic.org on September 24, 2014.

[38]Data are from the Annie E. Casey Foundation, 2013. *Kids Count Data Center.* Accessed on September 24, 2014 at http://www.datacenter.kidscount.org.

[39]Gary Orfield, Genevieve siegel-Hawley and John Kucsera, March 18, 2011. *Divided We Fail: Segregation and Inequality in the Southland's Schools.* The Civil Rights Project: University of California Los Angeles.

gion. Nearly one-third of African American students were in heavily racially segregated schools.[40] In addition to segregation, there are some alarming educational outcomes for African American and Latinos in California. In Los Angeles for the 2012–2013 school year, 21% of African American students and 17% of Latino students dropped out of high school. This is in sharp contrast to the low dropout rates of Asian Americans, 8.3%. Whites in Los Angeles had a dropout rate near the Latino rate, at 16.4%.[41]

As Asian Americans advance educationally, with large proportions graduating from the state's colleges and universities, the educational gaps between racial/ethnic groups are increased. While millions of African Americans and Latinos have also graduated from the state's higher-education system, there are large numbers who never make it out of high school. As these groups attain political office, however, it will be difficult to translate that political power to more successful education policy. Education governance in California is tremendously decentralized. Elected local school boards and local superintendents set local education policy, receive funding from state education dollars, and are subject to policies passed by the state legislature and Governor. At the same time, there is a state board of education and state superintendent of public instruction. With all of these policymaking bodies, it is very difficult for any group to direct educational policy toward their goals.

## Immigration and Affirmative Action

Immigration is perhaps the most visible issue connected to race/ethnicity in the state. A number of popular initiatives have been passed in response to the rapidly increased diversity of the state. One of these, proposition 187 in 1994, was so divisive that it galvanized a relatively disengaged Latino electorate, leading to increasing rates of Latino political involvement in the state. Matt Barreto and Ricardo Ramirez have argued that this initiative ultimately pushed Latinos away from the Republican Party and toward their strong identification with the Democrats.[42] The experience with proposition 187 has had a long-term impact on Latino politics in the state. More than 15 years later, 80% of Latino voters were seriously concerned that former Governor Pete Wilson—who led the campaign for Prop 187—was one of the co-chairs of the 2010 campaign for Republican gubernatorial candidate Meg Whitman.[43] As noted above, Latinos supported Whitman's opponent, Jerry Brown, by a strong majority.

Still, it is worth noting that proposition 187 passed with large margins. The immigration issue is of great importance to the state's largest racial/ethnic minority—Latinos—but the potential for building a broad statewide coalition in favor of more

---

[40]Orfield et al., 2011, "Executive Summary," pp. 1–2.
[41]Data calculated from California Department of Education, Data Reporting Office. "Cohort Outcome data for the Class of 2012–13: District Results for Los Angeles Unified." Accessed on September 24, 2014 at http://www.cde.ca.gov/ds/.
[42]Matt Barreto and Ricardo Ramirez, 2013. "Anti-Immigrant Politics and Lessons for the GOP from California." *Latino Decisions*. Accessed at http://www.latinodecisions.com/blog/2013/09/20/anti-immigrant-politics-and-lessons-for-the- gop-from-california/ on June 15, 2014.
[43]Ibid.

liberal immigration reform is tenuous. Moreover, the immigration issue itself, while mobilizing Latino voters, is not a strong mobilizing issue for African American voters. Some have argued that as the Latino population in the state has increased in size, African Americans have lost political power, and that immigration can be a potential "wedge" issue dividing these two otherwise potential coalition partners away from one another. Alternatively, there may be potential for Latinos to link with Asian Americans over this issue in the future, but a Latino-Asian coalition is difficult to achieve. As noted above, Asian Americans are generally more prosperous and less politically engaged than Latinos. How the diverse racial/ethnic groups in California forge majority coalitions around immigration or other issues will be a central concern in California politics.

## Conclusions: Racial/Ethnic Coalition Building in California?

While Latinos and African Americans have been more mobilized for participation and have been more successful in winning election to office, Asian Americans have done better economically and educationally. How can the successfully politically incorporated groups forge political ties with the least mobilized but most economically successful racial/ethnic minority group in California: Asian Americans? California's experience with two popular initiatives suggests potential for achieving this kind of political unity.

Affirmative action in education is an issue that divides these groups. Proposition 209 was passed in 1996, ending affirmative action in state and local government programs including admissions to the University of California system. It was strongly opposed by the Latino and African American political leadership. Since it went into effect, African American and Latino enrollment in the UC system declined precipitously.[44] A recent proposal by Latino state legislators to reinstate affirmative action in the UC admissions process has stalled, as Asian American Democratic legislators joined with Republicans to defeat the bill.

The potential for coalition building among African Americans and Latinos in support of affirmative action is there, but Asian Americans who have high rates of admission to the UC system are less likely support such measure.

However, the recent experience of proposition 30 suggests that the differences between Asian Americans and Latinos and African Americans can be bridged. Proposition 30, which passed in 2012 by a sizeable majority, temporarily raised taxes on the state's wealthiest individuals in an effort to close California's large budget deficit and to increase funding for public education. Although Asian Americans are more prosperous than Latinos and African Americans as a whole, large majorities of all three groups supported the measure: 61% of Asian Americans, 62% of African Americans, and 58% of Latinos were in favor of proposition 30 in September 2012, just before the election. Whites were

---

[44]Terry Christensen and Larry N. Gerston. 2008. "Initiatives as Catalysts for Racial Politics," Chapter 6 in Bass and Cain, eds, *Racial and Ethnic Politics in California*. Berkeley, CA: Berkeley Public Policy Press, Institute of Governmental Studies

less likely to support the measure at 47.2%.[45] As the initiative passed 55.4% to 44.6%, it is likely that the strong support of these three groups ensured its success. The capacity of this broad coalition to pass a tax increase for the purpose of balancing the state's budget *and* increasing spending on public education suggests that measures and candidates that can appeal to each of these three major racial/ethnic groups, for different reasons, will enjoy success. Proposition 30 may have been seen by Asian Americans as a reasonable way of balancing the state's budget, and thereby stabilizing the economy. For Latinos and African Americans, it may have been viewed as a measure that would improve the public schools and open up access to higher education. In the end, all supported the measure.

As California looks to a future where Latinos and Asian Americans will be the largest racial/ethnic groups, the immigration issue offers another opportunity to create a strong alliance. Policymakers eager to advance this issue will do well to consider the lessons from proposition 30. Any immigration reform will need to offer both groups an incentive to offer their support, if such a majority coalition is to emerge. More importantly, African Americans and whites will each need to find ways to forge partnerships with other groups—Latinos, Asians, each other—if they are to advance their policy interests. California's diversity requires that any policy proposals that require support from the majority of the state's voters be built on inter-ethnic/racial cooperation. Proposition 30 demonstrates that such a future is a real possibility.

---

[45]Data analyzed by author from California field poll, September 7–18, 2012. Data for this study, originally collected by the Field Research Corporation, were provided by the University of California Data Archive and Technical Assistance (UCDATA). UCDATA is not responsible for the analysis and interpretation of the data appearing here.

## CHAPTER 6

# Women in California Politics

*Valerie O'Regan*

"Toughness doesn't have to come in a pinstripe suit."
*Dianne Feinstein, U.S. Senator*

"My mother had a saying: 'Kamala, you may be the first to do many
things, but make sure you're not the last.'"
*Kamala Harris, California Attorney General*

Women are part of the political landscape in California. California voters have elected
women to the U.S. Senate and House of Representatives, the state Assembly and Senate,
as well as local and judicial offices throughout the state. In addition, women from various backgrounds have held leadership positions in both the national and state legislatures. Although there are still some political offices that have not been filled by women,
the number of these offices decreases every year. This chapter introduces the women in
California politics, from the national, state, and local levels of government.

## Women in the National Legislature

The general election of 1992 is often called "the Year of the Woman," and during that
election Californians elected two women, both Democrats, to represent their state in
the U.S. Senate. This was the first time that California had a female U.S. Senator. More
importantly, this was the first time that a state had two female Senators serving simultaneously, and both women were elected based on their own qualifications. Although both
women won their seats during the 1992 election, Dianne Feinstein's victory was in a special election to fill a vacancy due to Senator Pete Wilson's resignation from the U.S. Senate after he was elected governor of California in 1990. During the interim period from
1990 to 1992, State Senator John Seymour was appointed as U.S. Senator until the next
general election was held. Even though Senator Seymour was technically considered the
incumbent, Feinstein won the U.S. Senate seat with over 54% of the vote (Federal Election Commission, 1993) and assumed the seat on November 10, 1992, officially making
her the state's first female U.S. Senator. In 1994, when the Senate term originally won by
Pete Wilson in 1988 ended, Feinstein ran and won a full Senate term. The 1994 election
was much closer with Feinstein edging out Michael Huffington 46.7% to 44.8% to win

the seat (Federal Election Commission, 1995). However, Feinstein's re-election victories in 2000, 2006, and 2012 were far more decisive.[1]

Barbara Boxer is the other female Senator elected in 1992 although her term legally began on January 5, 1993. Boxer defeated her opponent Bruce Herschensohn, a conservative media commentator, by winning 48% of the vote to his 43% (Federal Election Commission, 1993). She won re-election in 1998, 2004, and 2010 with approximately 10% more votes than her opponents.[2]

Both women have built impressive political careers starting with getting elected at the local level of California politics. In 1969, Dianne Feinstein was elected to the San Francisco board of supervisors. During her eight years on the board she served as board president for 5 years. As a result of the assassinations of San Francisco Mayor George Moscone and Supervisor Harvey Milk on November 27, 1978, Feinstein was appointed mayor of the city making her the first female mayor of San Francisco. In 1979 she ran for the office of mayor and won, and was re-elected in 1983. In 1990, following her terms as mayor, Feinstein ran unsuccessfully for the office of governor; her opponent was U.S. Senator Pete Wilson. Two years later, Feinstein ran in the special election for the Senate seat previously held by Wilson (Wasniewski, 2006).

Similar to Feinstein, Barbara Boxer started her career as an elected official when she ran for and won a seat on the Marin County board of supervisors in 1976. In 1982, Boxer ran for an open seat in the House of Representatives; she defeated her Republican opponent with 52% of the vote. After five terms in the House, Boxer ran for the U.S. Senate seat she currently holds (Wasniewski, 2006).

Although it appears that women have been successful in getting elected to the U.S. Senate representing California, there was only one other viable female Senate candidate before the two current Senators. In 1950, California voters had their first opportunity to elect a female Senator when Democrat Helen Gahagan Douglas ran against Republican Richard M. Nixon. The 1950 race between Douglas, a singer, actress, member of the House of Representatives, and wife of actor Melvyn Douglas, and Nixon, the future Vice President and President, was considered one of the "dirtiest" in U.S. history. Nixon and his advisors employed fear-based tactics, such as overtly and covertly associating Douglas with Communism, as well as using sexist stereotypes such as questioning her toughness and dismissing her intellect, to campaign against his female opponent. During this race, Nixon referred to Douglas as the "Pink Lady" and Douglas referred to Nixon as "Tricky Dick" a nickname that would follow him throughout the rest of his political life. In the end, Nixon was the victor winning 59% of the vote and Douglas never ran for political office again (Denton, 2009).

Other firsts for women in California politics at the national level were when Nancy Pelosi was selected as the first female House of Representatives Democratic Whip in 2001, the first woman to be chosen by her colleagues to be House Democratic Leader

---

[1]According to the Federal Election Commission, Feinstein received 55.84% versus Tom Campbell's 36.59% in 2000, 59.43% versus 35.02% for Richard "Dick" Mountjoy in 2006, and in 2012 Feinstein won with 62.52 % against Elizabeth Emken's 37.48%.
[2]Based on Federal Election Commission data, in 1998 Boxer received 53.06% to Matt Fong's 43.01%, 57.71% to Bill Jones' 37.8% in 2004, and 52.18% versus 42.17% for Carly Fiorina in 2010.

in 2002, and the first female Speaker of the House of Representatives in 2007 (CAWP, 2014a). Prior to running for political office, Pelosi worked on political campaigns and held office in the California Democratic Party. In 1987, Pelosi won a special election to fill a vacancy in the House that resulted from the death of another female member of Congress, Sala Burton. To this day, Pelosi continues to represent her San Francisco district in the House and lead her party (Wasniewski, 2006).

Over the years, there have been 36 female members in the House of Representatives representing California, including 30 Democrats and 6 Republicans. The first woman elected to the House from California was Republican Mae Ella Nolan who was elected in 1922 by winning both a special election to replace her deceased husband, and a concurrent regular election. Nolan is one of seven California women who initially gained their seats in the House of Representatives by winning special elections to fill vacancies that were due to the death of their husbands (CAWP, 2014b).

Another important first in Congress occurred when Linda Sánchez was elected in 2002 to represent California's 39th Congressional District in the House of Representatives which meant that she would be serving in the House with her sister Loretta who also represents a district in California and was elected in 1996. This is the first time sisters have served simultaneously. Currently, California boasts of having 18 female representatives, all Democrats, out of the state's 53 seats in the House including Democratic Leader Pelosi (CAWP, 2014b).[3]

As we can see, California's political women have stood out at the national level. Dianne Feinstein and Barbara Boxer chair important committees in the Senate including the Senate Select Committee on Intelligence, the Committee on Environment and Public Works, and the Senate Select Committee on Ethics. Moreover, although Nancy Pelosi no longer holds the position of Speaker of the House of Representatives due to the Republicans holding a majority of the seats in the chamber, she continues to lead her party as the Democratic Leader of the House. All three of these women are widely recognized not only in California, but throughout the United States. However, as we focus on the state level, we note that women do not seem to be as successful in politics at this level in comparison to the success of California women in politics at the national level.

# Women and the State Executive

The top executive office at the state level is the position of governor. In California, the office of governor provides a level of name recognition and expertise that some have used to run for the presidency (Ronald Reagan, Jerry Brown, and Pete Wilson) or be chosen for the U.S. Supreme Court (Earl Warren). From the list of 39 California governors one notices that there has never been a female governor for the state. This is not for lack of trying.

Most recently in the gubernatorial election of 2010, Republican Meg Whitman ran against Democrat Jerry Brown for the coveted office of California governor. Although

---

[3] As of January 2015, the number of female representatives will increase to 19 with the addition of Republican Mimi Walters.

Whitman lacked formal government credentials, her business experience as the former chief executive officer of eBay provided the name recognition and wealth to fund the campaign that made her a viable candidate. Despite this, Whitman lost the election by obtaining only 40.9% of the vote to Brown's 53.8% (California Secretary of State, 2014).

Whitman was not the first woman to be a major party candidate for the office of governor in the golden state. Prior to the 2010 election, California had two other female gubernatorial candidates supported by the Democratic Party on the ballot: Dianne Feinstein in 1990 and Kathleen Brown in 1994. The race between Dianne Feinstein and Senator Pete Wilson was not expected. The year before the 1990 election, it was anticipated that John Van de Kamp would be the Democratic nominee for governor. Yet, Feinstein won the primary election in June 1990 with over 52% of the vote. Following the primary, with her experienced campaign staff and the hard work needed to reach out and raise the necessary funds, Feinstein was a contender. In the end, however, Wilson won the governor's seat with 49.3% of the vote to Feinstein's 45.8% of the vote (California Secretary of State, 2014), but the experience and network she developed made her ready to run for the Senate seat vacated by Wilson.

For the 1994 gubernatorial race, once again Pete Wilson's opponent was a woman. Kathleen Brown, the daughter of former governor Edmund "Pat" Brown and sister of current governor Jerry Brown, was the Democratic nominee to challenge Pete Wilson. Besides being part of the political "Brown" family, she was also elected in the 1970s to the Board of Education for the Los Angeles Unified School District, and appointed in 1987 to the Los Angeles Board of Public Works. Furthermore, in 1991 Brown was elected as State Treasurer for California (Earnshaw, 1994).

Even though Wilson was the incumbent and incumbents are expected to have an advantage at the polls, he was not a popular governor. With Brown's impressive political credentials, the outcome should have benefitted the challenger. However, Brown had her own problems including her inability to define herself and her key issues, and running out of money the weekend before the election (Scott, 1994). As a result, despite Wilson's unpopularity he was able to win re-election with 55.2% of the vote to Brown's 40.6% (California Secretary of State, 2014).

Although three women sought the position of California governor, none of them were successful leaving California as one of the 24 states which have never been governed by a woman. Early speculation is that current Attorney General, Kamala Harris, will seek the governor's office in 2018 when Governor Jerry Brown will be term-limited from seeking another term. However, 2018 is a long way off in the future and who knows what will happen during that time.

Besides the position of governor, the executive branch of California government also includes seven other elected positions: the Lieutenant Governor, Attorney General, Secretary of State, Controller, Treasurer, Superintendent of Public Instruction, and the Insurance Commissioner. In addition, there is a Board of Equalization consisting of four members who are directly elected by the voters. All of these positions have been filled by a woman at some time, except the office of Insurance Commissioner. In fact, the positions of Treasurer and Secretary of State have been filled by women more than once since the 1960s. There have been three female state Treasurers: Republican Ivy Baker Priest (1967–1974), Democrat Elizabeth Whitney who was appointed to fill a vacancy due to the death of Jesse Unruh (1987–1989), and Democrat Kathleen Brown (1991–1995). As for the Secretary of State, two women have been elected to this position: Democrat March Fong Eu who was the first Asian American woman to be elected to a statewide executive office in the United States (1975–1993) and Democrat Debra Bowen who has held the office since 2007 (CAWP, 2014b).

In addition to these offices, a woman, Democrat Mona Pasquil, was appointed to the office of Lieutenant Governor in an interim capacity (2009–2010) when John Garamendi left the office before his term was finished after he was elected to the U.S. House of Representatives. Pasquil was the first Asian American and first female Lieutenant Governor for the state. Moreover, Democrat Kamala Harris was the first woman, first African American, and first South Asian to be elected to the office of California Attorney General in 2011. Two other Democrats, Kathleen Connell and Delaine Easton, were the first and only women to get elected to the offices of State Controller and Superintendent of Public Instruction,[4] respectively. Both women served from 1995 to 2003 (CAWP, 2014b).[5]

## Women and the State Legislature

Although 34% of the current California members of the U.S. House of Representatives are women, the percentage of women in the state legislature is considerably lower. In fact, the female presence in the California state legislature has decreased since its high point in 2005–2006 and even at that point, it peaked at 30.8% (see Figure 6.1). Currently, there are 12 women in the 40-seat state Senate and 20 women in the 80-seat state Assembly resulting in 26.7% of the state legislators being women. This ranks California as 17th in the country as far as the percentage of female state legislators, well behind states such as Colorado and Vermont where women make up approximately 40% of their state legislators (CAWP, 2014c).

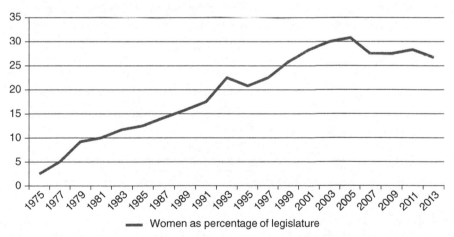

Women as percentage of legislature

**Figure 6.1**   Women as Percentage of California State Legislature

---

[4]Candidates for Superintendent of Public Instruction run as nonpartisans.
[5]In November 2014 Californians elected Democrat Betty Yee to be the next State Controller.

Women were able to get elected to the California Assembly earlier than they were able to get elected to the U.S. House of Representatives. As mentioned before, the first woman to represent California in the House was elected in 1922; however, in 1918 four women were successful in their efforts to become California Assembly members. Of those four women, three were Republicans (Grace S. Dorris, Elizabeth Hughes, and Anna L. Saylor) and one was a Democrat (Esto B. Broughton). It is interesting to note that women in California gained the right to vote and run for political office in 1911, 9 years before the ratification of the 19th amendment which granted women the right to vote in the United States. California was the sixth state to allow women the right to vote (Cooney, 2014).

As for the state Senate, the first woman to get elected to the chamber was Democrat Rose Ann Vuich in 1976. Even though this is 58 years after the year that the first women were elected to the state Assembly, it is 16 years earlier than the year that women representing California were successful in getting elected to the U.S. Senate. Two years later in 1978, the second woman and first African American woman, Democrat Diane Watson, was elected to the state Senate (California Legislative Women's Caucus, 2014). The number of female state Senators remained at two until 1984 when the number doubled and has continued to gradually increase over time.

Although over the years the percentage of women in the state Assembly has been greater than the percentage of women in the state Senate, in recent times this has shifted. As noted in Figure 6.2, since 2009 women make up a larger percentage of the state Senators in comparison to the percentage of female Assembly members. Another trend that has changed over the years is the gap between the number of female Democrats and female Republicans in the state legislature. Throughout the 1980s and up to the mid-1990s, the difference between the number of female Democrats and Republicans in the state Senate never exceeded two. In fact, in many of those years there were an equal number of female Democrats and female Republicans in the chamber. For the Assembly, the difference never exceeded three during the 1980s and up to the early 1990s. However, in the late 1990s for the state Senate and early 1990s for the Assembly,

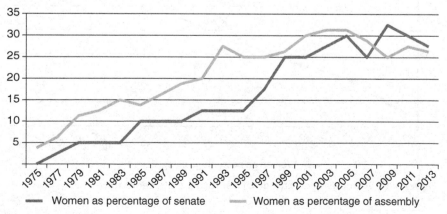

**Figure 6.2**  Percentage of Women State Senators and Assembly Members

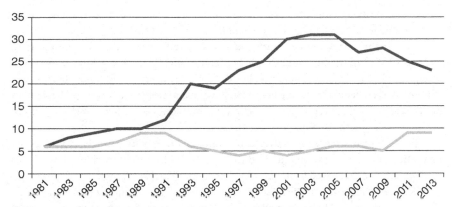

**Figure 6.3**   Number of Female State Legislators Based on Party Affiliation

the number of Democratic women began to increase substantially and the number of Republican women decreased or stayed at the same low level. As a result, most of the women who hold state legislative seats from the 1990s to the current time are Democrats (see Figure 6.3).

More firsts for women in the California state legislature include Republican Doris Allen becoming the first female Speaker of the Assembly, even though it was only for 3 months in 1995, and Democrat Karen Bass becoming the first woman of color to serve as Speaker of the chamber in 2008 (CAWP, 2014a). Currently, the Speaker of the Assembly, Democrat Toni G. Atkins, is the third female who has held the office; additionally, Atkins is the first lesbian to hold the position of speaker. As for the state Senate, there has never been a female President Pro Tem which is the main leadership position in the chamber.

Because there has never been a female governor in California and the percentage of women in the state legislature peaked at approximately 30% in 2005 but has decreased since that time, partisan and nonpartisan groups have been established to recruit and support female candidates for these state executive and legislative positions. Organizations and programs such as CALIFORNIALIST and Emerge California are recruiting and providing training for Democratic female candidates, while the California Federation of Republican Women encourages Republican women to get involved in the political process. Other nonpartisan organizations such as California Women Lead and Run Women Run have the same goals: to increase the number of female candidates and office holders in California.

# Women and the California Judiciary

Although some may consider the judicial branch as being politically neutral, justices in California acquire their judgeships through political means. They are either appointed by the Governor or elected by the voters at a general election. There are three levels of judicial authority in the state: the Supreme Court, Courts of Appeal, and the Trial Courts. The highest court in California, the Supreme Court, is composed of a chief justice and six associate justices. Out of the 114 Supreme Court justices since 1850, there have been only six female justices (Judicial Council of California, 2014a).

The first female Supreme Court justice was Rose Elizabeth Bird who served from 1977 to 1987. Bird was appointed to the Supreme Court by Governor Jerry Brown even though she had no judicial experience. Besides appointing Bird to the court, she was also appointed as chief justice making her the first woman to hold that position. Throughout her tenure as chief justice she was criticized for her views on crime, especially her opposition to the death penalty.

Because of her decision to overturn several death penalty verdicts as well as her reputation for being "soft on crime," Bird became the first California Supreme Court chief justice to be removed from office by the voters (Harris & Cohen, 2012).

As of April 2014, four of the seven justices are female including the chief justice, Tani Cantil-Sakauye. However, Justice Joyce L. Kennard who has served on the court since 1989 has announced her retirement; this may shift the female majority to a male majority on the court depending on the appointment of the next associate justice.[6] Chief Justice Cantil-Sakauye has the distinction of being the first Asian-Filipina American as well as the second female to hold the chief justice position (Judicial Council of California, 2014a).

Currently in the six districts of the California Courts of Appeal, women make up 31.9% of the appellate court justices; this percentage has fluctuated slightly over the last 8 years.[7]

As for the Trial Courts, 32.2% of the judges are female; here we find the percentage of female judges has increased gradually over the past 8 years (Judicial Council of California, 2014b). To be appointed or elected as a justice or judge in the state, a person must be a member of the State Bar of California or have served as a judge in California. We can anticipate that as more women complete law school and become lawyers in California, the number of female justices and judges will increase due to the expanded pool of qualified candidates for these positions.

# Women and Local Government

At the local level, mayors and city councils are the executive and legislative branches of city governments. It is predicted that women would be more likely to run for these positions and be more successful in their quests for these offices. These predictions are due to the local nature of the campaigns making them less expensive and more likely to be nonpartisan, which are benefits for female candidates who researchers have found lack the support of political parties. Since women are usually the primary caretaker in the home even when they run for and win political office, the proximity of the jobs to home and the likelihood that the jobs are part-time are also advantages of running for local offices. Additionally, there are more local political positions to run for in comparison to state and national level positions (Van Assendelft, 2014). However, even with the

---

[6]According to early reports, Governor Jerry Brown has announced that he will nominate another woman, Leondra R. Kruger, to replace Kennard.

[7]At the time of writing this chapter, there were 10 vacancies in the state Courts of Appeal.

benefits of seeking local political office, the number of women running for and winning these positions has not grown substantially, and in certain cases, has decreased in the past decade. For example, 14% of the mayors in the 100 largest U.S. cities were female in 2004; 10 years later, the percentage of female mayors in those cities was 13%. We do see a slight increase in the percentage of female mayors in the cities with populations over 30,000; in 2004, 17% of the mayors in these cities were female while in 2014, that percentage is up to 18.4% (CAWP, 2014d).

As we focus on the 10 most populated cities in California, we note that there has never been a female mayor in the most populated city, Los Angeles, even though former City Controller, Wendy Greuel, was a viable candidate for the office in 2013. However, women have been more successful in other California cities. The state capital and sixth most populated city in the state, Sacramento, has been led by three female mayors over the years. Cities such as San Diego, San Jose, Fresno, and Long Beach all have had two female mayors. Three cities, San Francisco, Oakland, and Bakersfield, have at some time elected a female mayor. The only other heavily populated city in the state that has not elected a female mayor is Anaheim.

Looking at the city councils of the same 10 cities we see variation in the percentages of women currently serving on the city councils. Women fill a majority of the city council seats in two of these cities: Anaheim city council is 75% female, and Oakland city council is 62.5% female. Women make up 44.4% of the city council positions in San Diego and Long Beach. In San Francisco, 36.3% of the board of supervisors is female, while 20% of the San Jose city council is female. On the low end we find Sacramento and Bakersfield where 14.2% of the city councilors are female. Lower still is Los Angeles where only one, or 6.6% of the city council members, is female. Finally, Fresno may currently have a female mayor, Ashley Swearengin, however, the city does not have any female members on the city council.[8]

Based on this information, we can see that women have been more successful in some city governments such as in San Diego and Long Beach. In other cities, such as Anaheim, women may not get elected mayor but they have a dominant presence on the city council. Finally, in large, powerful cities like Los Angeles, we may not see many women in city government due to assumptions on the part of potential female candidates that their chances of getting elected are almost nonexistent, or that the campaign will get too personal and dirty. There is also the possibility that voters may view female candidates as unqualified to lead a city the size and strength of Los Angeles and thus will not vote for them. Whatever the reason, the current Los Angeles city government is male-dominated.

# Conclusion

As we can see, women in California politics are not as rare as they once were. We have women representing the state at the national level and representing their districts at the state level. Women act as mayors of California cities and judges in the state's court system. Some women are the first to hold their political office, and hopefully they will not

---

[8]Ashley Swearengin was unsuccessful in her campaign for State Controller in November 2014 which would have required that she step down from the mayor's position.

be the last. Other offices have yet to be held by women. We also see that over the years the number and partisan affiliation of women officeholders have shifted. It is hoped by individuals and organizations, both partisan and nonpartisan, that more women will run for and win political office so that, eventually, women will reach parity with their male counterparts in California politics.

# References

California Legislative Women's Caucus. 2014. "Elected Women". Available from womenscaucus .legislature.ca.gov.

California Secretary of State. 2014. "Governor: Statewide Summary of County 2010". Available from www.sos.ca.gov/elections/sov/2010-general/.

Center for American Women and Politics (CAWP). 2014a. "Firsts for Women in U.S. Politics". Eagleton Institute of Politics, Rutgers, The State University of New Jersey, New Brunswick, NJ. Available from www.cawp.rutgers.edu/.

Center for American Women and Politics (CAWP). 2014b. "State Fact Sheet-California". Eagleton Institute of Politics, Rutgers, The State University of New Jersey, New Brunswick, NJ. Available from www.cawp.rutgers.edu/.

Center for American Women and Politics (CAWP). 2014c. "Women in State Legislatures 2014". Eagleton Institute of Politics, Rutgers, The State University of New Jersey, New Brunswick, NJ. Available from www.cawp.rutgers.edu/.

Center for American Women and Politics (CAWP). 2014d. "Current Numbers of Women Officeholders". Eagleton Institute of Politics, Rutgers, The State University of New Jersey, New Brunswick, NJ. Available from www.cawp.rutgers.edu/.

Cooney, Robert P.J. Jr. 2014. "California Women Suffrage Centennial: A Brief Summary of the 1911 Campaign". Available from www.sos.ca.gov/elections/suffrage/hist.

Denton, Sally. 2009. *The Pink Lady: The Many Lives of Helen Gahagan Douglas*. New York, NY: Bloomsbury Press.

Earnshaw, D. (ed.). 1994. "Kathleen Brown". In Davis, *California Women Speak: Speeches of California Women in Public Office*. California, CA: Alta Vista Publishing Company.

Federal Election Commission. 1993. *Federal Elections 92: Election Results for the U.S. President, the U.S. Senate and the U.S. House of Representatives*. Washington, DC: Federal Election Commission.

Federal Election Commission. 1995. *Federal Elections 94: Election Results for the U.S. President, the U.S. Senate and the U.S. House of Representatives*. Washington, DC: Federal Election Commission.

Harris, Gloria G. and Hannah S. Cohen. 2012. "Rose Elizabeth Bird: First Woman Chief Justice of the California Supreme Court." *Women Trailblazers of California: Pioneers to the Present*, 118–121.

Judicial Council of California. 2014a. "Past and Present Justices." Available from www.courts .ca.gov/supremecourt.htm.

Judicial Council of California. 2014b. "Demographic Data Provided by Justices and Judges". Available from www.courts.ca.gov/supremecourt.htm.

Scott, Steve. 1994. "Governor". *California Journal Weekly*, 25(12), 9.

Van Assendelft, Laura. 2014. "Entry-Level Politics: Women as Candidates and Elected Officials at the Local Level." In S. Thomas & C. Wilcox (eds.), *Women and Elective Office: Past, Present and Future* (3rd ed.). New York, NY: Oxford University Press.

Wasniewski, Matthew A. 2006. *Women in Congress, 1917–2006*. U.S. Government Printing Office.

**CHAPTER 7**

# The Governor of California and the American President[1]

*Scott Spitzer*

## Introduction: Executive Leadership in California and the Nation

The California governor and the U.S. president have become synonymous with leadership in their respective political systems. The similarities between them are many. Both are the center of the political process in their respective arenas, garner the majority of media attention, and are consequently our most visible political leaders. Both are the leading agenda-setters in politics and policymaking. The issues that dominate the work of the Congress and the state legislature, and which are featured as the top stories of the day in the media, are most often initially their issues. Both dominate their respective budget processes: while they may not get all that they for, the state's tax and spending priorities are essentially first set by them, and then reacted to by the legislature and other political actors. Both are also chief administrators in charge of huge, sprawling sets of executive branch bureaucracies, and charged with appointing and managing the leaders of these bureaucracies. Finally, both have the power to appoint judges to all levels of courts in their respective political systems.

Americans and Californians, however, are ambivalent about executive leadership. While we celebrate decisive and strong leadership from presidents and governors, we recoil at the idea of unlimited executive authority. Strong presidents and governors are lionized and revered: There is virtually unanimous praise reserved for the leadership from presidents Washington, Lincoln, and FDR; Governors Hiram Johnson, Earl Warren, and Pat Brown. But there is another side to this coin. Failed or corrupt presidents and governors receive strong repudiation from the public: consider the low approval ratings of President Nixon after "Watergate" or President George W. Bush's low ratings in the last months of his presidency, as the nation faced the worst economic crisis since the depression, and became increasingly frustrated with a widely perceived failed military effort in Iraq. Likewise, one need only refer back to the recent historic recall of Governor Gray Davis following an economic downturn and a major electricity crisis resulting in rolling blackouts, or to the low approval ratings for Governor Schwarzenegger in the final years of his governorship as the state confronted increasingly large budget deficits for examples of the public's repudiation of unpopular governors.

---

[1]This chapter builds on Vince Buck's original chapter for the fifth edition of this volume.

It turns out that while the public's expectations of executive leadership are increasingly high, the punishment for failure is severe. The contrasts between the recent experiences of President Obama and Governor Brown are instructive. After a series of highly public battles over the federal budget with the Republican-led House of Representatives and Republican minority leadership in the Senate, President Obama's legislative agenda has been stymied. He heads into the final years of his presidency with public approval ratings in the low 40s.[2] In sharp contrast, after facing one of California's worst economic and state budgetary challenges in many decades, Governor Brown led the state to projected billion-dollar surpluses over the next several years, and headed into the 2014 election year with approval ratings close to 60% (see Figure 7.1).[3] These contrasting political situations illustrate the wide range of public support that governors and presidents experience, highly dependent on cooperation from their legislature and good economic times, both of which are outside their capacity to fully control.

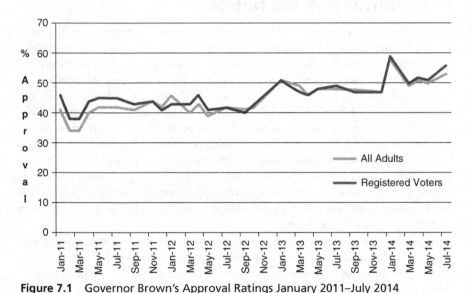

**Figure 7.1**  Governor Brown's Approval Ratings January 2011–July 2014

Data for Figure 7.1 from Public Policy Institute of California (PPIC), *Statewide Survey,* "Time Trend: Job Approval Ratings for Governor Brown, updated on 7/23/14." Accessed on August 8, 2014, at http://www.ppic.org/main/dataSet.asp?i=927.

---

[2]According to the Gallup polling organization, President Obama's overall public approval rating at the end of August 2014 was at 43%, and has been in the low 40 percentiles since July of 2013. See Gallup.com, *Presidential Job Approval Center,* at http://www.gallup.com/poll/124922/Presidential-Approval-Center.aspx, accessed on August 31, 2014.

[3]On the state's budgetary situation, see Michael B. Marios, January 9, 2014. "Brown proposes record $106.8 billion California budget." *Bloomberg,* at http://www.bloomberg.com/news/2014-01-09/brown-proposes-record-california-budget-of-106-8-billion-1-.html, accessed on August 31, 2014. On Governor Brown's approval ratings, see Melanie Mason, April 9, 2014, "Gov. Jerry Brown's approval rating climbs to high of 59%, poll finds," *Los Angeles Times,* at http://www.latimes.com/local/political/la-me-pc-jerry-brown-california-field-poll-20140409-story.html, accessed on August 29, 2014.

How do we account for effective leadership from our president and California governor? What are the common reasons for failures? What resources can these elected executives draw upon to ensure that they succeed? The answers to these questions are difficult to come by, and political scientists and historians continue to plumb the historical record for answers. Here we can begin to assess the resources that each bring to their task, beginning with an examination of the similarities and the differences in their formal and informal powers, turning then to the impact of their immediate political environment, and finally exploring how character and skill influence their success or failure.

## Formalizing Leadership: Executive Powers in the Nation and California

One of the great dilemmas that faced the founders of the nation, and the pioneers who chartered California's entry to the union as the 31st state, was how to provide for effective and strong leadership while protecting against the potential abuse of power. In both cases, there was a strong ambivalence toward executive power: on the one hand they feared unrestrained political power in the hands of a single man.[4] On the other hand, they also believed that strong executive leadership would be essential to the success of their nation and state. This ambivalence toward the executive was expressed in different ways in the national and state constitutions, and has evolved in both cases toward a far stronger executive than the original planners ever envisioned.

Both the U.S. and California Constitutions originally empowered their executives with broad grants of authority, while limiting them through a system of checks and balances (see Chapter 1 for more on California's Constitution). Still, there are some important contrasts to take note of here: the congress's checks on the president have been, from the start, far more limiting than the state legislature's checks on the governor. This contrast has been accentuated in recent decades. The President faces an increasingly strident partisan polarization in the Congress, coupled with a major upsurge in the use of the filibuster and other procedures for blocking the passage of legislation in the Senate.[5] In marked contrast, a relatively weak state legislature, coupled with Democratic Party majorities in both the Assembly and Senate, has resulted in an almost nonexistent check on a Democratic Party Governor (see Chapter 8 herein). This legislature's check on the

---

[4]While there are no formal prohibitions against women being President of the United States or Governor of California, there have been no women in either of these leadership positions as of 2014. Male pronouns are used throughout this chapter to reflect this history. It is worth noting that this is likely to change in the near term. Although California has yet to have a female governor, currently, there are five female governors in the United States, leading Arizona, Oklahoma, South Carolina, New Hampshire, and New Mexico. In addition, former first lady and Secretary of the State, Hillary Clinton is widely expected to be the front runner for the Democratic Party's presidential nomination in 2016. On women governors, see the Center for American women and politics, "statewide elective executive women 2014," retrieved from www.cawp.rutgers.edu, on August 31, 2014.

[5]On the development of extreme partisan polarization in the House of Representatives, see Dodd, Lawrence C. and Bruce Oppenheimer. 2013. "The House in a Time of Crisis: Economic Turmoil and Partisan Upheaval." In Dodd, Lawrence C. and Bruce Oppenheimer (eds.) *Congress Reconsidered, 10th Edition*, Washington, DC: CQ Press. On the increased use of the filibuster and other procedural blocks in the U.S. Senate, see Sinclair, Barbara, 2013, "The New World of U.S. Senators," in Dodd and Oppenheimer, eds.

governor has been weakened further since the 2010 election, with the elimination of a two-thirds requirement for passing the budget, and since the 2012 election widened the Democrats' advantage to a two-thirds majority in the state Assembly and a near–two-thirds majority in the Senate.[6]

Still, there are two other rather significant formal limits on the governor's powers. First, unlike the president who surrounds himself with his choice of the top executive branch leaders (his cabinet), the governor shares power with the state's leading executive officers, each of whom are independently elected in statewide elections. In addition, the state's instruments of direct democracy—the **initiative, referendum, and recall**—provide still another check on the governor's authority, while at the national level the public has no such direct capacity to legislate or remove officials from office. Neither of these checks has been strong enough to restrict the power of the governor relative to a fairly weak state legislature. Meanwhile, the president often faces an intransigent adversarial congress with one or both houses controlled by the opposition party.

In contrast, to the strong presidency of the 21st century, the presidents of the 19th century were largely restrained, with the exception of Washington, Jackson, and Lincoln. It was only with the presidency of Franklin D. Roosevelt, in response to the crises of the Great Depression and World War II, that the powers of the president were expanded to the point that we have become accustomed to today. However, the governor has been empowered to be the clear leader of the state's government nearly from the beginning of California's history.

## What Are the Formal Powers of the Governor Exactly?

As the state's chief executive, the governor is charged with implementing laws passed by the legislature or by citizen initiative. But there's more to his formal authority than simply this role. First, his formal powers can be understood best by taking a look at how they might be limited through the checks and balances designed in the Constitution. Beyond this, his formal authority can be divided into executive powers, legislative powers, and independent powers.

## Checking and Balancing

The U.S. Constitution empowered the president with broad grants of authority, but limited him with checks and balances, chiefly coming from the Congress. The governor is checked by the state legislature as well, but is limited further by independently elected executive officials—a **plural elected executive**.

We are all familiar with the separation of powers doctrine: the legislature—congress and the state legislature both—passes laws which must be either signed by the president or governor or vetoed. In both cases, their respective veto can be overridden by a two-thirds majority vote of the legislature. Beyond these more obvious checks and balances, it is worth noting that the president was not to be effectively checked by the power of the public. Presidents would be indirectly elected, with minimal involvement

---

[6]National Council of State Legislatures. 2014. "2014 State and Legislative Partisan Composition." at http://www.ncsl.org/documents/statevote/legiscontrol_2014.pdf, accessed on September 9, 2014.

of the general public. Presidential elections emerged in the mid-19th century as an informal, *extra-constitutional* development. Moreover, presidents were to be most powerful in their role as chief executive, nearly completely in charge of the federal government, except for their power to make appointments (and to remove officials) which would be checked by a majority vote of the Senate.

In California, by contrast, the state legislature was given a much weaker check on the Governor of California, especially in forging the state's budget (see below). By the 20th century, California's chief executive was seen by progressive reformers as an antidote to the political corruption in the state legislature. At the peak of their power nationally and in California, progressives elected Governor Hiram Johnson in 1911, and he led the state to institute a number of reforms designed to counter the dominance of big business (especially the railroads) and reduce the power of corrupt political parties, especially in the state legislature.[7] Most importantly, Johnson led the charge to inaugurate the state's system of direct democracy—establishing the initiative, referendum, and recall. These instruments of direct democracy empower the state's citizens to make state laws, amend the state's constitution, and remove elected political leaders without the involvement of any elected official.[8] In California, the public acts as a check on the powers of the governor, as well as the state legislature.

On the other hand, while progressives sought to expand the governor's power as an instrument of reform, they were cautious toward executive authority. California's progressives sought to check the power of the governor by expanding the number of other independently elected executives. Currently, California's **plural elected executive** consists of the Governor and seven additional state officials, all of whom are elected statewide: the **Lieutenant Governor (LG), Attorney General (AG), Secretary of State, Controller, Treasurer, Superintendent of Public Instruction, and Insurance Commissioner** (Table 7.1). In addition, there are also five members of the **Board of Equalization**: four are elected in single-member districts, and the State Controller serves as an ex-officio member.[9] This plural elected executive is a big contrast from the singular president, who appoints his own cabinet members with approval by a majority of the Senate, and many other top administrative officials on his own. In California, each of these executives is elected independently, some may be from the opposition party to the governor, and frequently they have ambitions of their own to run for governor. Of course, he also appoints his own cabinet.

What follows is a short description of each of the offices in California's Plural Elected Executive:[10]

---

[7]On the signature importance of the Progressives in shaping California's governance structure, see Kevin Starr, 1985. *Inventing the Dream: California through the Progressive Era.* New York: Oxford University Press.

[8]Of course the Secretary of State and the Board of Elections would be involved in certifying initiatives, referenda, and recall petitions, in placing these items of the state's ballot, and in certifying the results. This is a neutral, administrative role, not one designed to influence the outcome in any way.

[9]California Secretary of State, Debra Bowen. 2014. "Constitutional Officers." In *California Roster 2014.* Accessed at http://www.sos.ca.gov/admin/ca-roster/2014/pdf/00-2014-ca-roster.pdf, on August.

[10]This section is based on Renee B. Van Vechten. 2015. "The Executive." In *California Politics: A Primer,* Chapter 5, pp. 67–74. Los Angeles, CA: Sage Publications and CQ Press. Also, see Vincent Buck. 2008. "The Governor and the Executive Branch." pp. 111–113. See note 1.

**Table 7.1**    California's Executive Officers and Their Vote Percentage in the 2014 Elections*

| | |
|---|---|
| **Governor** | Jerry Brown (D): 60.0% (4,388,368 votes) |
| **Lieutenant Governor** | Gavin Newsom (D): 57.2% (4,107,051 votes) |
| **Attorney General** | Kamala Harris (D): 57.5% (4,102,649 votes) |
| **Controller** | Betty Yee (D): 54% (3,810,304 votes) |
| **Treasurer** | John Chiang (D): 58.8% (4,176,793 votes) |
| **Secretary of State** | Alex Padilla (D): 53.6% (3,799,711 votes) |
| **Superintendent of Public Instruction** | Tom Torlakson (nonpartisan): 52.1% (3,167,210 votes) |
| **Insurance Commissioner** | Dave Jones (D): 57.5% (4,038,165 votes) |
| **Board of Equalization** | George Runner (R), District 1: 57.8%; <br> Fiona Ma (D), District 2: 68.7%; <br> Jerome Horton (D), District 3: 62.4%; <br> Diane L. Harkey (R), District 4: 61.4% |

*Semi-Official Election Results California Secretary of State, Debra Bowen, December 5, 2014. Accessed at http://www.vote.sos.ca.gov on December 7, 2014.

**The LG:** Replaces the governor if the governor resigns, retires early, dies, becomes disabled, or is impeached. He also becomes the acting governor if the governor is out of the state. Like the Vice President of the United States, he presides over the state Senate, breaking any tie votes (which are highly unusual). He is also a voting member of the California State University Board of Trustees and the University of California Board of Regents, as well as other regulatory and advisory boards. Unlike the Vice President, he is elected independently of the Governor and is often from a different party.

**The AG:** Directs California's department of justice and oversees local district attorneys, county sheriffs, and local police chiefs; provides legal counsel to the state; defends the state in lawsuits; and sets the priorities for his powerful agency. This is a highly political office, as many AGs end up running for Governor (Jerry Brown for instance).

**The Secretary of State:** Oversees the state's elections—both state and federal. Oversees voter registration, publishes election pamphlets, monitors the integrity of voting machines, certifies initiative petitions, and certifies and publishes the results of elections. He or she also implements campaign finance rules and publishes campaign finance information according to state law, at http://www.cal-access.ca.gov. Finally, she oversees the records and archives of the state government, and charters corporations and nonprofit organizations.

*Beyond the setting of the state budget, which is negotiated between the Governor and the State Legislature, two state-wide elected officials and an elected Board are in charge of overseeing the state's finances. This reflects a fragmented governing structure that empowers the strong leadership of the Governor, who presents a unified budget while the other financial officers are divided in their responsibility for the state's treasury.*

**The Controller:** Chief fiscal officer for the state: oversees the collection of taxes, expends state funds, and monitors state's financial health. The controller also sits on the

Board of Equalization and Franchise Tax Board (which administers personal income and corporate tax laws).

**The Treasurer:** This is not a powerful office. The Treasurer essentially manages the state's funds after they are collected but before they are spent—managing state investments and the sale of bonds. His chief objective is to maintain favorable credit ratings for the state. He also sits on numerous boards that raise and spend state funds for infrastructure.

**Board of Equalization:** A four member board elected in districts, with a fifth ex-officio member (State Treasurer): oversees the assessment and administration of property, sales, and other excise taxes/fees.

*In addition, there are two other policy-focused state-wide elected executives:*

**The Superintendent of Public Instruction:** Chief administrator of the Department of Education and the State Board of Education. He is elected on a nonpartisan basis (unlike the other statewide offices), and shares power with an appointed Board of Education and a Secretary of Education (the latter is appointed by the governor). These arrangements produce a great deal of confusion over who is ultimately accountable for education policy in the state. The superintendent implements the state's high school exit exams, oversees data collection for education outcomes, and is responsible for the implementation of federal education programs like the move to Common Core standards in President Obama's *Race to the Top.*

**The Insurance Commissioner:** This is the only executive office established by citizen initiative (Proposition 103 in 1988). The commissioner regulates the insurance industry, which is a multi-billion dollar market for California. He/she licenses state insurance agencies and enforces insurance regulations, including those regulating health insurance providers.

# Formal Powers: Legislative, Budgetary, Executive

Although the governor's powers are shared with the other elected executives, and although the state legislature also places limits on his authority, his power is still great. When one considers the fragmentation of authority in governing the state's finances and education systems (K-12 and higher education), it is the Governor who gains in authority as he offers a singular program for governing in these, and other policy areas in the state.

Aside from the power he draws from his visibility and the size of the executive branch that he presides over, moreover, he has a set of formal powers which make him leader of the legislative process; leader of the budgetary process; and leader of the executive branch. Still, in each of these areas, the governor is limited by other elected officials, and by the constraints of contemporary political and economic circumstances.

## Legislative Powers

The Governor, much like the president, proposes the legislative agenda, usually outlining them in his annual "state-of-the-state" address.[11] The governor sets out his

---

[11]Governor Brown's 2014 State of the State address can be read in its entirety at his official website, at http://gov.ca.gov/news.php?id=18373, accessed on September 4, 2014.

administration's legislative priorities and calls on the state legislature to begin making his proposals into law. Governors have the power to call a special session of the legislature to address a specific issue, to veto legislation, and, in the case of spending bills (appropriations), the governor can veto or reduce single items in that bill without having to veto the entire piece of legislation. This is called the **line-item budget veto**, and is perhaps the governor's most significant power. It should be noted that this power is *not* available to the president. While President Clinton was given this power in 1996, in 1998 the Supreme Court declared the line item veto unconstitutional, as it gave the president legislative powers accorded to the Congress alone by Article I of the U.S. Constitution.[12]

> "I am here today to report on the state of our state . . .
>
> It occurred to me that these critics—who have long recited our state's decline—perhaps have nothing to say in the face of California's comeback—except, "please, don't report it." Well, I'm going to report it, and what a comeback it is: A million new jobs since 2010, a budgetary surplus in the billions and a minimum wage rising to $10 an hour!"
>
> Excerpt from Governor Jerry Brown's 2014 State of the State address, January 22, 2014

## Budgetary Powers

The governor, like the President, proposes a budget. But unlike the President, the governor must present a balanced budget, which is required by the state's constitution. This is not quite as restrictive as it might seem, since it doesn't include bond indebtedness and other borrowing measures. However, the national economic crisis that began in 2008 presented severe governing challenges. Although Governor Schwarzenegger sought a number of budget cuts and other measures to close repeated budgetary gaps associated with the 2008 recession, by the time he left office, there was a cumulative budget deficit of nearly $27 billion.[13] In 2011–2012, the budget shortfall was nearly as large –$25.4 billion. When one considers that the annual state operating budget in 2014–2015 is projected to be about $106 billion, these deficits represented nearly 25% of the state's total spending.[14]

The budget process in California is fairly typical of other state governments. The governor sets the state's budget agenda, and the state legislature finds it difficult to

---

[12]Clinton v. City of New York, 1998.

[13]On Schwarzenegger's fiscal challenges, see John L. Korey. 2011. "California: Failed State or Too Big to Fail?" *California Journal of Politics and Policy,* 3(2): 1–21. For estimates of the budget deficit inherited by Governor Brown, see Joel Stein. "How Jerry Brown Scared California Straight." *Bloomberg Businessweek,* at http://www.businessweek.com/articles/2013-04-25/jerry-brown-californias-grownup-governor, retrieved on September 5, 2014. Also see California Budget Project, 2011. *Governor Signs 2011–12 Spending Plan,* at http://www.cbp.org/documents/110630_201112_Spending_Plan.pdf, retrieved on September 5, 2014.

[14]On California's 2014–2015 budget, see Paul Warrant. 2014. "California's State Budget: the enacted 2014–15 Budget." *Just the Facts,* Public Policy Institute of California, at www.ppic.org, retrieved on August 29, 2014. Also, see Brian DiSarro and Wesley Hussey, 2012. "California's 2011–2012 Budget: Balancing the Budget Behemoth." *California Journal of Politics and Policy,* 4(3): 56–90.

challenge his priorities. The Governor sends the legislature his budget by January 10, and he is able to revisit it in May once there is a clearer sense of what the state's tax revenues will amount to, and how much the state's obligated spending will be. This "may revise" gives the Governor the chance to reclaim the budget agenda-setting power just two months before the beginning of the next fiscal year.

Until 2010, the budget required a two-thirds majority vote in each house of the state legislature. Once the legislature received the budget, the governor had a major challenge in getting the required two-thirds majority in each house. State budgets were routinely late because of the impasse that this supermajority requirement often created, especially as partisanship in the state legislature became more pronounced in the last two decades. Things became significantly easier for Governor Brown with the passage of Proposition 25 in 2010, which eliminated this requirement for spending measures but not for taxes. With the 2012 elections, Democrats achieved more than a two-thirds majority in both the Senate and the Assembly, enough to have permitted a disciplined governing Democratic party to pass both spending cuts and tax increases.[15] However, this was a short-lived advantage. Three of the 27 Democratic state senators were forced to leave office by a vote of their fellow senators, after being convicted or indicted for criminal charges.[16]

As a consequence, raising taxes continues to be a major legislative challenge. Given the staunch opposition of Republican legislators to tax increases and Democratic legislators' concerns about cutting programs important to their constituents, bargaining between Democrats and Republicans becomes necessary. While this slows down the budget process, it can place *more* power in the governor's hands. He is the essential crafter of compromises that are necessary to forge the state's budget. His influence in the budget process is therefore greatly enhanced.

One tool that significantly empowers the governor as he seeks to pressure the legislature to pass his budget is his **line item budget veto**. Once the legislature passes its budget, the governor can reduce any item, or remove any item completely, and then sign the changed budget into law. This line item veto, or its threatened use, is a powerful tool of persuasion (see informal powers below). Governors use it regularly and threaten to use it even more often.

In January of 2011, Governor Brown outlined his solution for the state's severe budgetary problems, including a wide range of spending cuts, a "realignment" of local and state spending responsibilities that would reduce the state's spending obligations, and a series of one-time savings and borrowing measures. After surprisingly vetoing a modified plan agreed to by legislative Democrats, the Governor signed a budget bill that achieved a temporary balance for fiscal year 2011–2012.[17] Moreover, in order to overcome the bitter partisanship that characterized Governor Schwarzenegger's budget

---

[15]Adam Nagourney. "With a Supermajority, California Democrats Begin to Make Plans." *The New York Times*, December 16, 2012, at http://www.nytimes.com/2012/12/17/us/politics/for-california-democrats-supermajority-is-a-new-challenge.html, accessed on September 4, 2014.

[16]Lou Cannon. "Corruption Costs Dems Their Supermajority in California." April 1, 2014, *Real Clear Politics*, at http://www.realclearpolitics.com/articles/2014/04/01/corruption_costs_dems_their_supermajority_in_calif_122125.html, accessed on September 4, 2014.

[17]Disarro and Hussey, 2012, pp. 77–83.

negotiations, Governor Brown proposed to put a set of ballot measures before the voters in June of 2012, whereby the state's citizens were asked to approve the extension of temporary tax measures enacted in 2010 to close that year's budget gap.[18] Brown recognized that this was an unusual step to take: "This is not a time for politics as usual. The stakes are too high," he announced in his State of the State Address several weeks after introducing his proposed budget.[19]

In 2012, proposition 30 passed, providing for a 7-year tax increase on the wealthy and a 4-year increase in the state sales tax. Combined with budget cuts and an overall improving economy, the state budget has been balanced, and the long-term debt is being reduced significantly.[20] Given the challenge of achieving a two-thirds majority in the legislature to raise taxes, Governor Brown exploited the state's system of direct democracy to overcome the resistance of the opposition party. The fact that such an approach was essential, and very difficult to achieve, elevated Brown's role in this budget process, as he achieved at least a temporary solution to the state's current and future budget problems.

The formal powers of the governor (the line item veto), and the formal requirements of the budgetary process (the two-thirds requirement for tax increases), act as limits on the governor's budgetary powers. His informal powers, however, are far more significant, and they act to expand his budgetary and political power (see below). The Governor dominates the state's news media; he can appeal directly to the public through high profile speeches like his State of the State address; and he has a unique capacity to utilize the initiative process to pressure the state legislature to pass his budget proposal.

## Executive Leadership

One more area of formal powers deserves discussion: the governor's leadership of the executive branch. Both the president and the governor head the executive branch of their respective governments. Both make appointments to top positions in executive agencies, the judiciary, and independent boards. Both have extensive staffs that help them manage the executive branch.

Over the course of his administration, a governor will appoint thousands of state employees. Like the president, who appoints the lead officials for each of the major federal departments—his cabinet secretaries—the governor appoints the secretaries of California's major agencies: business, transportation, and housing; corrections and rehabilitation; environmental protection; food and agriculture; health and human services; labor and workforce development; natural resources; state and consumer services; veterans affairs; and emergency management. He also appoints the next level down—most of the department heads, such as the directors of the departments of aging; alcohol and drug programs; and of child support services. In addition, the governor appoints

---

[18]"Governor's Message," "Introduction," and "Summary Charts." In *The Governor's Proposed Budget, 2011–12*, January 10, 2011. Department of Finance, California State Government at http://www.ebudget.ca.gov. Accessed on February 15, 2011.

[19]Governor Edmund G. Brown. "State of the State Address," January 31, 2011, full text at http//gov.ca.gov/news.php?id=16897. Accessed February 15, 2011.

[20]Adam Nagourney. January 10, 2013. "Back from the Fiscal Abyss, California Balances its Budget." *The New York Times*. At http://www.nytimes.com/2013/01/11/us/california-balances-its-budget, retrieved on September 5, 2014.

members to hundreds of independent boards and commissions, such as the Fair Political Practices Commission, which regulates campaign finance. Many of the terms on these boards and commissions overlap the governor's 4-year term, and so no one governor will appoint all board and commission appointments. Like the president, who has to submit all of his political appointees for approval by the Senate, the governor must have the state senate approve appointments to many of these high offices. Unlike the president, however, the governor must govern the executive branch with seven other elected executive officials, as well as the elected Bboard of Eequalization. This makes his ability to govern implementation of policies more complicated and politically challenging.[21]

## Summary of Formal Powers

In sum, the formal powers of the governor are significant. He sets the agenda for the legislative process, dominates the budget process by setting out a budget proposal for the legislature to react to, and by means of his powerful budget line item veto. In addition, the two-thirds majority requirement to pass tax increases ensures that the governor will be the leading broker of essential compromises between the majority and minority parties in the legislature. The governor is also the formal leader of the executive branch, and uses his power to make large numbers of executive and judicial branch appointments, all of which will shape the implementation of state policy. These formal powers are considerable. In the case of the line item budget veto the governor's power is perhaps even more potent than the president's. However, the fact that the governor shares power with a plural elected executive is a very important limitation on his power, one that is not shared by the president.

# Informal Powers

Formal powers, however, are only one set of resources for executive leadership. It is in the marshalling of these formal powers in skillful ways, using the vast informal resources that accrue to both of these offices, that the *real power* of these chief executives can be found. To the extent that the governor and president are effective in strategically marshalling their formidable formal and informal resources, they are effective as leaders. These same resources can be squandered ineffectively through poor political skill and strategic blunders. The informal resources for these executive positions come chiefly from their position as symbolic head of state, their high public visibility in the media, and from the weakness of other political actors.

## Symbolic Head-of-State and Head of the State

The presidency's role as head of state is an enormous resource for him in exercising power. Above and beyond his roles as leader of the legislative process and the executive

---

[21]On the Governor's significant appointment powers, see Ethan Rarick. 2013. "Governors and the Executive Branch." In Ethan Rarick, ed., *Governing California: Politics, Government, and Public Policy in the Golden State*, Chapter 9, *Third Edition*, Berkeley, CA: Berkeley Public Policy Press, Institute of Governmental Studies, pp. 228–229.

branch, the president is the symbolic representation of the nation's political identity. This gives him a unique resource to lead the nation, particularly when confronting foreign crises. As Aaron Wildavsky wrote, there are two presidencies, one in foreign affairs, where the legislative branch and the interest groups recede from power, and one in domestic policy, where both the congress and interest groups exert strong influence.[22] To complement this, one might think of two other kinds of presidencies, a head of state, and a head of government. In foreign affairs, the president becomes head of state and head of government, and faces an arena very conducive to his exercise of power. There are few competing political officials to the president in foreign affairs, and therefore presidents act without any significant check to their authority. This is all the more the case because of their symbolic head-of-state status: presidents enjoy tremendous public support whenever the United States is threatened, or our military is involved in conflict. Governors don't benefit in the same way from their role as head of their "small s" state, and certainly don't have an arena of policy where they face only token competition from the legislature or from the powerful interest groups in California politics.

And yet the governor is still the unique public leader representing the state when it faces a natural disaster, such as wildfires, earthquake, or the state's recent prolonged drought. His ceremonial and symbolic appearances boost public confidence, encourage rebuilding, and build political support for needed policy responses. In tough economic times, such as the dire situation facing California from 2008 to 2014, the governor's symbolic role as head of the state can be a particularly strong resource for exercising political leadership. Only the governor can speak to the interests of the state as a whole, over and above any special interests that have a particular claim on the state budget. Coupled with the weakness of the legislature, the two-thirds majority required to raise taxes, and the line item budget veto, the governor becomes the leading voice in the state's budget process.

## The Governor's Powers and the Weak State Legislature

Probably the most interesting formally defined difference between California's Governor and the President of the United States is found in the ways that they were originally intended to relate to their legislative branches. The presidency was to be limited by the Congress, who exercised this power effectively through the first 150 years of the nation's history, until President Franklin Delano Roosevelt, responding to the successive crises of the Great Depression and World War II, expanded the powers of the presidency and transformed his role in the nation's political system. California's Governor, however, was viewed early on as the disciplinarian of the state legislature. While the president was to be above public politics, the Governor was to be the great hope of the people. Governor Hiram Johnson epitomized this kind of leadership, as did other strong governors throughout the 20th century: Earl Warren; Pat Brown; and, in the view of many, Ronald Reagan. In the 20th century, strong presidents have become commonplace, but they have assumed this power *despite* the formal limits coming from the Congress. The situation is just the reverse in California: strong Governors are encouraged by the relatively weakly empowered state legislature.

---

[22]Aaron Wildavsky. 1998. "The Two Presidencies." *Society*, January/February.

The governor enjoys public visibility while state legislators are often unknown to the majority of their own constituents. Particularly in negotiating budget compromises, the fact that the legislature is often divided by partisanship means that the governor is by default the chief mediator, or the "negotiator-in-chief." When he reaches an impasse, he can use his prominent media profile to place pressure on the legislature to reach agreement. When they agree, the governor can claim credit for rising above partisanship and bridging feuding parties with statesmanlike leadership.

In addition, although the state legislature remains a professionalized legislature compared with many state legislatures across the nation, it has been considerably weakened by the passage of proposition 140 in 1990, which imposed term limits for the state legislature and the governor's office. Term limits reduced the collective institutional memory and experience of the legislature, and guaranteed that the new members of the legislature were focused on their next political move, rather than of a long-term career in the legislature. As well, the staff resources that these legislators could turn to assist them were cut by half as a result of proposition 140. Legislators often turned to interest group leaders in response (see Chapter 8 for more on the state legislature). The less experienced the legislature, the more influence the governor attained.

## Public Visibility and the Power to Persuade

Given the structure of a political system with separate institutions sharing powers, it is essential that the chief executive be effective at persuasion. If a governor or a president is to accomplish anything, he cannot just simply order people to obey, but rather must persuade others who control a share of the power to cooperate. This was the great insight of Richard Neustadt, in his classic work *Presidential Power*,[23] but it is no less applicable to the governor of California. Neustadt did not mean that the president should be a good public speaker so much as that he be skilled at bargaining with others, especially the Congress, the other leaders of the executive branch, and the public. Governors bank on the fact that legislators cannot achieve their goals for budget increases or tax cuts without his intervention, and that their priorities can be realized best by cooperating with the governor's agenda. These are his chief bargaining chips. With the executive branch, the governor is limited by the fact that many of the state's executive leaders are independently elected. This limits his ability to bargain with them. Still, the governor's dominance in budget politics gives him a distinct advantage with all members of the executive branch as well. Bottom line: when legislators and executive branch leaders go along to get along, they are no doubt going along with the governor.

## Going Public in California: A New Kind of Gubernatorial Leadership?

The linchpin in the governor's persuasive advantage over the other political actors in the system is his dominant profile in media coverage of state politics. Samuel Kernell observed that the modern presidency often uses his command of the television air waves

---

[23]Neustadt, Richard E. 1990. *Presidential Power and the Modern Presidents: The Politics of Leadership from Roosevelt to Reagan*, New York, NY: The Free Press. Originally published in 1960.

as part of a legislative strategy—to speak directly to the American people who will then pressure their elected representatives. President Reagan used this tactic perhaps better than any president before, or since.[24]

Until recently, however, many California governors have had relatively benign if not downright poor media personas. Californians will not remember Governors Deukmejian, Wilson, or Davis as persuasive or inspiring leaders. But with the historic 2003 recall election of Governor Gray Davis, the only successful recall of a governor in California's history, the era of dull governors ended. After Davis was recalled, there was a new gubernatorial election and Arnold Schwarzenegger, blockbuster movie star, easily defeated Lieutenant Governor Cruz Bustamante: 49% to 32% (Tom McClintock garnered 13% of the vote).[25] Schwarzenegger instantly made use of his media stardom in running for the governor's office in these unusual circumstances, attracting international news coverage.

Schwarzenegger attempted several times to use his heightened public profile to steer the state's agenda and priorities in his preferred direction. Facing an estimated $38 billion accumulated deficit, Schwarzenegger used his considerable persuasive skills to get voters to approve $15 billion in bonds to refinance the state's debt, while cutting a number of deals with Democratic Party constituencies—including unions and educators—to push through his first budget. Despite the fact that he later called this original budget deal "a mistake," because it created more debt, Schwarzenegger was enormously popular at this point, with 65% of the public approving of his leadership in the fall of 2004.[26]

Things quickly turned sour, however. Facing a budget stalemate with the legislature in late 2004, Schwarzenegger went directly to the public using the initiative process. This was a new kind of gubernatorial going public strategy, coming on the heels of the recall election that brought him to power. The governor was using the tools of direct democracy to bypass a legislature that he felt was being uncooperative, and holding a special election to enact his priorities into law. It was also a huge political gamble, and in the end Schwarzenegger was the loser. The voters rejected every one of his initiatives, and some by substantial margins. The rejection of the governor's agenda at the polls in November of 2005 corresponded with a tremendous drop in the "governator's" approval ratings.

Governor Schwarzenneger was able to rebound by moving to the center in 2006. He achieved the successful passage of a landmark anti-global warming law, pushed successfully for voter approval of huge new spending on infrastructure, and nearly passed a universal healthcare bill in California. Schwarzenegger also achieved some important political reforms: transforming the redistricting process from one dominated by the state legislative leaders to one controlled by a nonpartisan citizen-based commission; and seeing through a move from a closed- to an open-primary system (utilizing the initiative process to achieve these changes). Still, Governor Schwarzenegger left office with

---

[24]Samuel Kernell. 2006. *Going Public: New Strategies of Presidential Leadership*, 4th edition, Washington, DC: CQ Press.

[25]See A. G. Block and Gerald C. Lubenow. 2007. *California Political Almanac, 2007–2008*. Washington, DC: CQ Press, chapter 1, "The Political Scene," for a brief description of California's recent political history. The details for the remainder of this chapter are drawn largely from this account.

[26] For Schwarzenegger's candid admittance that his first budget deal was "a mistake" see Evan Halper, January 2, 2011, "The Governor's Wins and Losses," *Los Angeles Times*, p. A1.

poor public approval ratings and a budget gap that was worse than when he arrived in Sacramento, despite promising to be the reformer that would force state politicians to finally get a handle on structural budget problems.

Governor Brown, in his own way, is also an unusually high profile character in the governor's office. Brown entered office in 2010, winning an election as a Democrat in a year in which Republicans won widespread victories in elections everywhere else but California. This generated a great deal of media attention to California's unusual politics. Nationally, Republicans regained majority control in the House of Representatives, narrowed their deficit in the Senate, added five governorships to their total, and won majorities in "21 legislative chambers in 15 different states."[27] Contrast this with California: despite facing a billionaire opponent who spent millions on her campaign, Jerry Brown returned to the Governor's mansion—three decades after he first won election to the position in 1974, and democrats won the U.S. senate race, monopolized all of the elected executive positions in the state, and enlarged their majorities in both houses of the state legislature. This scenario was virtually repeated in 2014, when Brown won election with 60% of the state's vote, defeating Republican candidate Neil Kashkari easily. Although Republicans regained majority control of the U.S. Senate and increased their majority in the House of Representations in the 2014 elections, Democrats continue to have a large majority in the state legislature, just short of a two-thirds majority, and dominate the state's congressional delegation (39 to 14 republicans).[28]

Brown is the oldest sitting governor in the history of the state, and the longest-serving (he passed Earl Warren in October of 2013 as the longest-serving governor in the state's history). With his re-election in 2014 Brown became the only governor to have ever been elected four times.[29] His success in returning the state from record deficits to a surplus relied on powerful nonpartisan leadership: he vetoed a budget backed by democratic party majorities in 2011, and then returned to the promise of the state's direct democracy instruments, proposing to solve the difficult political challenges of the state's budget crisis by going public yet again with the successful proposition 30. While this kind of going public for Schwarzenegger led to defeat, Brown campaigned vigorously for his tax increase initiative and it passed easily in 2012. This suggests that the role of the Governor as a public leader has merged with the state's instruments of direct democracy and, in the right hands and under the right circumstances, can empower the Governor further.

## The Impact of Events

What separated Schwarzenegger's and Brown's experiences in pushing for ballot initiatives? One contributing factor was the very different political and economic contexts

---

[27]Ethan Rarick. 2010. "The Big Battle: Introduction." In Ethan Rarick, ed., *California Votes: The 2010 Governor's Race*, Chapter 2. Berkeley, CA: Berkeley Public Policy Press, Institute of Governmental Studies, p. 65.

[28]Bowen, Deborah C., California Secretary of State, 2014. "California General Election: Semi-Official Election Results." Accessed at http://www.vote.sos.ca.gov on December 7, 2014. CNN exit polls, at http://www.cnn.com/election/2014/results/state/CA/Governor#exit-polls. November 20, 2014, accessed on December 7, 2014.

[29]Because Brown served two terms as governor before passage of a two-term limit on the office in 1990, with proposition 140, he was eligible for two more terms: After winning re-election in 2014, he will be the only four term governor in the state's history, unless proposition 140 is overturned and a subsequent governor wins four terms—both highly unlikely events.

that they confronted. Political scientists have argued for decades that great presidents almost always emerge in the midst of a real crisis. Just think of Abraham Lincoln and the Civil War, or FDR and the Depression, and World War II. More recently Steven Skowronek has argued that transformative presidential leadership emerges when the dominant governing party is discredited and defeated, leading to a widened opportunity for a new way of governing.[30] Skowronek points out that presidentially led reforms of government and policy are often responses to the failures of the past, used by skillful presidents who take advantage of the opportunities presented by widespread dissatisfaction with current arrangements. Crises therefore empower presidents, but only if they take advantage of the moment.

Do crises also empower governors? It would appear that major crises are less significant in promoting gubernatorial leadership. However, governors who recognize major social and economic changes underfoot, and respond to those changes by shaping state governance for the long term, tend to be regarded as our most successful governors. The experiences of Governor Hiram Johnson, responding to the demands of the industrial revolution, and of Governor Earl Warren (before Brown, the only governor to serve three terms), responding to the massive economic and social changes during and after World War II both suggest this interpretation.

Looking at the events of the last decade, one might argue that Schwarzenegger's unusual ascent to power in 2003 was based on a thorough repudiation of the administration and electoral campaigns of Governor Davis. The rapid increase in demographic racial/ethnic diversity in the state in the 1980s and 1990s, coupled with the transformation of the state's economy, produced a great need for effective gubernatorial leadership. Taking Davis's leadership as a failure, the state looked to the public leadership of Arnold Schwarzenegger for a response. However, while Governor Schwarzenegger was able to achieve some meaningful long-term political reforms through initiatives, such as the new citizen redistricting commission (Proposition 11, passed in 2008), his efforts to create a more comprehensive set of fiscal and political changes for the state failed.

Governor Brown also faced a major crisis upon entering office, in the form of a major budget deficit. Brown responded by restructuring the state's budget and governance, and by relying on the voters' approval for a measure that significantly reformed the state's governance. Brown was somehow able to avoid the problems that afflicted Governor Schwarzenegger in 2005. What made the difference? Is there something about the personal qualities of the men that have led the state successfully that separates them from those who've not been as successful?

## Character and Leadership

Unlike legislatures, presidents are frequently evaluated from the vantage point of their personality and character. What sort of person is our nation's leader? How is that translated into leadership for the country? James Barber has identified a typology of presidential character, based on two simple dimensions: whether the president is active

---

[30]Stephen Skowronek. 1997. *The Politics Presidents Make: Leadership from John Adams to Bill Clinton, Revised Edition.* Cambridge, MA: The Belknap Press of Harvard University.

or passive, and whether he takes pleasure in his role—positive—or takes it on more as a kind of burden—negative.[31] Those presidents who are active-positive tend to be the most effective leaders, argues Barber. Those who are active-negative are our worst presidents. Barber predicted Nixon's failed presidency at the height of Nixon's popularity, right after his landslide 1972 election, calling him an active-negative. Whatever one makes of Barber's typology, his observation that character matters in shaping presidential leadership is an important one.

What can we learn about the success or failure of California's governors from a study of their character? It's a risky proposition to assess a man's character based on observations of his public activity, using information provided by the mass media. But one might argue that Gray Davis was a passive-positive governor, at a time when more active leadership was being demanded by the public.

Conversely, Schwarzenegger might be placed in the active-positive category. His effort to galvanize the public behind his reformist agenda in 2005 failed, but in 2006 he was able to make an extraordinary political comeback. After apologizing to the public for the unpopular special election, Schwarzenegger publicly broke with his own party over two major issues: signing a landmark global warming initiative and an increase in the state's minimum wage. Schwarzenegger easily won reelection in 2006, defeating State Treasurer Phil Angelides 56% to 39%.

One might take Schwarzenegger's successes in 2006 as evidence that his character was well suited for effective leadership. On the other hand, his critics argue that Schwarzenegger's character is faulty, noting that he could become combative and even insulting when he didn't get his way, and that his successes reflected not so much leadership as effective public relations. Indeed, his approval ratings began to drop as he became more combative in facing an increasingly intractable budget situation after 2008, falling to the same historic low of 22% that his predecessor Gray Davis faced just before he was successfully recalled in 2003.

Governor Brown's experience suggests that a governor's personal identity and leadership style is a political asset to him when it matches the public's mood. After souring on the ultimate outsider—movie star Arnold Schwarzenegger—perhaps the public sought an experienced politician to take on the fiscal crisis facing the state in 2010? Brown faced off in 2010 against Meg Whitman, who mirrored Schwarzenegger's strategy by portraying herself as a political outsider. Whitman had no experience as an elected official, having made her mark in the world of business, as CEO of Ebay. Whitman promised to shake up Sacramento with a business-minded practical leadership that the insider politicians couldn't provide. The voters instead elected a former governor, state attorney general, two-time presidential candidate, and mayor of Oakland: a consummate insider. His 2010 victory was a large one, defeating Whitman 53.8% to 40.9%.[32] He used the political momentum that his electoral victory provided to successfully challenge not only

[31]James David Barber. 2009 [1972]. *The Presidential Character: Predicting Performance in the White House, Fourth Edition.* New York: Pearson/Longman.

[32]California Secretary of State, Debra Bowen. January 6, 2011. *Statement of Vote, November 2, 2010, General Election.* http://www.sos.ca.gov/elections/sov/2010-general/complete-sov.pdf, accessed on February 15, 2011, p. 8.

republicans in the state legislature, but also leading democrats in the legislature, vetoing their 2011 budget. His success with the state's fiscal recovery, moreover, relied on a going public strategy where he positioned himself above the normal give-and-take of Sacramento politics to achieve the tax increases that would result in surpluses the following year. Brown had a 59% approval rating among registered voters in April of 2014, and his Republican challenger for the 2014 election struggled to gain simple name recognition among California voters.[33] Neil Kashkari, once again an outsider candidate—a businessman with no political experience—was easily defeated by Brown in 2014.

In either case, it is clear that we need to consider not only formal or informal powers of the governor's office in evaluating executive leadership in California. We need to also think hard about the political circumstances facing the next governor, and the character, political skills, and experience of the person in the office. Governor Brown's considerable experience in state government and his reputation for being willing to venture outside traditional solutions may have explained his appeal in the 2010 and 2014 elections.

Brown's experience may be what the voters were searching for, as he bucked a national trend toward the Republican party in the 2010 and 2014 elections, winning against an extremely well-financed Republican opponent in 2010, and easily defeating his opponent in 2014 as well.[34]

# Conclusions: Executive Leadership in California and the Nation

The governor faces a relatively weak legislature, filled with term limited politicians who have limited staff resources. The President, on the other hand, faces a Congress dominated by career politicians, with considerable resources to counter the power of the presidency, particularly in domestic policymaking. The Vice President of the United States is the President's campaign "running mate" and works to assist the President in fulfilling his agenda. The Lieutenant Governor of California, however, is elected independently of the Governor, and is frequently a political adversary of the Governor. Likewise, so too are the state's other executive officers. This "plural executive" has significant powers that can limit the Governor. The executive officers in the federal government, however, are appointed by the president, with the approval of a majority of the Senate, and can be removed at his will.

Probably the most significant differences in their formal authority can be found in the arena of the budget process. Both the president and the governor propose a unified executive budget to begin the process, and the legislative branch then goes to work on his proposal. The similarities end there. The Congress breaks up the federal budget into 15 appropriation bills, which the president must either sign as law or veto in

---

[33]Melanie Mason. April 9, 2014. "Gov. Jerry Brown's Approval Rating Climbs to High of 59%, Poll Finds." *Los Angeles Times,* at http://www.latimes.com/local/political/la-me-pc-jerry-brown-california, accessed on August 29, 2014. Also see Reid Wilson, May 19, 2014, "Republicans Worry Over California Governor's Race," *Washington Post,* at http://www.washingtonpost.com/blogs/govbeat/wp/2014/05/19/republican, accessed on July 18, 2014.
[34]Ibid.

**Table 7.2**  Comparisons between the Governor of California and the President of the United States

|  | California | The United States |
|---|---|---|
| **Designation** | Governor of California | President of the United States |
| **Shape/Design** | Plural Elected Executive | Single Elected Executive—appoints the Others |
| **Special Features** | • State's symbolic leader<br>• Line item budget veto<br>• $^2/_3$ requirement on tax increases strengthens governor<br>• Can use mass media & direct democracy to "go public" and legislate directly | • Nation's symbolic leader<br>• More powerful in foreign policy than in domestic policy<br>• Uses mass media to "go public" to persuade or pressure Congress |
| **Importance** | • Governor leads budget process<br>• Appoints many executive branch leaders<br>• Appoints state judges<br>• Responds to long-term social/economic trends | • Leader in national security<br>• Appoints all executive branch leaders<br>• Appoints federal judges<br>• Responds to economic and foreign policy crises |

their entirety. The governor's formal powers in this arena are more formidable. First, he responds to the state budget as a whole, and is given authority to reduce or veto any specific spending line in the budget, without vetoing the budget as a whole: a line-item veto. Moreover, in California, the legislature must pass any tax increases that are part of a budget package by a two-thirds super-majority, which makes it even more difficult for the legislature to offer a disciplined clear budget alternative to the governor's proposal. The U.S. Congress need only pass budget bills by a simple majority (Table 7.2).

But the real differences between the two offices run deeper than these institutional parallels and divergences. They are rooted in the very different founding impulses. While the Presidency was founded by men who were ambivalent toward executive authority, seeking to arrive at a functional executive that would be limited, the powers of the California governor were designed by reformers intent on empowering the public directly. The presidency was in fact established as a kind of bulwark against a rawer form of democracy, and the electoral college itself was adopted in great part to separate the public's voice from the choice of this powerful new executive. In California, the voice of the people was intended, as a result of the progressives, to be the dominant voice in the government. The governor, to the extent that he positions himself as the people's tribune, therefore, governs effectively against the perceived political class, embodied by the state legislature. When he ignores the people's concerns, or misreads them, he faces sure retribution in the polls.

# CHAPTER 8

# The California Legislature

*Matthew G. Jarvis*[1]

Broadly, the legislature is for the state of California what Congress is for the nation. It is the state's principal lawmaking body. Many features of the legislature are modeled on Congress: the California legislature has two houses, like Congress; its lower house, called the Assembly, is headed by a Speaker and the upper house (the Senate) by a President pro tempore. Yet there are plenty of differences, and in this chapter we will be concerned with comparisons, calling forth both similarities and differences. Great changes since 1990 mean that we begin with some differences.

## Great Changes in the California Legislature

No state government institution has changed more since 1990 than the California legislature. In that year, voters adopted Proposition 140, which amended the state constitution. Proposition 140 did three important things. First, it installed term limits for legislators. After 1990, members of the Assembly were restricted to three 2-year terms, after which they could not be re-elected to the Assembly. Members of the state Senate, similarly, were restricted to two 4-year terms. Second, Proposition 140 cut legislative staffs by about half, meaning that the number of workers who might supply research, advice, and general help to legislators was greatly reduced. Third, Proposition 140 cut off most legislators from retirement benefits that they previously could have received. In fact, in November 2000 California voters again said no to legislator retirement benefits, defeating a proposed constitutional amendment to allow legislators to participate in the state's public employee retirement system.

With these three extraordinary changes, California had turned its back on a *professional model* for state legislatures. It makes sense for us to explore that model, in order to understand what the California legislature once was, and where the California state legislature stands today.

## The Professional Model for State Legislatures

Proponents of a professional state legislature see strength in full-time, veteran, expert legislators. Making the legislative job full-time can mean more time studying issues and

---

[1]This chapter is an updated version of the same chapter in the previous edition of this book written by Harvey P. Grody and Keith O. Boyum.

staying abreast of constituents' wishes. Over time, legislators would have an opportunity to develop experience and knowledge, enormously helpful as lawmakers strive to grapple effectively with complex modern policy issues.

Those who want veteran, expert legislators, therefore, would favor a system that built in encouragement for talented people to build legislative careers. Good salaries, generous pensions, and other benefits make sense in that framework. Such things attract people to careers. Without them, people would not want to stick with the legislative job. Legislative staff also support the general idea. If veteran lawmakers were given a large, expert, and secure staff to help them, there would be still more knowledge and perspective available. The legislature as an institution might be an appropriate match or balance to the governor—who has a very substantial staff. The state could have the benefit of careful scrutiny—by experts—of the governor's proposals for new laws.

When California adopted these concepts in 1966, this professional model made California's legislature more like Congress than any other state's legislature. It seemed a great reform. Indeed, in the next decade other progressive states sought to follow California's lead, moving away from the part-time, amateur legislatures that many small states still maintain. It seemed that modern, complex issues would be better addressed by strong institutions.

## Why California Spurned the Professional Model

Why, then, did California voters abandon the professional model in 1990? What might be the virtues of a term-limited legislature with a smaller staff? And were the voters wise or foolish in the choice that Proposition 140 represented?

Notice first that Americans—Californians very much included—have changed a basic orientation toward all institutions of government in the years since 1966. In the mid-1960s, roughly three-quarters of Americans, when asked in a survey, would *agree* that government was made up of people who usually tried to do the right thing. Confidence in government was high. But there had been a virtual turn-around in attitudes by the 1990s. In the mid-1990s, roughly three-quarters of Americans, when asked in a survey, *disagreed* that government is made up of people who are competent and well-motivated. Politicians were equated with incompetence and venality in the American (and Californian) mind. Amid all of this, few institutions drew more scorn than legislatures. Thus California's voters in 1990 were ready to express their dissatisfaction by voting for Proposition 140.

Proponents of Proposition 140 also argued that term limits would keep legislators oriented to the people "back home" whom they represented. Fresh faces regularly would be drawn from the district, they argued, as term limits required incumbents to retire. The argument was that these new people would better understand the needs and interests of the district. The proponents, in essence, were arguing that legislators should behave as *delegates*—legislators who simply vote the way their constituents prefer, rather than exercising the legislator's own judgment. The new people would not be as reliant on Sacramento lobbyists for either information or campaign donations, it was said.

Opponents of Proposition 140 raised several concerns, in addition to the loss of institutional strength that came with abandoning the professional model. The most basic was democracy. How can it be appropriate to forbid voters from electing the people they wish to elect, opponents asked? "Stop me before I vote again!" some joked. Furthermore, the opponents of Proposition 140 argued that amateur legislators would be *more* dependent on interest groups and bureaucrats. Where professional, long-time members of the legislature could develop real expertise in public policy, both in them and in their staffs, amateurs would have to look to the governor, to the state bureaucrats, and to organized lobbying groups for basic information and perspectives. A weak legislature rather than a strong one was the real outcome of Proposition 140, opponents argued. The opponents of Proposition 140 supported a legislature composed of *trustees*—legislators elected to craft legislation that *they* saw as being in the best interests of their district, state, or country.

As the 21st century began, it was clear that a weak legislature was California's fate. The governor stood tall in state policymaking, while the Assembly was especially hobbled by fast turnover of members and even faster turnover of leadership. A weak legislature, then, indeed seemed to be in California's future for some time to come. On one hand, the federal appellate courts have refused to find Proposition 140 unconstitutional. On the other hand, California voters, mistrustful of politicians, seem to be in no mood to change things. In 2002, for example, the voters rejected a proposed constitutional amendment to allow some legislators to extend their legislative tenure by one term, and in 2008 voters rejected another constitutional amendment to allow legislators to serve 12 years in either chamber as opposed to six in the Assembly and eight in the Senate.

However, one must question whether the second decade of this century will lead to a turnaround for the legislature. Voters did approve a constitutional amendment allowing legislators to serve a combined 12 years in either or both chambers in 2012, as well as propositions changing the redistricting process in 2008, adopting a "top-two" primary system in 2010, and lowering the threshold to pass the budget by a simple majority in 2010 (though any bill that raises taxes still requires a two-third vote in both chambers). Put simply, a lot of the fundamentals of our legislature have been tinkered with recently; it remains to be seen how all the consequences of these changes will shake out.

# Basic Characteristics of California's Legislature

## The Essential Functions of Legislatures

Generally, of course, legislatures do for the states what Congress does for the United States: they enact legislation (i.e., new laws) via *statutes*. Beyond this *lawmaking* function, political scientists usually define three other functions that legislatures perform: representation, oversight, and the so-called constituent functions. *Representation* is the notion that policy choices are made with our interests in mind, either those interests that we have communicated to the legislator or those interests that he or she can recognize without being told. *Oversight* amounts to keeping watch on the implementation of policies and programs that already are on the books. That is, legislators try to (1) insure that government employees (especially within the executive branch) carry out the wishes of the legislature as expressed in the laws that were adopted and (2) review policies and programs to see whether or not they need to be altered in some way so as to more efficiently achieve their intended goals.

The *constituent* function involves individual casework, that is, investigating and trying to resolve problems that ordinary citizens may have with government bureaucracies. State legislators and members of Congress perform some of this function, for example, helping with a Social Security problem or trying to resolve a mix-up with the Veteran's Administration.

## The Essential Structures of Legislatures

Congress and the legislatures of every state except Nebraska are bicameral (composed of two houses). The larger of California's two houses is the Assembly, which is composed of 80 members elected to 2-year terms. Under the terms of Proposition 140, each California Assembly member was restricted to serving only three terms, or 6 years. The state Senate includes 40 members elected to 4-year terms, with half of the members elected every 2 years. State senators represent about twice as many constituents as do members of the Assembly. Under the terms of Proposition 140, senators were limited to two terms, or 8 years. Proposition 28, passed in 2012, changes these limits to a total of 12 years combined, but allows for those years to be served in any combination of the two chambers. The differences in size and term lengths invite comparisons to the U.S. Congress, where the House of Representatives consists of 435 members each elected for a 2-year term, and the Senate consists of 100 members elected for 6-year terms. There are no term limits for members of the U.S. Congress. In both the California legislature and the U.S. Congress, the larger house elected for a shorter term is considered the "lower house." Each Senate is considered the "upper house."

Most observers consider the upper house to be a better job. In the first place, running for re-election is hard work, and in any given election voters might, after all, choose one's opponent. Thus, politicians like it when they must run for re-election less frequently. Second, longer terms seem to connote greater trust in senators. Some see in this an implication that senators are expected to use their own judgment in reaching decisions more than members of the lower house, who are expected to pay closer attention to the views and opinions of constituents. That implication is reinforced by some differences in duties. For example, U.S. senators and California state senators are asked to vote to confirm (or not to confirm) some high-level appointments proposed by the president or by the governor, respectively. By and large the lower houses are not asked to offer their judgments about nominees. Third, as a member of a smaller body, the influence of one person increases, for example, one California state senator is one of 40 whereas one Assembly member is one of 80.

Legislative careers often begin in the lower house and conclude in the upper house in most bicameral systems. It makes sense: begin with a smaller constituency, take a short term in office, and let the voters and your colleagues take your measure. At the same time, however, some elected members of the U.S. House of Representatives keep seeking reelection to that body, and often seek leadership jobs as their careers mature. Here we see the professional model. Veteran leadership and expertise can be found. The same was true for California—until Proposition 140 brought in term limits. Until 1990, the Assembly had its share of veterans whose careers and essential orientations were to that body. Facing being termed out in 1996, many of these "veterans" began looking toward other political careers.

As of 1996, when the term limits adopted in Proposition 140 fully took effect, no members of the Assembly elected in 1990 could run again for that body. Some key Assembly veterans, however, ran for and were elected to the state Senate, a pattern that continued through the 2002 elections. By 2004, however, all of the long-term, pre–Proposition 140 legislative veterans who had moved to the Senate were termed out of the Senate.

The new term limits seem likely to lead to legislators serving longer careers in one chamber, with less "jumping" to the other chamber. In turn, this should, ironically, move the legislature back toward the professional model discussed earlier, even though many individual politicians will spend less time as a state legislator (12 years is less than 14), because those legislators will have more invested in the robustness of their current institution and be less focused on running for the next job (California Senate, US House, large city mayor, etc.)

## Elections and Redistricting

California legislators, as in most states, are elected from single-member districts. The geographical boundary lines for the 80 Assembly and 40 state Senate districts are created every 10 years (after the national census), and are based roughly upon equal numbers of people per district.

However, while obeying the principal constitutional requirement for essential population equality, it is possible to draw district lines favorable to Republicans or to Democrats. Thus politicians regard the drawing of district lines—the process is called redistricting—as enormously important. It is no surprise that Republicans and Democrats have had some bitter fights about redistricting over the years. Where Democrats cried foul after the redistricting, which followed the 1950 census, the redistricting that followed the 1980 census left Republicans grumbling. Governors (who have the power to veto a redistricting bill) and often the courts (with the power to judge constitutionality) are important players in the redistricting game, too.

In fact, courts had the last word following both the 1980 and the 1990 censuses. With the governor and large majorities in both the Assembly and Senate in the hands of the Democrats after the 2000 general elections, control of the next decennial redistricting was securely in their hands.

Term limits, however, also impacted the 2001 redistricting. With little opposition from the Republican minority, a bipartisan redistricting was accomplished with very few competitive districts created at any level (Congressional, Assembly, or Senate). State legislators in both parties seemed more interested in creating safe districts not only for their next election, but also for where they could run when they were termed out of their current seats.

The consequences of redistricting and term limits combined are rather severe. Long-serving legislators have the ability to cultivate name recognition and goodwill among their constituents; term-limited legislators are deprived of these advantages and must cater to the majority in their districts. At the same time, these term-limited legislators have to keep an eye on the next job they might run for, whether it is the Assembly, Senate, or Congress. However, since the last wave of redistricting created districts that are safe for each party for all three, what this means is that legislators have to worry about the primary election for their current seat and their next one. Either one will cost a great deal of money, which will have to come from interest groups located on either end of the political spectrum.

In 2008, Californians voted for Proposition 11 to create an "amateur" redistricting commission to create new districts for the 2012 elections and beyond. The hopes of supporters are that private citizens don't care about protecting any particular legislator's interests. Opponents charged that Proposition 11's requirements for commissioners (no electoral experience and no large campaign contributions, among others) would lead to a commission made up of people who had no idea how to satisfy the many constitutional requirements on redistricting. Opponents tried to repeal the measure, but voters were in no mood to change the policy before it went into effect, and retained it at the ballot in 2010. The districts drawn by the Citizens Redistricting Commission have withstood legal challenges so far, and the first election with the new lines elected a two-third supermajority of Democrats to both the Assembly and Senate, though that was likely only a temporary phenomenon.

## Primary Elections

The first task of a candidate for the legislature is to win nomination in the March primary election. The winner of a primary election becomes his or her party's nominee in the November general election. California saw changes in the rules for primaries, and then a return to the previous rules as the 1990s closed, and finally, completely different rules go into effect in 2012.

For over a century, in most of the nation, party voters in closed primaries have chosen general election candidates. In closed primaries, voters who registered as Democrats choose Democratic candidates, while voters who registered as Republicans choose Republican candidates. Voters who "decline to state" a political party for themselves may not vote in a partisan primary election. California, though, has often been just a little different than other states. Cross-filing from 1913 to 1959 allowed candidates to run for the nomination of multiple parties; the blanket primary in the late 1990s allowed voters to vote for anyone they wanted in any party's primaries; and in 2010, voters approved Proposition 14, where the top two vote-getters in the "primary" election, regardless of party, would be the only candidates in the general election (for more on the history of nominations in California, see Chapter 5). The argument for Proposition 14 was that, in very partisan districts, moderates or members of the opposite party have little voice, and this system will force candidates to "run to the middle." Opponents noted that voters, robbed of knowing which party a candidate is from, actually know very little about the candidates; the information that is likely to swing them would come from campaign ads, and this would increase the influence of moneyed interests.

Election scholars tend to find both sets of claims dubious. State legislators are polarized mostly because our residential patterns give us fairly homogenously liberal and conservative districts. Moreover, in primary elections, only the most motivated voters tend to show up, and these are people with strong opinions. Nothing about the top-two primary system changes these realities, and California is likely to see two candidates facing each other in the general election who are either a conservative and a liberal, or both on the same side of the aisle with an established incumbent and a fringe challenger.

Neither of these scenarios produces moderation. However, one scenario that is possible with the odd math of the top-two primary system has come about already, and likely will again in the future: two candidates in the general election from the same party, neither of whom would have been able to win in a "normal" general election in that district. For example, in 2012, Gary Miller, a staunch conservative Republican won the election in the 31st Congressional district over a "tea party" challenger—in a district that voted for Obama over Romney 57–41% and Brown over Whitman 57–37%. This happened because turnout among the Democratic voters in the primary election was much lower than Republican turnout (as there was no contest for the Democratic presidential contest and Republicans often have higher primary turnout in California than Democrats do) and because there were four Democratic candidates who split up that vote among themselves, while both Republican candidates only split their vote two ways.[2]

## Organization

Both legislative houses are usually organized by the political parties in terms of committee memberships and leadership positions. As with the U.S. Congress, California's legislature does most of its significant work through its many standing committees, the most important of which are the committees that screen the budget and other money bills. Although partisanship traditionally had been less important in the organization of the state Senate than in the Assembly, since the late 1960s the role of political parties in both houses has increased. Political party organization in California's legislature, especially in the Senate, however, remains less significant than in some other states or the Congress.

Bills must be introduced by a member of the legislature. Once introduced a bill is referred to an appropriate committee, which reviews and frequently amends the original version before recommending passage by the full house. Most bills never make it past the committee stage. To become law, a bill must be passed in identical form by an *absolute majority* in both houses (i.e., 21 in the Senate and 41 votes in the Assembly) and signed (or not vetoed) by the governor. This process is essentially similar to that of the U.S. Congress except no absolute majority of either house is required. Another major difference is that an "absent" or nonvoting California legislator has his or her vote tabulated as a "nay" vote. Legislative critics point out that nonvoting is a way for legislators to avoid taking positions on controversial subjects and that many bills are defeated as a result of nonvoting.

California required a two-third majority vote on passage of the annual budget bill from 1933 until 2010, a provision that enhanced the bargaining position of the minority party. In 2008, for example, minority Republicans refused to vote for budgets that had tax increases, while majority Democrats wanted to balance the budget with a mixture of spending cuts and tax increases. During the budget negotiations, Republicans even wanted the Democrats to revoke nonbudgetary legislation that had already passed! In 2010, voters passed Proposition 25, however, which made the budget a majority decision again. In the very same election, however, voters also strengthened restrictions on

---

[2]This same thing almost happened again in 2014 in the same district! In addition, there was a 0.4% vote difference between the candidates in second through fourth place in the state Controller race: less than 1,200 votes out of nearly 3.5 million cast!

the ability of legislators to raise revenues, passing Proposition 26, which requires that fee increases receive a two-third vote in the legislature. Thus, the new legislature should be more amenable to majority party control, if only for measures that don't increase revenues. Perhaps an indication of this is that previous discussions that used to involve the "Big Five" (the governor and leaders of the majority and minority parties in both chambers) are now meetings of the "Big Three" (Governor Brown and the heads of the Democrats in both chambers).

## Senate Leadership

One significant difference between the leadership positions in the two houses is found in the different roles played by the Senate president pro tempore and the Speaker of the Assembly. Many significant *formal powers* held by the Speaker are not held individually by the Senate leader. The president pro tempore shares the leadership power and management functions of the Senate with the Rules Committee. The president pro tempore, a member of the majority party, chairs the Rules Committee, which among other things assigns members to Senate committees, appoints the chairs and vice chairs of committees, and refers (assigns) bills to committees. Although the Rules Committee majority reflects the partisan alignment in the whole Senate, in the past chairs of other committees were not always members of the majority party. In recent years, however, this pattern has changed as partisanship has increased in both legislative houses.

One similarity between the state Senate and the U.S. Senate is that formally each body is presided over by a nonmember, the lieutenant governor and the vice president, respectively. The functions of the formal presiding officer are limited, with the most significant item being the rare casting of a vote to break a tie.

## Assembly Leadership

As is the case with the Speaker of the U.S. House of Representatives, prior to term limits, clearly the most significant political figure in the California legislature was the Speaker of the Assembly. The Speaker is elected formally by a majority of the entire Assembly: the winning candidate must receive 41 votes. In practice this usually means the majority party selects one of its members in a party gathering (a *caucus*), and then votes as a unit for that candidate.

With one party firmly in control of the Assembly, the politics of who should become the Speaker is restricted to members of that party. Assembly members do political favors for each other, bargain with each other, and make agreements—and a winner emerges. This bargaining and agreement-making process happens frequently in this era of term limits, and the job of Speaker turns over every couple of years or so.

## The Power of the Leaders

Even though the Senate president pro tempore has become a more powerful political figure in recent years, the Speaker is not necessarily a politically weak leader. Depending upon rules agreed to by one's party caucus and then adopted in a vote on the Assembly floor, Speakers can exercise varying degrees of power. Speakers typically have the significant power to assign bills to the committees of their choice. Speakers also commonly determine committee memberships, and these powers taken together—to assign bills to committees and to determine who will serve on committees—mean that the Speaker is in charge of legislation. The Speaker also controls all Assembly space in the Capitol building, meaning he or she can award good offices to friends and bad ones to adversaries.

Given these formal powers, it is not surprising that interest groups as well as Assembly members pay special attention to the Speaker. Because these groups pay such attention, Speakers can also find ways to encourage campaign contributions to their friends, or to discourage contributions to those who are not so friendly. Imagine, then, that you are a member of the Assembly. The Speaker might (1) help you win election by helping you to raise money for your campaign, (2) help you be effective in your job by giving you choice committee assignments, and (3) through his or her influence upon other members, help you win passage of legislative proposals that you consider important, especially for your home district. Or the Speaker might withhold any or all of this help. How likely would you be to do what the Speaker wants you to do whenever you could? In addition, the Speaker and Senate president pro tempore are two of the "Big Five," which also includes the governor and the leaders of the minority party in each chamber. This informal group meets often to discuss pending legislation, especially the budget. Party leaders can represent their party in these informal negotiations, where it is often easier to make concessions and deals.

In some other states, strong political party organizations compete for influence with legislative leaders. Legislators in those states may look to their parties, not to their legislative leader, for such things as help with campaign contributions. In California, however, statewide political party organizations are weak (see Chapter 5). The Speaker's power is thus not as frequently or effectively challenged. Note, however, once again the importance of term limits. Speakers came and went every couple of years in the era of limited terms. This had two very important consequences. First, leaders lacked experience and contacts that might have given them more power. More importantly, though, because leaders were going to be replaced soon, others (legislators, interest groups, and the governor) didn't have to worry about how the leaders might react in the future, and the leaders couldn't promise any future actions. In contrast, a governor elected twice can serve 8 years. The advantage was decidedly to the governor, and he or she, not the Speaker, was the principal leader and spokesperson for the governor's party. The open question now is what will happen with the new "relaxed" term limits; smart money would bet that Speakers will no longer be sophomores serving one term, but we will see more experienced Speakers serving longer. Thus, expect some moderate growth in the power of the Speaker, but the days of strong Speakers like Jesse Unruh and Willie Brown are not likely.

# Money and Elections to the Legislature

Californians, like most Americans, have a hard time figuring out what they would prefer for a relationship between politics and money. Ordinary citizens know that it costs a great deal of money to run for political office, and even alert 11-year-olds know that people who want something—for example, interest groups (see Chapter 6)—are typical sources of that money for candidates for office. Americans hate that system. It seems like selling the government to the highest bidder. On the other hand, ordinary citizens are not willing either to donate the money themselves, or to support legislation that would provide public money—tax dollars—to candidates for office. Remember, in our times, ordinary citizens have little respect for politicians. Who would give money to those they scorn?

In that context, Californians have been ready to say yes to initiative constitutional amendments that would artificially limit the influence of money on politics. Propositions 208 in November 1996 and 34 in November 2000 both won by wide margins. Yet the limits are relatively generous. And in any event, such limits will not end the link between money and politics. Campaigning will always take money.

Let us note just one reason why campaigning takes money. Most ordinary citizens get most of their news from television, but California television stations do a remarkably poor job of covering politics in the state capital. This is true partly because ordinary citizens have little interest in policymaking in the legislature. They prefer local television coverage of weather, sports, crimes, fires, lost children, and pets. The result, however, is an electorate that rarely knows the name of its member of the Assembly or of the Senate. To break through that inattention requires campaign advertising, and advertising takes money. In California, this is very costly, as our legislators are competing over very many voters and media costs are very high, as our higher disposable income and large media markets mean politicians have to compete with commercial advertisers to reach the same ears and eyeballs.

It also is crucial to note that the courts are certain to have the last word on campaign finance restrictions. The principal reason for that is American freedom of speech. Individuals and interest groups alike cannot be prevented from telling the world their point of view, through advertising or in any other way, even if laws may limit direct contributions to political campaigns beyond certain dollar limits. Freedom of speech means that interest groups will continue to be able to spend any amount at all to tell the world whom they support as a candidate for office.

The 21st century thus began with Californians unhappy about the perceived influence of money on politics and willing to vote for restrictions on campaign donations. Yet these restrictions could not end the money and politics relationship, given fundamental needs to communicate with inattentive voters, and given freedoms of speech. At the same time, Californians are a long way from being willing to spend tax dollars to take the place of willing interest groups in writing large checks to support campaigns for office. Thus, dissatisfaction with legislators, the campaigns they run, and the funds they raise to run them is destined to continue into the foreseeable future, with no solution in sight.

# The Governor and the Legislature

The governor of California has both political strengths and weaknesses when it comes to dealing with the legislature as state laws affecting public policy are produced. Significant strengths include the governor's initiative in proposing the annual budget, the item veto on money bills, and a strong position in making appointments. Furthermore, although the governor cannot formally introduce bills (his major weakness, as constituents often behave as if executives can simply dictate new policies), he often requests the introduction of bills, which initiate major policy proposals to which the legislature must react.

The legislature primarily reacts rather than takes the initiative in preparing the annual budget proposal. As in all states and in the United States, the chief executive takes the lead in proposing the budget. There are also some specific, constitutionally mandated deadlines—regularly ignored in recent years—on the legislature for getting a budget measure enacted. Note also that the governor has the power to reduce or eliminate through item veto any appropriation made by the legislature. Some other states also give their governors the item veto. The U.S. president does not have this authority.

The key point is this: budgets are the most important policy documents considered by legislative bodies, and executives dominate the budget process. We can say that the governor of California is "the most important legislator," even though he is not a member of the legislature. The same point is true for the president: he is the most important person in congressional deliberations, even though he is not a member of Congress (see Chapter 7). The potential for discord between a legislative body (a state legislature or Congress) is also more likely when the political parties of the chief executive and the legislative majorities differ.

## A Concluding Perspective

For about 25 years, it seemed that a professional California legislature had a genuine opportunity to tackle the problems of the nation's largest state. Not that the legislature ever was triumphant or preeminent. On one hand, the policymaking function was never fully conceded to the legislature, as in normal American style the governor sought leadership and vigorously advanced his ideas, and the courts and the bureaucracies exercised extremely important influence over laws and policies at the point of implementation. On the other hand, new departures in public policy for California were frequently enacted via the initiative route, using ballot propositions to gain the lawmaking consent of ordinary voters.

Still, even while hobbled by internal weaknesses—importantly, the lack of discipline brought about by the astonishing weakness of California political parties—most observers thought the California legislature worked. The legislature accommodated large changes, some like property tax cuts or mandates on state spending brought about via ballot propositions (13 and 98 in these examples). The legislature grappled with changing demographics and changing economics in the state. The legislature responded to earthquakes, fears of crime, recessions, and more, never pleasing everybody (no one ever does in politics) but at a minimum creating a real dialogue in the state capital. Interest groups and the governor had a legislature armed with a strong staff, long memories, and expertise to engage these issues. It seems likely that California public policy was better for having had 25 years of a strong, competent legislature.

As the state began the new century, however, its legislature had been weakened by term limits and sharply reduced staff. Feeble political parties were no support for a legislature of newcomers. The inexperienced, understaffed legislators had few incentives to learn about complex issues, term limits and uncompetitive districts encouraged them to be very liberal or very conservative as they ran for the primary in the next seat, and with supermajority budget rules, this ended up paralyzing the legislature in partisan gridlock.

**Table 8.1** Comparisons Between the California Legislature and the United States Congress

|  | California | The United States |
|---|---|---|
| Designation | • The California Legislature | • Congress of the United States of America |
| **Shape/ Design** | • Composed of two houses, or "bicameral": a *Senate* (40 members, 4-year terms); and an *Assembly* (80 members, 2-year terms) | • Bicameral: a *Senate* (100 members, 2 from each state, 6-year terms); and a *House of Representatives* (435 members, 2-year terms) |
| **Special Features** | • Both houses apportioned by population<br>• *Speaker of the Assembly* is important figure; state *Senate president pro tempore* has become as important, if not more so<br>• Absolute majorities to pass bills and two-thirds vote on budget bill<br>• Absent member's vote counts as a "nay" vote | • No term limits<br>• Only the House of Representatives is apportioned by population<br>• The *majority leader* is the most important figure in the U.S. Senate; the *Speaker* is the most important figure in the House of Representatives<br>• Only a simple majority of members "present" needed to pass most bills |
|  | • Chairs of standing committees are powerful figures in both the California legislature and the United States Congress | |
| **Importance** | • Takes up key state and local issues, including education, transportation, crime, and environmental quality<br>• Proposition 13 shifted key decision making about many issues, such as education, away from the local level to the state, because the state must supply the money<br>• By weakening the legislature, Proposition 140 increased the influence of the governor, bureaucrats, and interest groups | • Both houses of Congress play a major role in making domestic policy, including taxing and spending decisions<br>• The U.S. Senate is much more influential than the House of Representatives in making U.S. foreign policy |
|  | • The chief executive—the governor or the president— although not a member of the legislative branch, is much more influential than any other figure inside or outside of the legislature or Congress | |

The influence of governors, bureaucrats, and interest groups had increased, and governors and others running for office increasingly joined interest groups in mounting public relations campaigns on behalf of ever more ballot propositions. Within less than a year of his election as governor in 2003, for example, Arnold Schwarzenegger became a regular advocate of initiative proposals. With a weakened legislature, the public policy conversation in California seemed likely to be lean rather than abundant, mean rather than generous, and too frequently imprudent rather than wise.

As a new decade dawned in 2011, the legislature has again been born anew. Redistricting is now in the hands of a supposedly nonpartisan commission, primaries now yield the top two vote getters and the budget rules have changed for the first time in nearly 80 years. In 2012, voters continued to make fundamental changes, modifying term limits in a way that should lead to longer service, but within one chamber. It remains to be seen what the effects of these changes will be; the first two changes are argued to reduce partisanship, whereas the budget change empowers the majority party, and the term limits change should marginally increase professionalism. So far, redistricting changes seem to have had no impact on partisanship; the top two primary system hasn't reduced partisanship, either (though it does seem to occasionally lead to the "wrong" party winning in November); the impact of changes in the budget rules are unclear, because the Democrats managed to get a two-third majority anyway, but also passed tax increases at the ballot box and have an improving economy helping to balance the books in Sacramento; and term limit changes will take many years to observe, as everyone elected before 2012 is still governed by the older Proposition 140 limits.

# CHAPTER 9

# The Courts of California

*Pamela Fiber-Ostrow*

## Introduction

Most students have seen the judiciary depicted on popular movie and television shows, and increasingly, reality TV. Therefore, students may feel familiar with courts, and it is likely through the courts that most Californians will interact with government (either through resolution of a civil matter like suing for damages or a criminal matter). While some of these depictions capture parts of our justice system, like all good movies and TV they suspend reality and glamorize what can be a mundane and/or complex system. For example, TV depicts a trial as having a judge, a lawyer on each side, a jury, bailiff, and witnesses while costume and sets call for a black robe for the judge, jury boxes, and evidence. However as we will discuss, different types of trials require different types of actors and sets. Furthermore, many cases do not even go to trial, while others face a judge without a jury; moreover, appellate hearings (appeals) require an entirely different set of actors and sets. But starting with the basics, courts were established to resolve disputes between parties. These parties may be private citizens, a citizen, and a public entity like a city or state or government agency, or even the public against a person accused of a crime.

The role of the courts is to *apply* the laws that legislatures and others enact. State courts apply state laws and constitutions, while Federal courts apply national laws and the national constitution. This is not as simple as it sounds. Every state in the union has a justice system as does the Federal government, but the operation of each is unique, as are the rules and laws that govern its establishment and practices. This separation of authorities, known as *judicial federalism*, allows states to determine various aspects of their justice system, but also makes discussions of different states' court systems more difficult; while they may share a lot in common, they will also have many differences. From time-to-time under some circumstances, Federal courts may enforce state laws and state courts may enforce national laws.

An important area of overlap involves the Constitution of the United States. The Constitution stipulates that "Judges in every State" shall be bound by its provisions. During the early part of the 20th century the United States Supreme Court began to apply the rights and liberties guaranteed in the U.S. Constitution to the states through the Fourteenth Amendment, known as selective incorporation. This incorporation expanded into the 1960s and state judges put national constitutional requirements into practice. Fundamental liberties that most Americans prize are among these, including freedom of speech and freedom of religion. Guarantees of certain standards of fairness in criminal proceedings in the Bill of Rights and the Fourteenth Amendment, which also require that all persons be equally treated in crucial ways, were also applied to the states changing the way state judicial proceedings were conducted in a variety of ways.

When questions of law that turn on national constitutional provisions arise in state proceedings, the Federal courts can ultimately override state courts' rulings. This, then, amounts to a limited oversight that the Federal courts may exercise over state court decisions. However, two key points should be kept in mind as we seek to understand the relationships between the two systems:

1. Most cases do not raise constitutional issues.
2. Most cases in which national constitutional issues are raised in fact never reach the Federal courts, but instead are finally decided in state courts.

The most important lesson in this is that state courts are substantially autonomous and independent of Federal courts—because very few issues raised in state courts are subject to Federal court review, and even when such issues are subject to review, they are usually not reviewed. It follows that if the state courts are essentially autonomous, state constitutions and laws are also fairly independent of any Federal court intervention providing they do not violate the national constitution or laws.

# Kinds of Law: Criminal and Civil

California courts review two types of laws and cases: criminal and civil. In both civil and criminal cases, the law as contained in California's codes guides the court process. Criminal law is contained in the penal code, created by statutes from the state legislature and/or the voters through the initiative process. In criminal cases the goal is to determine whether a crime occurred by deciding whether someone is guilty of a crime (violating a section of California's penal code), and making decisions based on the facts presented to the courts (or the absence thereof). When criminal laws are broken—when I hit you on the head—the public via the government considers itself aggrieved. The civil law is also created by statutes but the cases are different from criminal. Civil cases decide if the facts are strong enough to support the claim that a person is responsible for something like damages to property or person, settling the estates of deceased persons, or protecting citizens' rights from state or local government (California Legislature, n.d.). Civil law covers disputes between private parties in which the government usually has no direct involvement (although it may be called upon to enforce outcomes in civil cases). In addition, a civil suit may arise if a citizen feels aggrieved by a state law or city ordinance. The standard for finding a defendant guilty in a criminal trial is guilt beyond a reasonable doubt. In a civil case, the plaintiff enjoys a lower standard and must merely show that they deserve the judgment based on the preponderance of the evidence.

# Kinds of Law: Public and Private

A second distinction useful for this discussion is between public law and private law. Public law involves general rules for broad classes of people, and typically the state is either a party to public law transactions, or considers itself substantially affected by the outcome. Technically, criminal law is in the public law sphere, but better modern examples include civil rights laws, welfare laws, antitrust laws, environmental laws, and social security laws. Governments secure civil rights for people, and thus are involved in the transaction.

Governments provide welfare to people in need, and thus are involved in the transaction. Private law, on the other hand, manages relationships between individuals, in which usually it is thought that the government has no direct stake. Most contract law is private—a name change is considered a private law matter.

# Structure of the Courts

Like the federal government, California's courts are considered adversarial common law courts where judges serve as referees to ensure both sides are given equal opportunities to present their cases and the law is faithfully followed. Adversarial indicates that parties at trial are on opposite sides; common law refers to the use of previous case law to help guide the current case. It also indicates that when a court makes a decision (in trials a verdict and in appellate cases hands down an opinion or a ruling) it becomes part of California's body of law. California's courts were modeled after the federal system and are divided among trial and appellate jurisdiction (Table 9.1).

Trial courts are the fact-finding courts because their jobs are to determine the facts of a case; this may include determining whether a crime occurred (criminal court) or settling disputes between two parties or individuals, like whether a person is responsible for damaging another's property (civil court). These courts have original jurisdiction; this means that they will be the first court to hear a case. The *courts of appeal*, which include the California Supreme Court, review questions of law and due process and have appellate jurisdiction, hearing cases on appeal, and in certain limited cases may have original jurisdiction. *Jurisdiction* here refers to the authority of a court to interpret and apply the law. Article VI of the California Constitution creates trial and appellate level courts and authorizes the state legislature to fill in some details. The legislature, however, does not have as much discretion in the creation of state courts as is given to Congress regarding the creation of the Federal courts. The national constitution authorizes the creation of courts in two places. Article I authorizes Congress to create "tribunals" (sometimes called legislative courts). Such courts have limited jurisdiction (i.e., limited authority to hear cases). The national constitution in Article III creates "one Supreme Court," and authorizes Congress to create other courts inferior to the Supreme Court. These Article III courts (sometimes called constitutional courts) exercise "the judicial power of the United States," and have been given general jurisdiction (i.e., broad authority to hear cases).

**Table 9.1**   The Organization of Courts in California and in the United States

|  | California* | The United States** |
|---|---|---|
| Constitutional Varieties | California has no "legislative" courts comparable to those created by Congress. Article VI of the state constitution provides for all California courts. | The U.S. Supreme Court and the lower Federal courts are based upon Article III of the U.S. Constitution. Congress also creates Article I "legislative" courts to hear some administrative matters. |
| Trial Courts General Jurisdiction | 58 Superior Courts with 1,872 judges; about 9.5 million cases/year. | 94 U.S. District Courts (including territories & Puerto Rico) with approximately 678 judges; about 300,000 cases/year; in addition over 300 bankruptcy judges are assigned to districts. |
| Intermediate Appellate Courts | 6 District Courts of Appeal with 105 authorized justices; nearly 25,000 case filings/year. | 13 U.S. Courts of Appeal with approximately 179 judges; about 60,000 cases/year. |
| Courts of Last Resort | California Supreme Court composed of Chief Justice and 6 Associate Justices; about 9,000 filings and dispositions year. | Supreme Court of the United States composed of Chief Justice and 8 Associate Justices; about 10,000 cases filed/year but most denied review. |
| Judicial Selection and Terms of Office | All trial court judges appointed by the Governor or elected in nonpartisan election; 6-year term Appellate and Supreme Court Justices are nominated by the Governor and confirmed by Commission; retained by nonpartisan, noncompetitive election; 12-year terms. | All Article III judges nominated by the President of the United States and confirmed by U.S. Senate; these judges serve during "good behavior" (i.e., for life unless impeached). "Legislative" (Article I) court judges serve varying fixed terms. |
| Methods of Removal | Impeachment, or by Commission, or by defeat at election, or recall election. | Impeachment for Art. III courts; nonreappointment for Art. I "legislative" courts. |
| Formal Qualifications | Member of the Bar for a number of years (varies with court level); certain residence requirements. | No constitutional criteria. |
| Informal Qualifications | Political background; appellate justices often have trial court experience. | Political background; by tradition only attorneys have been appointed; "Senatorial courtesy" often applies to trial court nominees. |

In both systems, the chief executive normally selects judges from his own political party and of similar philosophy and ideological persuasion.

*California data: Judicial Council of California, Annual Report, 2008.

**U.S. data: Administrative Office of the United States Courts, Annual Report, 2008.

## Trial Courts: Fact Finding

California follows the hierarchical, pyramid pattern of the national system and most states. There are fact finding trial courts, appellate courts, and a Supreme Court in both systems. California's trials take place in superior court. Superior courts cover nearly all of the works of the courts and most cases begin and end at trial. They are established in each of the 58 counties in more than 450 locations, with more than 2,100 judicial officers to deal with both civil and criminal matters (California Courts, 2013). Civil disputes occur when citizens or legal entities sue each other, either for damages (usually money) or to prevent harm or to ask someone to stop doing something; criminal cases involve violation of criminal laws, ranging from misdemeanors, such as vandalism, to serious felonies, such as murder. Both the federal district courts and California's superior courts require juries in order to meet the U.S. Constitutional demands of the Sixth and Seventh Amendments, and call upon citizens to serve as jurors: before-hand to decide whether probable cause exists to indict (accuse) individuals or corporations on criminal charges based upon the evidence presented (grand jury), and in trial (petit jury). Both Superior Court and District Court juries require a 12-person panel. Although both Constitutions protect a defendant with the right to a jury, a defendant can waive this right.

Not all cases that go to court are seen by a jury. Depending on the desires of the litigants (in criminal cases the defendant chooses) superior court cases can be heard by juries or by the judge in a *bench trial*. The number of judges assigned to each jurisdiction varies according to population and caseload. Further, in both civil and criminal law, cases can be settled out of court (plea bargain in criminal court and different settlement agreement in civil), discussed more below.

Although all 58 counties must follow the Constitutional demands, many differences exist among the 58 counties' court operations. Each has a unique budget; budgets depend on caseloads, voters, population, and the economy both in the counties and in the state and the nation as a whole. This makes the operation of each court system unique despite all residing in the same state.

California has created specialized subdivisions of superior courts to ease the burden on the superior court. *Traffic court* deals with all traffic violations except those committed by juveniles. Under civil law, several subdivisions have been created. Private citizens may use *small claims court* to sue each other over damage to property, landlord/tenant disputes, collection of money owed, and many other types of claims if the amount involved is $10,000 or less; however, these courts do not employ lawyers or juries. According to the California Courts official website, the $10,000 limit applies to a "natural person (an individual);" government and corporations may only ask for $5,000 in small claims courts. Further, the limit is $7,500 in a suit over a car accident with an insured motorist (California Courts, n.d.b.). *Probate court* involves the administration of wills and estates. *Family law courts* settle domestic disputes; they are concerned with divorce and child custody.

In criminal cases California has established several additional specialty courts to address specific needs of its citizens. These include domestic violence courts, DUI/drug courts, juvenile drug courts, mental health courts, veteran's courts, and community and homeless courts to address the needs of both offenders and scarce judicial and prison resources. In addition, juvenile courts deal with matters affecting accused persons under the age of 18 years. However, prosecutors may try minors accused of particularly heinous crimes as adults. There are no juries in juvenile proceedings. In all these specialized courts the mission includes public safety, efficiency of both time and resources of the courts and judicial officers as well as best practices for addressing the needs of the offenders and any victims.

The Federal trial court of general jurisdiction is the U.S. District Court. Congress has created 94 U.S. District Courts including at least one district in each state, the District of Columbia and Puerto Rico, the Virgin Islands, Guam, and the Northern Mariana Islands. In total, there are 677 authorized judgeships (not including bankruptcy) (2012 Judicial Facts and Figures). In addition Congress has established several specialized courts. The U.S. Court of Claims hears cases over most claims for money damages against the United States, disputes over federal contracts, and unlawful "takings" of private property by the federal government. The U.S. Court of International Trade addresses cases involving international trade and customs issues. Finally, U.S. Bankruptcy Courts handle bankruptcy cases since bankruptcy is a federal issue; therefore the federal courts have sole jurisdiction over bankruptcy issues, and cannot be heard by a state court.

In criminal cases, defendants are guaranteed certain rights under both the United States Constitution and California's Constitution. The rights of the accused are listed in Article I, Declaration of Rights of California's Constitution. Like the federal rights guaranteed under the United States Constitutions' Fourteenth Amendment, Section 7 of California's Constitution guarantees due process and equal protection of the laws, and like the Fifth-Eighth Amendments of the United States' Constitution, Sections 14–17 of California's Constitution include guarantees of rights to a speedy trial, a preliminary hearing before a magistrate, counsel, be advised of the charge against the accused, trial by jury, confront witnesses, and to summon witnesses on his or her own behalf. California's justice system must, at minimum, adhere to the Federal Constitution's provisions but may provide greater protections for the accused.

There are several distinctions among the types of criminal cases that get processed through California's courts, reflecting the types of crime that are codified in California's penal code which include infractions, misdemeanors, and felonies.[1]

## Caseloads

While the courts of every state hear both civil and criminal cases, the ratio of criminal to civil filings and disposition will vary from state to state. Most civil cases are private law matters. Smith may sue Johnson about a contract, or Mrs. McGregor may sue her husband Mr. McGregor for divorce. A moment's thought makes it clear that there are more of these private law transactions in society than there are public law transactions. If we

---

[1] Felonies are the most serious crimes and include crimes such as murder, possession of dangerous drugs for sale, rape, and armed robbery. In a felony the judge may impose a sentence of one year or more in state prison or a heavy fine or both. Lesser crimes called misdemeanors carry less severe penalties of up to, but not more than, one year in county jail or a fine of not more than $1000 or both. Misdemeanors include petty theft, prostitution, and vandalism.

add to that insight the knowledge that regulating private transactions is overwhelmingly state business, and if we further remember that criminal law is overwhelmingly the business of the states, we can correctly conclude that state courts hear more cases than do Federal courts. Indeed, in any given year the state trial courts located in Los Angeles County alone do more business than all of the Federal trial courts in all of the states combined! A fair conclusion is that when ordinary citizens find themselves involved in court cases, those cases are very likely to be heard by state courts.

By way of summary, we can explain the large number of cases brought to California courts by remembering these points:

1. Ordinary "private law" transactions are numerous, and are brought primarily to state courts rather than to Federal courts.
2. Criminal cases nearly always go to state courts.
3. California (unlike many states) is active in the public law area, and thus California courts hear state-level cases based on such laws.

In contrast, the central business of the Federal courts is public law. Comparatively few private law and criminal cases are heard there. Even though substantial growth has been experienced in Federal case loads over the past three decades, the numbers are dwarfed in comparison with state court case loads. Note, too, that the cost of operating the California courts is no small matter: 3.6 billion dollars for 2014–2015 (California Budget 2014).

# The Players in Court

The players in a criminal trial include the judges, prosecution, defense, and juries. Judges have a variety of different duties in the court process. Generally speaking, the judge listens to the evidence presented and makes a determination of the law based on the application of these facts to the legal code. In cases involving a jury, judges make decisions about what types of evidence will be presented to the jury. In a criminal case, if a defendant is found guilty, the judge determines the sentence for the offender. Most importantly, they preside over the legal process as an independent representative of the system, meaning that they do not have a bias toward the prosecution or the defense. When judges make rulings, they have the force of law.

The process for selecting judges is straightforward. *Superior court judges* are elected countywide on a nonpartisan ballot for 6-year terms. Candidates must be attorneys who have been members of the California bar for 10 years. If the incumbent is unopposed, then his or her name will not appear on the ballot. If a vacancy occurs between elections, the governor may appoint a qualified replacement to be voted on by the electorate at the next general election. Often as the workload of a court exceeds the capacity of the existing staff, the judges appoint attorneys to serve as temporary judges, called *commissioners*.

In the remaining 49 states, judges may be elected or appointed, though the details of the election or of the appointive process vary substantially from state-to-state. All Federal judges are appointed. They are nominated by the President of the United States, and confirmed by the U.S. Senate as directed by the Constitution.

## Attorneys

Lawyers present their most persuasive arguments to the finders of fact (either jury or judge) hoping to exploit the weaknesses of the other side. The role of the lawyer is to best represent the needs of the client (the state or the defendant in a criminal trial) in order to convince the triers of fact. In a criminal case the prosecution represents the people of the state of California and is the authority of the *District Attorneys* to prosecute cases in superior courts. They are elected in each county on a countywide, nonpartisan ballot. Their offices include numerous deputy district attorneys who prosecute the cases. In some cases defendants will hire private defense attorneys to represent them in court; however, indigent (poor) defendants will be assigned an attorney. *Public defenders* are appointed by the county boards of supervisors to represent defendants who cannot afford a private attorney. Many counties have public defender offices although in some cases the court appoints a private attorney to provide legal services.

## Juries

Trial by jury is a right protected in the federal Bill of Rights in both criminal (Sixth Amendment) and civil (Seventh Amendment) trials and in California's constitution. The framers of the United States Constitution provided for trial by jury to protect defendants from a government that might abuse its powers. It is the jury that must find a defendant guilty (or a party responsible for something), not a government actor. It is the job of a jury to review facts and make decisions in legal proceedings. There are two types of juries: a grand jury and a trial jury.

Every county in the state has a *grand jury* of voluntary members who serve two functions. The first and primary responsibility is to investigate and examine ways to improve county governance. The second and less frequently used is to issue criminal indictments based on the grand jury's determination if a crime has been committed and there is enough evidence to charge. Most of us are more familiar with *trial juries* whose responsibility is to review the facts of a case and determine whether there is reasonable doubt that a defendant committed a particular crime. The jury pool is drawn from both Department of Motor Vehicles registration and voter registration lists. To serve on a jury in the state of California, prospective jurors must be U.S. citizens and at least 18 years old. In addition, jurors must be able to understand English enough to understand and discuss the case; be a resident of the county in which the summons was delivered; have completed jury service more than 12 months prior; and not be serving currently on a grand jury or on another trial jury. Over 8.6 million Californians who were summoned to jury service completed their service in 2011, but this does not mean they all served as jurors. Completing service could mean that they phoned in each day and were never asked to appear at a court. The better representation is the number of Californians sworn to serve as jurors: 164,512 (California Courts, 2013). Once seated at trial, jurors must listen to both sides of the case, during which time they cannot discuss the case with anyone until deliberations begin, and then only with fellow jurors. During deliberations, jurors must consider only information and evidence presented in the courtroom. If the jury is not able to agree on a verdict, the judge may dismiss the jury as a "hung jury," and call for a mistrial. This may also mean the case will go to trial again with a new jury.

There is certainly controversy surrounding the United States' requirements for trial by jury including the ability of a jury to come to an impartial decision. Bias that pervades our understanding of society is likely to creep its way into the court room; lawyers may exploit those biases in their presentations of witnesses and evidence. For example, in attempting to make a female defendant more sympathetic, the defense team may appeal to the juries' understanding of women as mothers or society's belief that women are typically more nurturing. Conversely a prosecutor may reverse that by exploiting our understanding of women as more caring and nurturing by showing how much a woman has violated that norm.

In response to thinning ranks of prospective jurors, California adopted "a one-day-or-one-trial" system in which a juror reporting for service is either assigned to a trial on the first day he or she reports or is dismissed from service for at least 12 months. Failure to report for jury service in California may result in a fine up to $1,500, and although unlikely, it is possible to face jail time in addition to the fine. It is against the law for an employer to prevent an employee from serving on a jury by threatening to fire or terminating employment on that basis. California pays jurors $15 a day, and reimburses them at least 34 cents per mile starting on the second day of service.

## Alternate Dispute Resolution

A defendant in a criminal case may opt to enter a guilty plea in lieu of a trial or enter into a *plea bargain*. In a plea bargain, the prosecutor and defense agree to reduce the charge in return for a guilty plea to the lesser offense. The practice of plea-bargaining serves several purposes and those in favor tend to cite the ability of courts to save money and time. Since trials are costly to the county by using resources of judges and juries, plea bargains are helpful to county budgets. In addition, where the evidence may produce an unfavorable outcome for the prosecution, a plea bargain ensures them of a "win" with a guilty plea, over a "loss" at trial or dismissal. Moreover, they clear the docket for another case and lessen the load on the superior court. In terms of defendants' rights, under the terms of a plea bargain defendants are granted a lesser charge than they would have received had they gone to trial and been found guilty. Under certain circumstances felonies may be reduced to misdemeanors or serious felonies reduced to felonies, which carry lesser penalties.

Some critics of criminal case plea bargaining worry that persons accused of crimes may be pressured unfairly into guilty pleas. In addition, a trial may produce fairer outcomes with a chance for a jury's finding of not guilty. In these cases advocates for defendants' rights argue prosecutors lure the accused in with a lesser charge but the accused may not fully understand the options or may not have the opportunity to fully understand the possibility of being found not guilty in a trial. Others express the concern that some accused persons escape too lightly, by offering to plead guilty to a lesser crime than in fact they committed. For example we all have heard criticisms about the "revolving door of justice" or the criminals that get a "slap on the wrist." In the two decades ending the 20th century it was clear that critics of criminal case processing were persuading voters. The popularity of getting tough on crime occasionally spills over to proposals for taking all persons accused of crime to trial. Yet negotiations are the only possible way that cases can be moved through trial courts. American states take about 5% of all cases to trial. California is right in line with this figure.

Critics worry that at least some civil settlements are unfair, as when one injured party feels it necessary to settle for a smaller payment than might have been won at trial. Monthly bills may have begun to pile up, and parties cannot afford the cost or time involved in fully pursuing the suit. A tenant, for example, may be at a particular disadvantage versus a landlord in this regard.

# Courts of Appeal and the Supreme Court

Trial courts decide questions of fact: does the evidence support the charge that the defendant murdered the victim in cold blood? Is Mr. Lopez responsible for the damage to Mr. Garcia's car? Appellate courts decide questions of procedure or law: were the rights of the accused violated by the police for failure to produce a warrant to search his or her home? Does California's law violate an individual's guarantee of free speech or equal protection of the laws? Here the focus of the court is not the facts but the law. There are no juries, and lawyers do not produce evidence and witnesses. Instead, lawyers submit written briefs and may also appear before the appellate court in oral argument. The process is adversarial like the trial courts, but in the appellate courts, the attorneys are questioned by the judges during their oral arguments whose goal is to persuade the court that their interpretation of the law is the most accurate. California has two levels of appellate courts: the courts of appeal and the state supreme court.

## California Courts of Appeal

California has six district courts of appeal, with 105 justices serving in the courts. Judges sit in a panel of three to hear appeals from superior courts or certain state agencies. Cases are appealed from the superior court to review the decision of that court by a party who is challenging that decision. Decisions of the panels (opinions) are published in the California Appellate Reports. Opinions will be published if they establish a new rule of law, involve a legal issue of continuing public interest, criticize existing law, or make a significant contribution to legal literature (Judicial Council of California, 2011). Each of the six courts selects one of its members to be the presiding justice, who is the administrative head of the court. The six courts are located in San Diego (with divisions in Riverside and Santa Ana), Los Angeles (with a division in Ventura), Fresno, San Jose, San Francisco, and Sacramento.

Courts of appeal have both appellate jurisdiction (hearing appeals) and original jurisdiction (first court to hear a case). Like the Supreme Court, the courts of appeal have original jurisdiction in habeas corpus, mandamus, certiorari, and prohibition proceedings (California Constitution, Article VI, Section 10). Habeas corpus proceedings are used when a person believes he or she has been unlawfully denied freedom to appear before a court or a judge. A writ of certiorari is the term used when the court grants a case on appeal from a lower court. A writ of mandamus and a writ of prohibition are prerogative writs available in civil proceedings to appellate courts in California. A writ of mandamus is issued by a court to order a government agency to perform an act as required by law. A writ of prohibition is issued to stop a lower court from proceeding in a specific case.

Generally, a criminal or civil defendant who loses in superior court has the right to appeal to the court of appeals for a reversal of the decision. In civil cases, however, if a party appeals a monetary award and loses, interest will be added to the amount to cover the extra time consumed on appeal. The six appellate courts had 13,498 filings of records of appeal; of those, 6,145 were criminal cases. In addition there were 6,150 criminal cases filings of original proceedings (Judicial Council of California, 2013).

There are 12 regional circuit courts of appeal, distributed throughout the country and one for the District of Columbia in addition to the Federal Circuit which hears cases on subject matter and not by geographic location. The number of judgeships for the Circuit Courts is established by Congress in Title 28 of the U.S. Code, Section 44. The current total is 179, with the Ninth Circuit (includes California) the largest with 29 (United States Courts website 2014). In 2013 there were 56,475 filings in the U.S. Circuit Courts.

## California Supreme Court

The Supreme Court of California is the state's highest court. Its decisions are binding on all other California courts. The court conducts regular sessions in San Francisco, Los Angeles, and Sacramento; it also occasionally holds special sessions elsewhere.

Most of California's Supreme Court caseload is appellate, usually decided in superior court, and then reviewed by one of the courts of appeals. The court has discretionary power to hear cases, so in most cases, the state Supreme Court may decide which cases it chooses to hear. In cases where the death penalty has been imposed, however, the California Supreme Court must hear the case on appeal. In these cases the state Supreme Court hears the case directly from the Superior Court. In all cases, the decision by the court is final unless the federal courts are asked to review a federal constitutional issue in the case.

The state constitution gives the California Supreme Court the authority to review decisions of the state courts of appeal. This reviewing power enables the Supreme Court to decide important legal questions and to maintain uniformity in the law. The court selects specific issues for review, or it may decide all the issues in a case. In 2011–2012, the Supreme Court issued 87 written opinions. There were 4,620 petitions seeking review from a Court of Appeal decision and 3,417 of these were from appeals in criminal matters. There were 18 automatic appeals filed from Superior Court following a sentence of the death penalty; in addition to these, the Supreme Court disposed of 29 automatic appeals by written opinion. The court's opinions are made accessible in various ways, including publication in the *Official California Reports*.

According to the California Commission on the Fair Administration of Justice (2008) between 1992 and 2002, the California Supreme Court upheld the death penalty 90% of the time, compared to 14 other death penalty states who combined have a 73.7% average. Additionally since 1978, 70% of the cases upheld by the state and then appealed to federal courts have been overturned. For Californians, this means the most populous state has the largest population of death row inmates but the longest time waiting on appeal. The Commission reports that the California Supreme Court is so backlogged that just one appeal from a conviction after 1997 has been resolved. Among the recommendations made by the Commission, one would be to permit intermediate courts of appeal to decide capital cases, but this would require a Constitutional Amendment. Posing the question before the voters would likely open a floodgate of debate, not over the rights of the courts to resolve death penalty sentences, but on the death penalty itself.

# Membership and Qualifications

The California Supreme Court is composed of seven justices: a chief justice, who is appointed specifically to that position, and six associate justices. While all justices and appellate judges are eventually voted on by the public during regular elections, their appointments begin earlier than that. The governor forwards the names of potential justices to the Commission on Judicial Nominee Evaluation (JNE). This 25-member commission includes 19 members elected by the bar, which is the association of attorneys admitted to the practice of law in California. The other six are public members appointed by the governor. This commission considers the qualifications, including the character, of each proposed nominee, and rates him or her exceptionally well qualified, well qualified, qualified, or unqualified. Following the JNE ratings, the governor chooses whom to nominate to the Supreme Court or courts of appeal. This nomination is forwarded to the Commission on Judicial Appointments, which is composed of the chief justice of the state supreme court (or an associate justice if the vacancy is the office of chief justice), the senior (longest serving) presiding justice of the court of appeals, and the attorney general. The commission holds public hearings and receives testimony about the nominee in both oral and written form from anyone who wishes to submit it. The three then vote. If two vote to confirm the appointment, the nominee becomes a justice and takes his or her place on the bench. The new justice is either confirmed or rejected by the electorate at the next election, running unopposed. If a majority of the voters affirm the selection, the justice serves the rest of the 12-year term. Subsequently the justice must run for another 12-year term. If a majority of California voters do not support the justice, the office becomes vacant and the process begins again. Judges are removable through recall as well. In most cases however, justices simply retire! California Supreme Court Justice Marvin Baxter is the most recent justice to retire, announcing he would not seek re-election in the 2014 November elections after 24 years on the California Supreme Court. His retirement becomes effective January 4, 2015.

The November 2014 ballot asked voters whether to retain three justices of the California Supreme Court. All three were retained but two of the three are newly appointed while the third will begin her third full term. Justice Kathryn Mickle Werdegar, was retained for the third time, originally appointed and confirmed in 1994 by Republican governor Pete Wilson.

The newest member of the Court has an unusual profile for a Supreme Court justice, but one that is increasingly familiar to Californians. Mariano-Florentino Cuéllar, who at age 42 will be the youngest justice on the bench. Before his appointment to replace Justice Baxter, he was a law professor at Stanford University. But notably Justice Cuellar was born in Mexico and with his family crossed the Rio Grande and later moved to California. He holds degrees from Harvard, Yale and Stanford (Editorial Board, Sacramento Bee 2014).

Justice Goodwin Liu, the second youngest at age 43, was appointed by Governor Brown and confirmed in 2011 and faced his first retention vote as well. He had been a professor at U.C. Berkeley's Boalt Hall law school. Prior to his confirmation to California's Supreme Court, he had been nominated by President Obama to serve in the Ninth Circuit but was filibustered by Republicans in the Senate (Editorial Board, Sacramento Bee 2014). Governor Brown will have one more replacement to fill for Justice Joyce Kennard, who retired earlier in 2014. In total that he will have chosen 3 of the 7 justices.

## "Discipline": Handling Judicial Wrongdoing

The state Commission on Judicial Performance is responsible for the discipline of judges. The Commission is composed of a majority of lay (nonlawyer) members plus judges and lawyers. In 2013, there were 1,817 judgeships within the Commission's jurisdiction. In addition to jurisdiction over active judges, the Commission has the authority to impose certain discipline upon former judges. While Commission actions ranged from reprimand to removal from office, in fact very few complaints led to disciplinary actions of any kind, and removal from office was especially rare. In 2013, 1,209 new complaints were filed about active and former California judges. The 1,209 complaints named a total of 1,504 judges (908 different judges) alleging legal error not involving misconduct or expressed dissatisfaction with a judge's decision.

In addition to action by the Commission, California judges may be removed in three further ways: re-election loss, impeachment, and recall. In a small move toward such a system at the national court level, Congress has provided for procedures for investigating complaints of unfairness or incompetence against Federal judges. Providing methods other than formal impeachment for removing Federal judges, however, would take an amendment to the U.S. Constitution. Informal avenues, however, exist for dealing with errant Federal trial judges, for example, reducing of caseloads or assigning minor matters to them.

The United States Supreme Court is comprised of a Chief Justice and eight associate justices. This number was established in 1869. Over 10,000 cases were filed in the Supreme Court which includes petitions for certiorari. According to the United States Supreme Court website (2014), oral arguments is granted in about 100 cases per term and formal written opinions are delivered in 80 to 90 cases. The Court will dispose of 50 to 60 additional cases without granting plenary review.

## Jobs of Appellate Courts

As described above, the appellate courts generally review issues of law. This is called judicial review, which involves judgment as to whether a law or action by government is constitutional. A complex society generates complex laws that require judicial untangling. As new technologies emerge, laws and their implementation do not always keep pace. For example, while law enforcement must obtain a warrant before using a wiretap on a telephone,[2] must they also obtain a warrant to track a cellphone through the International Mobile Subscriber Identity (IMSI) that a mobile phone emits to connect with a cellphone tower in order to receive service even though the individual took precise measures to ensure their privacy? Moreover, many statutes tend to be written ambiguously

---

[2] See *Katz v. United States* 389 U.S. 347 (1967).

open to question and judicial interpretation. As discussed above, Californians' use of the popular initiative often results in enactment of law that is constitutionally suspect or just poorly drafted. This means California's courts must reconcile the meaning of the statute with California's constitution and the federal constitution; in some instances, the federal courts become involved in these cases as the losing party has a right to be heard in federal court regarding matters arising under the United States Constitution.

# Issues and Value Conflicts

## Judicial Participation in Private Law Issues

Marriage is ancient. The rules about marriage, however, can be marvelous examples of value conflicts surrounding private law. One of the most contentious issues in California has been over the definition of marriage, involving every branch of California's government, the initiative process, and the federal district, appeals and Supreme Court as well as. Same-sex marriage is an ongoing legal battle in the United States, only recently guaranteed for Californians by a decision handed down by the United States Supreme Court in 2013.

The story regarding California's embrace of same-sex marriage began in 1993 when Hawaii's Supreme Court declared that denying the right for same-sex couples to marry constituted discrimination and sent the case back to trial court for a rehearing. The trial court judge ruled that denying gays a right to marry could not be supported by the Hawaiian Constitution. However, the decision unleashed a tremendous backlash and voters in the state passed a Constitutional amendment defining marriage between a man and woman only. But the Hawaii legislature passed a landmark "Reciprocal Beneficiaries" law that created some of the protections same-sex couples could not access through marriage. This created a ripple effect throughout the states including California. The United States Constitution declares that states must honor contracts from other states, known as the Full Faith Credit Clause of Article IV, Section 1. This clause means that traditional marriages must be recognized in the states, even if the marriage license was issued in another state. So in other words, what happens in Vegas doesn't stay in Vegas if two people said "I Do."

However, with regard to same sex marriage, fearful that couples would soon have the right to marry, Californians picked up the debate in 2000, passing Proposition 22, denying through statutory law the right of same sex couples to marry by defining marriage as "a personal relation arising out of a civil contract between a man and a woman." However, in 2004, then- San Francisco mayor Gavin Newsome began to issue marriage licenses to same-sex couples, which were nullified in August 2004, (*Lockyer v. City and County of San Francisco*) by the state Supreme Court. Then in May 2008, the California Supreme Court overturned Proposition 22 in a 4–3 ruling declaring that the state Constitution protects a fundamental "right to marry" that extends equally to same-sex couples. In response to the ruling, in November 2008, voters passed a Constitutional amendment to California's Constitution defining marriage as a union between a man and a woman only. The California Supreme heard challenges to Proposition 8 under Constitutional procedural grounds and held that the proposition had been passed constitutionally. However, the Court's ruling did not settle the question of gay marriage in California;

instead it merely continued an ongoing state and national debate. In August 2010 a Federal district court struck down the law under the Equal Protection Clause of the U.S. Constitution's Fourteenth Amendment and the ruling was upheld by the Ninth Circuit. Finally in 2013 the United States Supreme Court was asked whether Proposition 8 was constitutional. The Supreme Court never gave an answer as to the constitutionality of a constitutional ban on same sex marriage in California. Essentially the majority of the court found that the case was not properly before the court as governmental officials in California had refused to appeal the trial court's decision. When deciding whether a law is constitutional, only the government can represent the "law" before the United States Supreme Court, even though the backers of Proposition 8 were entitled to represent the law in the district court's trial proceedings. Since the proponents of proposition 8 were not entitled to step into the state's shoes to appeal the decision, the court found it could not issue a decision as to the constitutionality of the law, leaving in place the federal trial court victory for two same sex couples who had sought to marry.

The point is not to argue that same-sex marriages are good or bad. The point is that courts interpret as well as change the rules about private law. Some observers, mostly on the conservative side of politics, thought that courts probably weakened the institution of marriage  and had done great mischief. Others, mostly on the liberal side of politics, thought that the courts had advanced the cause of justice. Let us notice that courts had taken a side, had made rules, and had supported some values while turning away from other values. The short label for all of that is politics. In ways just like these, courts can be regarded as significant participants in the American political process.

## Judicial Participation in Public Law

Courts have a critical role to play in at least some of the political issues of our times. Examples include how races should get along (consider *Brown v. Board of Education* 1954), and how society should treat illegal immigrants. Surely the participation of state and Federal courts in resolving the November 2000 presidential election disputes in Florida sharply illustrates the point. The point is that California and many other state courts exercise a state-based constitutional judicial review function very similar to that of the Federal courts. One should also note that when courts exercise the judicial review authority, it often generates political reactions. This is especially true where the issues at hand are emotionally charged. These cases illustrate the authority and role of courts as the final interpreters of state constitutions and the constitutionality of any statutes or other enactments by local governments. Consequently, we will say it again, reader: state and Federal courts are significant participants in the American political process.

## The Nonpartisan Tradition of Judicial Politics

Californians no less than other Americans prize a notion that judges are and ought to be uninfluenced by partisan political considerations. There is no conflict in that with the dimensions of judicial politics that we identified earlier. Although values surely conflict and though that surely amounts to politics by any reasonable definition of the word, there is no necessary fight between Democrats and Republicans implied.

Ways of insulating judges from partisan politics are consciously present in California as well as U.S. judicial structures. Strong tradition is a part of this: judges and other observers alike agree that partisan elections are inappropriate for California. Furthermore, long terms of office help to insulate judges from partisan fights. Schemes like retention elections usually insulate judges from electoral challenge, too.

For all of this, there are some traditional political elements found in the judicial selection process that have been accepted if not always cherished. These include such things as making judicial appointments that reward former legislators or other political party supporters for faithful service, or indeed other friends, like former law partners or law professors. But other political activities, for example, using the ballot initiative process, have appeared to be attempts at lessening the traditional independence of the judiciary.

## Judicial Politics in the 21st Century

From the mid-1970s to the mid-1980s, conservative political groups mounted serious efforts to unseat both trial court and appellate court judges in California. In the most remarkable assault, Governor George Deukmejian, other Republican candidates for office, and a remarkable variety of ad hoc groups joined a campaign in 1985 and 1986 that resulted in the landslide defeat of Chief Justice Rose Bird (who received a 66% "no" vote), and Associate Justices Cruz Reynoso and Joseph Grodin. The incumbent justices and their supporters were out-spent in the campaign by roughly $5.5 million to $2 million (Wold and Culver, 1987: 350).

Observers differed on the question of whether the incumbents deserved to be cashiered by the voters. But the process, which relied on large amounts of money and heavily negative television advertising, disturbed professional observers. The inability of judges to engage in heated, high-priced election contests, and indeed, the view that they should not even try, dominated the arguments of those who were critical of the 1986 judicial retention elections. But others not critical of the contests responded that this was just the kind of situation for which retention elections were designed. The people spoke—as the system was designed to allow them to speak. By 1988 it was clear that the newly constituted court led by Chief Justice Malcolm M. Lucas was deciding cases differently from its Rose Bird-led predecessor. With the exception of several decisions that affirmed sentences of death imposed by trial courts, the changes were subtle, in most instances gradual yet discernible.

## References

California Courts. 2013, September 13. *Court Filings Decrease for Fiscal Year 2011–2012.* Retrieved from http://www.courts.ca.gov/23492.htm.

California Courts. n.d.a. *About California Courts.* Retrieved from http://www.courts.ca.gov/2113.htm.

California Courts. n.d.b. *Resolving Small Claims Cases.* Retrieved from http://www.courts.ca.gov/20129.htm.

California Legislature. n.d. *California's Legislature, Chapter V: Judicial department.* The Judicial Department California's Legislature. Retrieved from http://www.leginfo.ca.gov/pdf/caleg5.pdf.

Editorial Board Sacramento Bee. 2014 "Endorsements: Three California Supreme Court justices deserve a thumbs up from voters" The Sacramento Bee 10/08/2014--next to judicial-2011

Judicial Council of California. 2011. *Court Statistics Report: Statewide Caseload Trends 2000–2001 through 2009–2010.* Retrieved from www.courts.ca.gov/12941.htm#id7495.

Judicial Council of California. 2013. 2013 *Court Statistics Report: Statewide Caseload Trends 2000–2001 through 2011–2012.* Retrieved from http://www.courts.ca.gov/12941.htm#id7495.

Wold, John T. & John H. Culver, 1986. The Defeat of the California Justices: The Campaign, the Electorate, and the Issue of Judicial Accountability, 70 JUDICATURE 318.

# CHAPTER 10

# California Local Governments

## Yuan Ting and Samuel B. Stone

## Introduction

In addition to being a citizen of the United States and California, an average Californian also lives within the jurisdiction of perhaps 10 or more local governments. Residents in the city of Fullerton, for example, are governed by a municipal government, a county government, two school districts (elementary and secondary), and several special districts including air quality management, community college, sanitation, transportation, vector control, and water. These local governments are given responsibility for providing the most basic public services such as health, public safety, education, water, public transit, recreation, and commerce, to name just a few.

The importance of local government increases as more people settle in urban areas. At the beginning of the 20th century, 60% of the American population lived in rural areas and most of them lived their lives without too much involvement with government. By 2010, 81% of the population lived in cities. This urbanization trend is even more startling in California, where 95% of Californians lived in cities as of 2010 (see Table 10.1). As more and more people moved into urban areas, people living in close proximity had

**Table 10.1**  Rural and Urban Population in the United States and California, 1900–2010

|  | 1900 (%) | 1950 (%) | 1990 (%) | 2000 (%) | 2010 (%) |
|---|---|---|---|---|---|
| **United States** |  |  |  |  |  |
| Rural Population | 60.4 | 36.0 | 24.8 | 21.0 | 19.3 |
| Urban Population | 39.6 | 64.0 | 75.2 | 79.0 | 80.7 |
| **California** |  |  |  |  |  |
| Rural Population | 47.7 | 19.3 | 7.4 | 5.6 | 5.1 |
| Urban Population | 52.3 | 80.7 | 92.6 | 94.4 | 94.9 |

Source: Census Bureau (1995). *Urban and Rural Population: 1900 to 1990*. Retrieved January 18, 2009. <http://www.census.gov/population/www/censusdata/files/urpop0090.txt>; Census Bureau (2011). *Statistical Abstract of the United States: 2011*, Table 29. Washington, DC: U.S. Department of Commerce; Census Bureau (2010). *Percent Urban and Rural in 2010 by State*, retrieved 2/20/14, http://www2.census.gov/geo/ua/PctUrbanRural_State.xls.

to work together to provide their communities with fresh water and waste management. They had to create police and fire departments to protect lives and private property from crime and natural disasters. So we have to create local governments and hire people to provide more public services as our communities grow.

As we entered the 21st century, the needs and problems of our communities have become more complex and require governmental solutions across political jurisdictions. For example, the cars that leave the suburban communities in the morning produce traffic jams and pollution for major employment centers in other cities later in the day. The crime in a central city affects suburban residents who travel to see a baseball game or a concert. Intergovernmental cooperation has become more important as governments from different jurisdictions and levels seek solutions to solve their problems jointly.

In addition to the impact of population change on the growth of local governments, there is a long history of grassroots democracy in our country. Many Americans believe that government closest to the people governs best. Therefore, we arrange our local governments in small units and divide responsibility and authority among many governmental units in the same area. This is called decentralization. We try to coordinate public policies among these separate governments. The result is a complex maze of many jurisdictions with different duties and powers, and a system that makes coordination and common policies difficult to achieve. Behind these conflicts are differences over basic perspectives on how to create the best kind of government to serve the needs of people.

This chapter will discuss the origin and constitutional basis for local governments, the relationship between the federal, state, and local governments, the particular features of California local governments, major issues facing local governments, and political values that affect the way decisions are made in local governments. The chapter will attempt to answer one key question: can local governments be held accountable to deal with the needs of an increasingly complex urban society?

# The Nature of Local Government in the United States

The American Revolution of 1776 has been called a revolt against a strong central government: revolutionaries sought to create governments that citizens could directly influence. Throughout American history, prominent thinkers have argued that the most basic governmental functions should be handled by governments physically close to the citizens they serve. Thomas Jefferson, for instance, believed strongly in the principle of local control. The gentleman farmer from Virginia and the author of the Declaration of Independence envisioned small units of local government in which every citizen becomes ". . . an acting member of the government, and in the offices nearest and most interesting to him, will attach him by his strongest feelings to the independence of his country, and its republican constitution" (Jefferson, 1999, p. 213). In Jefferson's view, small areas like five miles by ten miles are the ideal size for the most important unit of government. In these neighborhoods, all important decisions can be made in a meeting of the people living in that territory, where issues can be decided by a show of hands.

The Jeffersonian tradition features faith in local government and distrust of the national government. Local governments are thought to be more responsive to the interests and desires of the people in a given area and easier to change if significant numbers of residents object to the ways things are done. Moreover, the idea of community held by Jefferson and others included not just physical proximity, but also common values and feelings of those who live near one another. Such common values, interests, and desires would be shared by local government officials and reflected in governmental decisions.

When a French political thinker, Alexis de Tocqueville, visited America in 1831, he observed this unique tradition of grassroots democracy and wrote:

> These Americans are the most peculiar people in the world.... In a local community in their country, a citizen may conceive of some need which is not being met. What does he do? He goes across the street and discusses it with a neighbor. Then what happens? A committee begins functioning on behalf of that need. All of this is done by private citizens on their own initiative. The health of a democratic society may be measured by the quality of functions performed by private citizens." (1956, p. 201)

This tradition is shown in the U.S. Bureau of Census' count of local government. According to Table 10.2, there were more than 90,000 local governments in the United States as of 2012. Between 1982 and 2012, the number of county governments has remained relatively constant, decreasing by only 10 or 0.3%. In 2012, there were 443 more municipal governments than in 1982, a 2.3% increase. Township governments have decreased by 374 or 2.2% in the same period. However, counts of special-purpose governments have undergone greater changes than general-purpose governments. The number of school districts has decreased by 13.3%, from 14,851 in 1982 to 12,880 in 2012. This decrease reflects a continuing trend since the 1950s resulting from school district consolidation and reorganization. The number of special districts has increased by 36.3% from 1982 to 2012, which is in response to the increasing demands for services that traditional governments (townships, cities, and counties) cannot provide. The large number of local

**Table 10.2**   Local Governments in the United States

| Type of Government | 1982 | 2012 | % Change 1982–2012 |
|---|---|---|---|
| All local governments | 81,780 | 90,056 | 10.1% |
| County | 3,041 | 3,031 | − 0.3% |
| Municipal | 19,076 | 19,519 | 2.3% |
| Township | 16,734 | 16,360 | − 2.2% |
| School district | 14,851 | 12,880 | − 13.3% |
| Special district | 28,078 | 38,266 | 36.3% |

Source: Census Bureau. 2006. *Statistical Abstract of the United States: 2006*, Table 415. Washington, DC: U.S. Department of Commerce; Census Bureau (2013). *Government Organization Summary Report: 2012*.

governments reflects the Jeffersonian tradition of grassroots democracy, but it raises an important question about the financial burden local governments place on citizens.

The U.S. Constitution of 1789 was also endorsed by those who saw too much state and local power in the Articles of Confederation. Its authors, James Madison and most particularly the influential Alexander Hamilton, wanted a powerful central government capable of defending the borders and regulating the economy. Madison, the most important voice in crafting the Constitution and the principle of separation of powers, feared the evil power of the "mischiefs of faction" that he felt were common in smaller governmental units (1787). Only a central government with sufficient checks and balances could protect individual rights and liberty.

Hamilton believed that the Articles of Confederation clearly demonstrated the weakness of decentralized government, and argued for a powerful national government. In his view, Americans need a national government strong enough to protect their interests and fulfill their dreams.

At the same time, Hamilton, himself a New Yorker, was a proponent of industrialization and foresaw an urbanized future for America. Jefferson, a Virginian, was suspicious of large cities and envisioned a nation of farms and small towns. These contrary attitudes are reflected in the ambivalence toward cities that many Americans feel today.

These traditions created the constitutional government in the United States, and they both support and are leery of strong local governments. This explains the reason why our history is one of conflict over these traditions of how best to make governmental decisions and serve the needs of citizens. Should we divide our country into small local units that may represent the view of the average citizen more effectively, or should we be more concerned with the potential tyranny of such small units? Can those small governments adequately handle concerns that may span beyond the boundaries of local jurisdictions? Will larger urban governments be sensitive to the needs of individual neighborhoods and communities? California local governments can be described as conflicts over these perspectives.

# Local Governments and State Government

The U.S. Constitution leaves to the states all governmental functions that are not assigned to the federal government. Local governments are nowhere mentioned in the Constitution, even though local governments existed when the Constitution was drafted in 1787. The organization of local governments was left for each state and its people to determine. State constitutions and laws can create local governments and can abolish them. State-level legal provisions determine what local governments can and cannot do. Local government officials must operate within those constraints.

In the early years of California's history, cities were dependent on the state for their powers, and the legislature was accused of running the state for the benefit of large companies, like the Southern Pacific Railroad. The railroad company forced many local governments to pay subsidies for the privilege of having a station built in their communities. The state's meddling with local governments produced a backlash that led to the drafting of a new state constitution in 1879. The 1879 constitution included a number of reforms to the laws relating to local governments as well as more explicit limitations on the state's power to interfere in local matters. These were followed by further reforms to make government more responsive to the people through the Progressive movement in the early 20th century (see Chapters 3 and 4 for further discussion of the Progressive movement), the adoption of the Brown Act, and other state laws in the 1960s, and most recently the reinvention reforms to make government more accountable for performance and results.

## Charter Versus General Law Cities

Local governments are often described as "creatures of the state" as state law regulates many of their actions. School districts, for instance, are regularly inspected by state education agencies to ensure uniformity of standards that the state law requires be met. There are two kinds of cities in California: charter and general law. As part of reforms to maximize local control, the state constitution gives cities the power to become charter cities. The charter city provision in the state constitution, popularly referred to as the "home-rule" provision, is based on the principle that a city, rather than the state, is in the best position to know what are the needs of its people and how to meet them. A city charter is a special document that, in many ways, acts like a constitution for the city. By adopting a charter, the home-rule provision allows the city greater autonomy to make its own decisions and enhanced ability to conduct municipal affairs, such as election matters, land use and zoning, and how to spend its tax dollars. In practice, however, general law cities may exercise most of the same powers of charter cities if their councils vote to do so. To become a charter city, a city's voters elect a charter commission to draft the charter, which has to be ratified by a majority vote of the city's voters. A city charter can be changed only by a vote of the city's voters, not by the city council. Of 482 cities in the state, only 121 of them are chartered. In general, charters are more common for larger cities than smaller ones.

The 361 cities that have not adopted a charter, called general law cities, are bound by the state's general law with respect to municipal affairs. These general law cities are permitted to do only those things prescribed by the state law and little else. The state law governing general law cities is clear because it has been subjected to judicial scrutiny and tested over many decades; however, city charters can be more complicated, and it is not always a straightforward process to determine what can and cannot be done under the state law.

# The Impact of Federal Government Programs on Local Governments

The federal government influences local governments in several ways. Congress provides direct financial aid to local governments, and the amount of federal aid has varied in different periods of time. The federal government has become active in assisting local governments, and by the 1970s it was common for 10%–15% of a city's budget to come from Washington, DC. Generally speaking, cities with larger numbers of poor residents were more heavily dependent on federal funds. During this period, costs for providing public services might be shared among the federal, state, and local governments, with state and local officials working within federal guidelines to provide many public programs. And the federal government began to increase its influence on state and local governments. For example, public education is considered traditionally a state and local responsibility—to establish schools, develop curricula, and determine requirements for teacher qualifications, enrollment, and graduation. The Cold War stimulated the first comprehensive federal education legislation, when in 1958 Congress passed the National Defense Education Act in response to the Soviet launch of Sputnik. As a result, the federal government began supporting public elementary and secondary education to improve science, mathematics, and foreign language instruction. In 1965, Congress passed the Elementary and Secondary Education Act, which provided federal aid to disadvantaged children from poor urban and rural areas. In the same year, Congress passed the Higher Education Act to provide federal aid for needy college students. Today, the federal government's influence in public education is everywhere. Almost all school districts receive some federal aid, which requires them to comply with federal rules and regulations.

The relationship between the federal government and local governments took a turn during the Reagan presidency. Reagan wanted to end the federal government's role in domestic programs and shift some responsibility back to the states. As a result, the Reagan and subsequently George H. W. Bush years brought a significant reduction in federal funds for local government programs, and little increase occurred during the Clinton administration. One consequence of this shift of responsibility is that we find that older central cities are facing the problems of declining city life with fewer resources. During the George W. Bush presidency, the role of the federal government expanded significantly after the terrorist attacks in 2001. The passage of the Patriot Act greatly increased the surveillance powers of the federal government. President Bush also expanded the role of the federal government in domestic policy areas such as education and social services. For example, Congress passed the No Child Left Behind Act in 2001, which introduced further federal involvement in public education, traditionally the responsibility of the state and local governments. In addition, since the September 11 attacks, the federal government has expanded its role in emergency management. For example, Congress has authorized several assistance programs, including grants, training, technical assistance, equipment, and exercises to help first responders in local governments—such as fire service, emergency medical service, and law enforcement personnel—prepare for potential terrorist attacks.

The federal court system also influences local governments. The U.S. Supreme Court has been asked frequently to determine the constitutionality of local government practices. Since local governments are considered creatures of the state, many of their actions, such as police practices, zoning laws, and restrictions on commerce, are frequent subjects of state and federal court cases. For example, in 2003 California passed a law to establish the medical marijuana program, which is administered through county governments. The program allows patients, upon obtaining a recommendation from their physicians for use of medical marijuana, to apply for and be issued a medical marijuana identification card. The program allows qualified patients and their caregivers to possess, grow, transport, and use medical marijuana in California. In the Supreme Court case *Gonzales v. Raich* (2005), the court ruled that the federal government has the power to arrest and prosecute patients and their suppliers even if the marijuana use is permitted under state law, because of its authority under the Federal Controlled Substances Act to regulate interstate commerce in illegal drugs. This ruling has an important impact on local governments enforcing the medical marijuana program because such practice is subject to federal prosecution. On the other hand, in 2008 the U.S. Supreme Court refused to review a landmark decision in which California state courts found that its medical marijuana law was not preempted by federal law and that it was not the job of local enforcement to enforce the federal drug laws (*City of Garden Grove v. Superior Court* (Kha), 2007). This example shows how the federal court can influence the actions of local governments.

# California Local Governments

All of the various kinds of local governments in California share some common characteristics:

- They are governed by elected officials.
- They have the authority to raise money through taxes and fees.
- They can borrow money, hire people, and administer certain public services.
- They have the power to enforce certain laws made by state or local elected officials.

We can divide California local governments into counties, cities, and special districts.

## Counties

Counties' Boards of Supervisors delegate their executive activities to hired managers, sometimes referred to as Chief Executive Officers. These executives function like city managers.

California is geographically divided into 58 counties of varying sizes and shapes. Originally counties were the primary vehicle through which the state performed many important functions including law enforcement, public health, welfare, transportation, and the administration of elections. Generally speaking, California counties don't have the broad powers of self-government that cities have. The state legislature has more direct control over counties than cities and may delegate to the counties any function that belongs to the state itself. For example, if the state legislature passes a law to require land use zoning by a certain method, it will be binding on all the counties. On the other hand, the county may adopt its own if the state didn't require a method. Counties can also be more than simple agents of the state government. At the direction of elected county officials, other functions beyond those mandated by the state can be undertaken.

The state constitution recognizes two types of counties: general law and charter. General law counties stick to the state law as to the number and duties of county elected officials. Charter counties have a somewhat greater authority to determine the election, compensation, terms, removal, and salary of the governing board and other officers. Currently, there are 44 general law counties and 14 charter counties. In California,

**Table 10.3**   Ten Most Populated Counties in California

| County | Population (2013 Estimate) | Type |
|---|---|---|
| Los Angeles | 10,017,068 | Charter |
| San Diego | 3,211,252 | Charter |
| Orange | 3,114,363 | Charter |
| Riverside | 2,292,507 | General Law |
| San Bernardino | 2,088,371 | Charter |
| Santa Clara | 1,862,041 | Charter |
| Alameda | 1,578,891 | Charter |
| Sacramento | 1,462,131 | Charter |
| Contra Costa | 1,094,205 | General Law |
| Fresno | 955,272 | Charter |

Source: California Department of Finance. 2008. *California County Population Estimates.*
Sacramento, CA: Department of Finance; Census Bureau (2014). *State & County QuickFacts*,
retrieved 20 February, 2014, http://quickfacts.census.gov/qfd/states/06/.

charters are more common for larger counties than smaller ones—of the 10 most populated counties, 8 of them are chartered (see Table 10.3).

The governing board of each county is called the Board of Supervisors. Counties
typically have five supervisors, elected from separate districts. County residents also
elect other officials including the assessor, auditor-controller, clerk-recorder, district
attorney, public administrator, sheriff-coroner, and treasurer-tax collector. Unlike the
separation of powers that characterizes the federal and state governments, the Board of
Supervisors is both the legislative and the executive authority of the county. The board
performs its executive authority by setting policy priorities for the county, overseeing
county departments and approving their budgets, supervising county employees, and
appropriating money for programs to meet the needs of county residents. As the legislative body of the county, the board may pass and enforce within its limits all police,
sanitation, public health, social service, and other ordinances that do not conflict with
the state's general law.

County government also mirrors California's great diversity. For example, Los
Angeles County is one of the nation's largest counties with 4,084 square miles and has
the largest population (over 10 million in 2013) of any county in the nation. It had a
budget of $24.7 billion for the 2013–2014 year, which is more than the expenditures
of 20 states. San Bernardino County is larger than any other county in the nation with
20,160 square miles and is larger than nine states. Alpine County, on the other hand, had
only about 1,200 residents in 2012.

Counties have major responsibilities for many social services as required by state
and federal laws, including health care and public defenders for the indigent, aid to
the homeless, and welfare to the poor. They are major providers of jails and juvenile
halls. They are the assessors and collectors of property tax. They keep and issue official

records and administer elections. In recent years the demands for these services have increased, just as the economy has declined. This has presented a tremendous challenge to local governments seeking solutions to meet increasing demands with fewer resources. In particular, counties in urban areas have faced considerable financial problems in recent years as the need for these services increased while state funding declined. Orange County declared bankruptcy in 1994, sending shock waves throughout the nation's local governments and financial community. How could one of the nation's wealthiest counties have insufficient resources to cover its expenditures? One reason was the increasing pressure placed on county officials to pay for social services while state and federal funds for these services declined and the numbers of people in need increased. Another reason was the reluctance of Orange County officials, responding to voters' perceptions of high government spending, to increase taxes. To solve these problems, the county treasurer's office tried to raise needed funds through speculative investments, which seemed to be a "low-cost" solution at the time. Many cities and school districts in the county found the temptation similarly promising and added some of their money to the Orange County investment pool. Eventually this high-risk investment led to one of the largest local government bankruptcies in the United States history. More recently, Los Angeles County has faced serious fiscal problems, and elected officials have threatened to close the county-run hospitals and drastically curtail medical and social services to the poor.

## Cities

There are 482 cities in the state. Cities are formed at the request and consent of the residents in a given area. Normally, residents create cities when a settlement of people becomes large enough to need more public services than the county government can reasonably provide. Since the advent of Proposition 13, however, the incorporation of new cities has become more infrequent because a city's property tax apportionment is based on the city's share of property tax revenue it generated when Proposition 13 went into effect. Figure 10.1 displays the frequency of municipal incorporation over the state's history. It shows that there are two periods during which the incorporation of municipalities peaked. The first period was prompted by a ballot measure known as the Separation of Sources Act of 1910, which established that local governments could tax property and granted local governments the exclusive control over the use of property taxes. The Act was also in response to the rapid population growth and the increasing pace of urbanization in the state. The second period began in the late 1950s when several state-level reforms like the Lakewood Plan and the Bradley-Burns Act created powerful incentives for municipal incorporation in the state.

In order to incorporate, residents in the proposed city must prove that their new city can provide adequate services to themselves without county support. The city of Jurupa Valley in Riverside County was incorporated in July 2011 after decades of growth and became the youngest city in California. There are also examples of cities formed by major landowners, like the cities of Irwindale and Industry in Los Angeles County, which contain large industrial properties and less than 2,000 residents. Incorporation as a city permits these industries to be served by local governments without significant changes or taxes. Other cities such as Villa Park in Orange County and several small

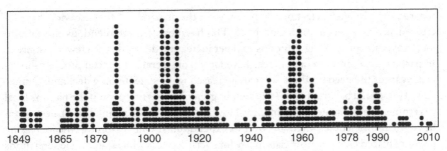

**Figure 10.1**  Frequency of Municipal Incorporation in California

cities on the Palos Verdes peninsula in Los Angeles County consist of small numbers of wealthy homeowners. Incorporation as a small city allows these residents to avoid being burdened with the costs of serving poorer residents.

The residents who want their community to incorporate as a city usually are looking for more local control. As we have discussed earlier, the state constitution, under the "home-rule" provision, gives cities greater authority for self-government by adopting their own charters. The state law giving cities their legal authority provides for two different forms of municipal government: the mayor-council form and the council-manager form. Residents can choose their own form of government and elect people from their own community to run it.

## Council-Manager Government

The most common form of city government in California is the council-manager government in which most administrative responsibilities are delegated to a professional manager. In the council-manager form of government, residents elect a city council of five or more members, which is the legislative body of the city. Often a mayor is also elected. He or she is a voting member of the council and presides at council meetings and performs ceremonial functions, but has no specific executive duties. Council members and the mayor are generally part-time officials. They are paid salaries varying from nothing to several hundred dollars per month or meeting. Some cities elect their council members in small districts designed to represent different sectors of the population. More commonly, council members are elected citywide or at large. Other cities employ some combination of these two methods, electing some council members by districts and some at large or requiring council members to live in various districts but be elected at large. The council meets frequently to enact local laws, adopt the budget, and give policy direction to the city manager.

The city manager is appointed by the city council and acts as the chief executive officer. The day-to-day tasks of running the city government are placed in the hands of the appointed city manager. She or he is guided by the council but is given the responsibility of hiring employees, seeing that the work of the city is being carried out, and providing plans for future growth. City managers serve at the pleasure of the council, which means that they can be fired by a majority vote of the council, and the council is free to determine their salaries. Their relationship to the council is similar to that of a chief executive officer to a corporate board of directors. City managers may have learned about municipal government and management skills in graduate programs like the Master of Public Administration and on the job as a department head or assistant city manager. Ideally, in the council-manager form of government, different departments are coordinated and led by the city manager, and the entire city government is responsive to the city council and, through these elected representatives, to the people.

### Mayor-Council Government

This form of government rules Los Angeles, San Diego, San Francisco, and Oakland. Citizens in the strong mayor-council cities elect a city council, which is the legislative branch of municipal government, and a mayor, who is the executive head of the government. The mayor and administrators who report to the mayor are responsible for executing council-approved policies. The mayor is also involved in legislation and normally can veto bills passed by the council. He or she appoints department heads with the advice and consent of the council. The strong mayor-council system has the advantage of clearly defined political leadership. A directly elected mayor with executive powers can more easily introduce innovations in city policy. In theory, a mayor's position with respect to the city council is analogous to a governor's position with respect to the state legislature or to the President of the United States' position with respect to Congress. But, historically, a mayor's powers compared to the city council are typically weaker in California than those of the President compared to Congress. The city of Los Angeles, for instance, is usually referred to as having a weak mayor-council form of government. The mayor does not have direct authority over several important operating departments such as police, fire, and public works. Commissioners appointed by the mayor and confirmed by the city council directly govern these departments. Los Angeles city council members also have considerable control over public decisions that are made concerning their districts.

## School Districts

School districts are common in most of the United States and seem best explained by a widespread feeling that school decisions should be made locally and separate from other governmental decisions. School districts are units of local government that are completely separate from other local governments such as counties and cities. They have their own elected boards of three, five, or seven members. California has 546 elementary school districts, 83 high school districts, and 334 unified school districts (California Department of Education, 2010). School districts receive some of the property tax revenues generated in their counties, but the bulk of their funding comes from the State of California.

## Special Districts

Special districts are the most numerous form of government in both the nation and the state. As the community becomes more densely developed, more special districts are created to provide separate services. In California, there are about 2,200 special districts, not including the nearly 1,000 school districts. This number is far greater than all the counties and cities combined. Special districts are governmental units created to perform a single or limited set of services to the community. Although school districts may have received the most public attention, other districts provide air pollution control, coastal management, fire protection, libraries, mosquito control, recreation and parks, waste management, and other important services.

As independent governmental units, special districts may have the power to levy taxes and issue bonds. Special districts have no specific boundary requirements. Some cover only portions of a city, while others may cut across several cities and counties, resulting in a layered public sector of considerable complexity. The Metropolitan Water District of Southern California, for example, serves 26 cities and water agencies with nearly 19 million residents in six different counties in Southern California, which allows the district to achieve economies of scale and avoid problems of coordination between cities and counties with respect to their need for water. Special districts are occasionally created as a response to problems common to several cities or counties. Air quality management, transportation, and water districts are good examples, since traffic congestion, smog, and water problems do not stop at city or county boundaries. Other special districts are formed to provide services before a city is created.

Special districts may be governed by elected boards or by boards appointed by elected officials. Most special districts have five-member boards, but some special districts are governed by a large board. The Metropolitan Water District, for example, is a consortium of 26 member cities and water agencies, and each member is entitled to elect at least one director to its governing board. In most cases, board members do not receive any compensation or receive only a nominal salary. While special districts are created to provide specific services and promote local control, the increase of special districts in a densely populated area may create a fragmentation of government and make it difficult for citizen participation because overlapping boundaries and different layers of local governments are likely to make special districts less visible than city and county governments. This explains why voter turnout in special district elections is usually lower than in municipal elections.

# Local Government Finance

Given the increasing demand for public services, elected officials and city managers spend much of their time searching for new sources of revenue. Local government finance changes frequently as new state laws, court decisions, and initiatives alter their revenue sources. Generally speaking, local governments are low on the food chain of government revenues. As problems occur at other levels of government, sources of revenue are taken away from local governments. As a result, city officials are adept at finding new sources.

Proposition 13 of 1978 severely limited the property tax, which is the major source of revenue for local governments (see Chapter 11 for further discussion of property tax and revenue changes in California). It limits property tax liability to a maximum of 1% of assessed value of property and caps the rate of increase in assessed value to 2% per year. Following its passage, local government property tax revenues were cut by half and cities and counties had to raise user fees and local taxes, as well as lobby the state to divert significant state funds to local governments to make up much of the property tax loss. As a result, local governments have relied more heavily on the state general fund and have seen a shift of power from local jurisdictions to the state. As the state economy went into a pronounced recession and schools were required by the courts and voters to increase educational funding, local governments lost significant amounts of state revenue and had to look for other revenue tools to finance local services. For example, in the mid-1990s taxes on utilities were popular in California cities.

Most cities also used the authority granted under the state constitution to impose other local taxes like hotel and business licenses as well as a variety of fees like those for sewer connections, building permits, and development impact. In response to the perceived abuses in the use of local taxes and fees, California voters passed an initiative in 1996 to prohibit new utility taxes and other special assessments and fees without the support of two-thirds of voters in the community.

## Bankruptcies

Local government bankruptcy is an exceedingly rare occurrence in modern U.S. history. It has, however, occurred with startling frequency in California. Local government bankruptcy refers to a process by which a federal bankruptcy judge grants a local government the power to enter into Chapter 9 bankruptcy, which allows it to renegotiate its obligations to its creditors, vendors, and other parties to which it is otherwise contractually obligated to make payments. During the term of bankruptcy protection, the local government is often taken over by an emergency financial manager who is typically appointed by the state government or by the court. This period is known as receivership. Bankruptcy is both highly undesirable and extremely difficult to secure. Federal bankruptcy judges only grant bankruptcy to governments that can prove that it is impossible to meet their current financial obligations. It is undesirable because drastic cuts in services must be made and local governments become essentially unable to borrow money for a long time.

The most high profile local government bankruptcy in the state was that of Orange County in 1994. The Orange County Treasurer at the time, Robert Citron, had been using the county's power to issue debt in order to reinvest those funds in investments that carried a substantial interest rate risk. When interest rates began to rise and these investments lost money, Citron issued more debt to cover the losses. In order to accomplish this, Citron falsified financial documents and made a number of false statements to the board of supervisors. He pled guilty to these charges the following year. In the meantime, the county had no money to pay back the debts or cover the losses. Additionally, Citron had been investing the cash assets of many other local governments in these risky investments and they, too, suffered financial losses. The county filed for bankruptcy and subsequently cut services, laid off employees, and began the long slow process of recovery.

A number of California cities have filed for bankruptcy more recently. These include the major cities of San Bernardino, Stockton, and Vallejo along with the smaller cities of Desert Hot Springs and Mammoth Lake. Vallejo filed bankruptcy in 2008, while San Bernardino and Stockton filed for bankruptcy in 2012. These bankruptcy filings have largely been used by local governments as a means to renegotiate pension and other employee retirement benefits in order to put their fiscal house in order.

## The Rise and Fall of Redevelopment Agencies

In 1945, the state legislature passed the Community Redevelopment Act which authorized cities to create redevelopment agencies (RDA). These RDAs were special districts whose purpose was to channel reinvestment to blighted areas of cities. The agencies had a variety of powers including the ability to issue debt and the condemnation powers of eminent domain. These powers were soon augmented by an additional one. In 1952, California voters passed Proposition 18, which established tax increment finance (TIF). TIF is an economic development tool whereby increases in property tax revenues within a redevelopment district are retained by the district rather than shared with the other local governments that also service that area. These retained property tax revenues are then reinvested in the district and represented the principal revenue stream for the RDAs. In the typical arrangement, the RDA makes infrastructure improvements to the blighted area and pays for these improvements by issuing bonds. The bonds are then paid back over several decades by the retained property tax revenues (referred to as the "increment"). The infrastructure improvements are used to incentivize private sector reinvestment in the district. Property values within the district then rise due to this reinvestment. As property values rise, this produces higher property tax revenue, which goes to pay back the bonds which were used to pay for the infrastructure. For this reason, TIF is sometimes referred to as "self-financing."

This cycle of financing and reinvestment, however, is predicated on a number of assumptions. One of these assumptions is that a lack of new infrastructure is the only thing keeping the private sector from reinvesting in an area. Another assumption is that the RDAs will only spend their money on projects within the district that will attract reinvestment. In the case of California redevelopment districts, there were many cities and projects where these assumptions did not hold. Until the 1970s, there were few RDAs and those that existed were relatively small. Rapid suburbanization in the 1960s led to blight in older areas and fiscal pressures on cities forced many of them to turn to TIF to address these problems. This was accelerated in 1978 when Proposition 13 was passed. The extremely strict limits on property taxes imposed by Proposition 13 left California cities with very little revenue. Many cities attempted to make up that loss by creating redevelopment districts which could recapture some of the revenue that would have gone to other local governments. The number of RDAs exploded and by the late 2000s, their share of property tax revenues statewide was six times what it was in the mid-1970s (Taylor, 2012). Many RDAs had used TIF and their other powers to finance city government activities not directly associated with redevelopment of blighted areas within the redevelopment district. The state legislature, in turn, had imposed a number of strictures on RDAs over the years in an effort to curb these practices. These included requirements that RDAs spend at least 20% of their revenues on affordable housing, that the proposed district not contains mostly vacant land, and a more precise definition of blight.

Nevertheless, many of these practices continued and the state legislature faced with its own fiscal crisis turned to RDAs to help fund K–12 schools and community colleges. In 2011, the legislature passed ABX1 26 and ABX1 27, which dissolved RDAs. The tax increment revenue generated by the redevelopment districts is still pledged to pay off bonds and meet other contractual obligations. Any additional revenue is returned to the other local governments with jurisdiction in that area with a claim on property tax revenues: counties, school districts, and community college districts. The redevelopment districts' assets are also taken and sold with the proceeds being directed toward school districts. Unsurprisingly, municipal governments are at odds with the state government over this policy and fighting it in the courts.

## Prison Realignment

In 2009, a federal court decided that the overcrowding in California's prisons violated the constitutional prohibition of cruel and unusual punishment (*Plata & Coleman v. Schwarzenegger*, 2009). The court gave the state 2 years to comply with the decision. In order to reduce overcrowding in the state's prisons, the state undertook a series of reforms to its corrections and rehabilitation system. One of these reforms was prison realignment. The term "realignment" refers to a shifting of responsibilities from one level of government to another. In this case, the state shifted responsibilities for incarceration and post-incarceration supervision for some prisoners to the counties, which had more capacity in their jails. In order to do this, the state legislature essentially created two categories of felonies: crimes that were nonserious, nonsexual, and nonviolent, and all others. Offenders that were convicted of nonserious, nonsexual, and nonviolent crimes could now be sentenced to serve their time in county jails instead of state prisons. The state also enabled county probation departments to supervise parolees of these crimes. Realignment thus significantly devolved administration of the state's corrections and rehabilitation system to the county level while the rules and policies are still made at the state level. Practitioners and researchers in the criminal justice field hope the realignment would reduce recidivism and criminal justice costs.

# Local Governments and Voting

We praise local governments as the place in our political system where citizens have the most influence. However, voter turnout in city elections is usually quite low. Less than 30% of the registered voters participate in the average city election in California. In contrast, over half of those registered to vote typically cast ballots in presidential elections. Why are most local elections ignored by their residents? Several reasons are frequently given. Media attention is sporadic, given the large number of elections and the fact that most cities represent a small portion of the media's circulation. Therefore, voter knowledge about local elections is quite limited. Also, little effort is made in our society to interest the average citizen in local government. School children, for example, seem to learn a great deal about the national government but little about local government. Beyond this, several unique characteristics of local elections tend to encourage low voter turnout.

Local elections in California are carried out on nonpartisan ballots. Candidates may be members of a political party, but party designations will not be put on the ballot. For most people, political party is an important clue to the nature of the candidate. It provides the voter with a general idea of how the candidate feels about certain important issues and how the candidate relates to other elected officials. A nonpartisan ballot thus deprives the voter of important clues to the candidate's positions. Lacking such knowledge, the citizen may prefer not to vote. (For a further discussion of California's party tradition, see Chapter 4.)

At-large elections, where several city council members are chosen over the entire city, make it more difficult for the candidates to know the voters personally. In smaller districts, often the candidates can campaign door to door, and they know many of the voters personally. At-large elections, however, distance elected officials from their local constituencies and discourage personal candidate-voter contact, and therefore voters' interest in the election is likely to decline.

Studies also show that cities providing more services in-house by their own employees, as opposed to those contracting out their services, are likely to have a higher voter turnout in local elections because city governments "have more direct control over some of the basic issues that affect residents' quality of life," and therefore generate more interest in voters when local officials are up for election (e.g., Hajnal & Lewis 2003, p. 658). Based on this argument, as cities and counties continue to contract out public services, voter turnout in local elections is unlikely to improve.

## Local Government Officials and Ideology

Holders of power have the ability to make public policy. To what end this policy is made depends on the values, beliefs, and feelings of those with power. Usually people who wield power have a general set of values in mind when decisions are made. We call this series of interrelated values an ideology. An ideology organizes one's attitudes and helps one make sense of the world of politics. It also shapes one's view of the appropriate scope of government. Currently, most attitudes toward politics at the national, state, and local levels are related to two dominant ideologies: the conservative view generally associated with the Republican Party and the liberal view related to the Democratic Party.

Conservatives generally believe that government is at best a necessary evil. Society operates well when government does only those things that are absolutely necessary, and the private sector is permitted to operate without too much governmental interference.

Conservatives are pessimistic about the ability of government to accomplish significant changes in people or ways of life. They tend to rely on private institutions such as businesses, churches, and private charities rather than government to assist needy individuals. To conservatives, government should be limited and play a secondary role to private institutions. For example, conservatives favor fewer governmental regulations and a greater reliance on the market to provide jobs and health care. However, conservatives do not always oppose governmental intervention, such as using governmental power to restrict abortion.

Liberals, on the other hand, believe that government should be a positive force in society. Liberals argue that government should be used to improve social conditions and redistribute wealth through taxation. They also feel that the private sector must be controlled and steered by government to best promote the general welfare. Consequently, liberals favor a larger government and one that is geared toward advancing the interests of the lower and middle classes. Liberals do not always favor governmental actions, such as those allowing prayers in public schools.

The ideologies of local officials, however, seem to tell us less about the practice of government. Often local governments that maintain very extensive services are located in areas where the citizens support conservative officials in state and national elections. Anaheim, for instance, elects mostly conservative state legislators and congressional representatives. Yet the city is involved in major expenditures and projects that seem to be associated with a greater governmental role in the local economy. The city owns a major league baseball stadium, an indoor events center that hosts major league hockey, a convention center, and two golf courses. The city also operates the only municipal electric system in Orange County and owns part of the San Onofre nuclear power plant. City officials were instrumental in luring Disneyland to the city and are paying some of the costs of a major addition to the park.

This expansive view of the role of government, common in an otherwise conservative environment, suggests a third ideology that may more accurately be described as community conservationist (Agger, Goldrich, & Swanson, 1964). Supporters of this position see government as a partner with the private sector in helping the development of the community. Government expenditures that attract business or enhance the desirability of industrial or commercial interests are supported. Therefore, baseball stadiums and transportation systems are built for the purpose of increasing trade and commerce in the cities. Proponents of this position view officials like city managers as a source of innovation leading to enhanced business opportunities and commercial activities. Such enhancement may include some measures usually defined as social interventions in nature, such as low-cost housing and public transportation. These policies are supported by local constituents, however, only if they enhance the economic health of the community.

## Regional Governance

All urban areas contain a council of governments, a voluntary body that is responsible for coordinating transportation and land use plans for the region and has significant input into the actions of other area-wide districts. The Southern California Association of Governments, for example, is the largest council of government in the United States. The association prepares plans for air quality, growth management, transportation, and waste management in the region encompassing six counties: Los Angeles, Orange, San Bernardino, Riverside, Ventura, and Imperial.

The state legislature has also created Local Agency Formation Commissions (LAFCOs) whose job is to regulate the boundaries of cities and special districts. LAFCO boards are appointed by the county and existing cities. They do not make decision directly involving land use, but rather have authority over actions such as the incorporation of new cities and special districts and whether cities and special districts are able to annex new territory. Communities wishing to incorporate must prove to their LAFCO that they can provide their residents and businesses with the basic public services that have been provided by the county, but must be provided by the new city if incorporation occurs. Other actions that must be approved by LAFCOs include detachments (when territories wish to break away from existing jurisdictions), disincorporations and dissolutions (when a local government ceases to exist), consolidations (when two or more governments join together into a single one), and mergers (when a city takes over a special district that was formerly independent) (Bui & Irhke, 2003).

Urban counties also contain transportation agencies, which are responsible for developing major transportation networks for automobiles and mass transit. The Orange County Transportation Authority, for example, provides countywide bus, paratransit, and Metrolink commuter-rail services to county residents. Recent initiatives have required many of these agencies to prepare congestion management plans that require cities to control traffic congestion when they decide on future growth and development. For example, Orange County voters approved Measure M in 1990, a 20-year initiative funded by a half-cent sales tax to improve the county transportation infrastructure. In 2006, the county voters approved the renewal of this initiative for another thirty years.

The California coast is governed in part by the statewide Coastal Commission, which was first established by Proposition 20 in 1972 and later made permanent by the California Coastal Act of 1976. Working with coastal cities and counties, the commission plans and regulates the use of land and water in the coastal zone. Land use changes that potentially affect access to beaches and the coastal environment must be approved by this commission or the local government.

Last, an air quality management district regulates all major urban areas. These governments can enforce regulations that affect air quality. The South Coast Air Quality Management District, for example, is the air pollution control agency for all of Orange County and parts of Los Angeles, Riverside, and San Bernardino counties—one of the most populated and smoggiest urban areas in the United States. The authority of these agencies includes controlling and regulating moving sources of pollution (primarily cars), in addition to the traditional stationary sources, such as factories and commercial areas that emit pollutants. The emphasis on mobile sources has led to a concern for car travel in the greater Los Angeles area. Therefore, the local air quality management district has encouraged carpooling, bicycling, and land use patterns that better coordinate jobs and residences.

All of these regional governments generate conflict with cities and counties as they attempt to assume authorities and powers traditionally thought to be those of the city and county. Land use decisions, for example, what each resident can do with his or her own property, now must meet the approval of several regional agencies. City officials often do not take direction from regional governments willingly. Therefore, conflict between the regional agencies and cities and counties has increased in recent years and will most likely become more significant in the years ahead.

# Conclusion

California local governments operate within a conflicting environment. As weak actors, politically and legally speaking, they must constantly react to court rulings and the decisions of other governments. The Jeffersonian tradition of strong local government may clash with the need to promote livable regions where traffic flows freely, air is clean, natural resources are preserved, and all citizens have equal access to public services. The interest in having more centralized authority reflects the Hamiltonian tradition of larger governments capable of solving the problems that small governments have difficulty coping with and agreeing on with one another. Just as Madison feared the factional nature of small government, regional governments frequently find local officials insensitive to the problems of society that span city boundaries.

Some fear that the cost of regional governments in regulations and fees will ruin the economy. Others believe that failure to handle the problems of traffic congestion and environmental degradation will lead to economic decline in the region. They argue that strong regional government is needed to plan, coordinate, and work out compromises between different cities with competing goals. On the other hand, other people see stronger governments in local communities and neighborhoods where citizens could be partners with public administrators seeking better ways of attacking the problems that directly affect the public. To proponents of this perspective, regional governments distance citizens from local governments and encourage conflict between public administrators and citizens. Therefore, the conflict represented in the ideas of Hamilton, Madison, and Jefferson is still with us, as local governments face the problems and prospects of an increasingly populated urban society.

# References

Agger, R., Goldrich, D., and Swanson, B. 1964. *The Rulers and the Ruled: Political Power and Impotence in American Communities*. New York, NY: John Wiley & Sons.

Bui, T. and Irhke, B. 2003. *It's Time To Draw The Line: A Citizen's Guide to LAFCOs California's Local Agency Formation Commissions, Second Edition*. Sacramento, CA: Senate Publications.

Bureau of Census. 2006. *Statistical Abstract of the United States: 2006*. Washington, DC: U.S. Department of Commerce.

Bureau of Census. 2010. *Percent Urban and Rural in 2010 by State*. Retrieved 20 February, 2014 from http://www2.census.gov/geo/ua/PctUrbanRural_State.xls.

Bureau of Census. 2013. *Government Organization Summary Report: 2012*. Washington, DC: U.S. Department of Commerce.

Bureau of Census. 2014. *State & County QuickFacts*. Retrieved July 3, 2014 from http://quickfacts.census.gov/qfd/states/06/.

California Department of Education. 2010. "History of School District Organization in California." In *District Organization Handbook*. Sacramento, CA: School Fiscal Services Division.

California Department of Finance. 2008. *California County Population Estimates*. Sacramento, CA: Department of Finance.

*City of Garden Grove v. Superior Court* (Kha), 2007 S.O.S. 6933.

*Gonzales v. Raich* (2005), 545 U.S. 1.

Hajnal, Z. and Lewis, P. 2003. Municipal Institutions and Voter Turnout in Local Elections. *Urban Affairs Review*, 38(5), 645–668.

Jefferson, T. 1999. Jefferson: Political Writings. In Joyce Appleby and Terence Ball (eds.), *Cambridge Texts in the History of Political Thought*. New York, NY: Cambridge University Press.

Madison, J. 1787. *The Same Subject Continued: The Union as a Safeguard Against Domestic Faction and Insurrection*, Federalist No. 10.

Tocqueville, A. 1956. *Democracy in America, edited by Richard D. Heffner*. New York, NY: New American Library.

Taylor, M. 2012. *The 2012–13 Budget: Unwinding Redevelopment*. Sacramento, CA: California Legislative Analyst's Office.

# CHAPTER 11

# Budgetary Politics in California

*Paul Peretz*

"Money is the mother's milk of politics."
*Jesse Unruh (California Assembly Speaker 1961–1969)*, L.A. Times,
*March 31, 1963*

While at first sight nothing might seem more boring than examination of budgetary spreadsheets, politicians understand that decisions about money, where it comes from, who pays it, how it is spent, who receives it, and who does not receive it, is the heart of the political process. Whatever policies one wishes to pursue, the crucial decisions are how much money is spent on those policies and who has to pay for that spending. Governments that can raise large sums of money are more powerful and more likely to meet their aims than governments with less in the way of financial resources. Governments that directly control the sources of funding are more powerful than governments that depend on other governments for their funding. Governments that have freedom to move money from one use to another are more powerful than those who are constrained in how they raise money and how they are allowed to spend it.

This chapter looks at federal, state, and local budgetary decisions that affect Californians. We will start by laying out how these budgets are made and then go on to examine the differences in what the federal government, California State, and California local governments do, and how budget outcomes have changed over time.

## Budgetary Processes

The United States has one of the most complex budgetary systems in the world. First, it is complex because of the federal system and secondarily because American governments are designed so that each part of government is checked and sometimes contradicted by other parts. This checks and balances system, sometimes, leads to the budgetary compromises that its builders hoped for, but just as often leads to dysfunctional gridlock.

### California Local Budgeting Process

A typical Californian is affected by federal government policies, by state government policies, and by the policies adopted by a variety of local governments. Someone in Fullerton for example is affected by Orange County decisions, City of Fullerton decisions, Fullerton School District decisions, Southern California Metropolitan Water District of Southern California and Orange County Water District decisions, and decisions by the South Coast Air Quality Management District. Finally the people themselves are a government and periodically pass propositions that make budgetary decisions and constrain or expand what each of these bodies can do.

Most of the local governments are organized rationally, with one group making the basic decisions and one appointed administrator carrying them out. Federal and state governments, however, divide power between an elected administrator and two separately elected bodies. This system generally prevents rash decisions, but just as often, prevents necessary decisions from being made and/or leads to suboptimal compromises.

Because budgetary decisions are the most important decisions made in most years, every group attempts to influence budgets. Figure 11.1 gives a simplified view of how local government decisions are made. While in many states elected mayors have the main say in budgeting, in California an appointed city manager (or his equivalent in other local bodies) has the most power, with the council (or its elected equivalents in other local governments) setting the broad parameters and having the final word. Figure 11.1 shows how it works. Programs within departments propose budgets with guidance from department heads. The departments then submit these budgets to a finance group whose job is to reconcile the budgets with available revenues and enforce the priorities of the city manager and the Council. In smaller cites the assistant city manager may take the pace of the finance department.

The city manager then checks that the resulting budget can be paid for with available funds, fits his or her priorities, and will be acceptable to the council. It is then generally looked at by a subcommittee of the council before being passed by the full council. Typically the budget takes about 6 months to produce and the resulting budget is similar to the previous year's budget. Most of the change from year to year occurs because revenues are lower or higher than in the previous year, a result of the requirement that local government budgets must be balanced. Changes in who is city manager and in the

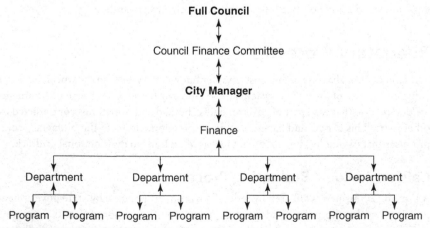

**Figure 11.1**   Municipal Budget Process

political complexion of the council also result in changes in the budget. In larger cities or counties the department heads and the elected officials have more say, while many smaller and poorer cities are dominated by the city manager or his equivalent.

## California State and Federal Budgeting Process

As we move from local to state and federal government the budgetary system gets more complex and more political. Figure 11.2 shows the California budgetary system. I have not drawn the bureaucracy in the detail I have shown in Figure 11.1, but the readers should note that it is organized in much the same fashion, except that the increased size often results in one or more extra layers of bureaucracy. The other two things missing from the chart are the influence of the federal government, which supplies the bulk of the funds for California's health and welfare programs, and the role of Assembly and Senate minority and majority leaders in years when the formal budget process breaks down. In such years these four often huddle with the Governor to produce a compromise budget.

When compared with the local level both the federal and the California state budgetary decisions are more complex and generally more dysfunctional. The basic process of making budgets is very similar at the federal and California state levels. Budgets are initially proposed by the people administering the policies. These proposals go through a winnowing process within the administrative branch, with proposals from geographical subunits being aggregated into program proposals, then moved up the chain of command until they reach the departmental level. These proposals are then examined by budget experts gathered in the Office of Management and Budget at the federal level and the Finance Department at the state level. These bodies form a unified budget which is then submitted to both chambers of the legislature. Once in the legislature the budget is

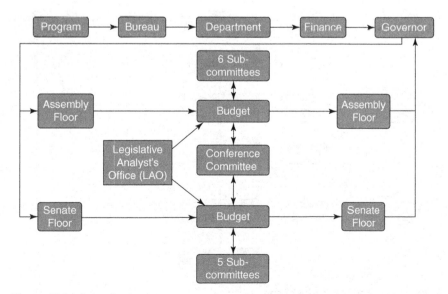

**Figure 11.2**   State Budget Process

examined by the legislature's own analysis unit (the Congressional Budget Office at the federal level and the Legislative Analyst's Office at the California level) and referred to committees and subcommittees in both branches that "markup" (change) the budget. The two legislative bodies then use conference committees to iron out differences, before sending the budget to the chief executive (the President at the federal level and the Governor at the state level). Figure 11.2 illustrates the basic steps at the California state level and Figure 11.3 is a simplified version of the steps at the federal level.

When looking at Figure 11.3, the reader should note that the revenue portion of the federal budget goes to the Ways and Means committee in the House and the Finance committee in the Senate and the spending part goes to the Appropriations committees in both branches. I have left this out of the diagram as major tax changes during the budget process are rare. Also left out is the fact that around 60% of the budget consists of entitlement programs such as Medicare and Social Security which are set by Congress as a whole when the programs are instituted.

At both the state and federal levels the major influence on big decisions are the positions of the two political parties, the position of the Governor or President, and the views of major interest groups. For more detailed decisions, the California Finance Office at the California level or the Office of Management and Budget at the federal level are most influential in the executive branch and the subcommittees of the Budget Committee in California and the subcommittees of the Senate and House Appropriations Committees at the federal level have the most influence in the legislative branch.

Although the basic process is the same at both levels there are a number of differences that sometimes have serious effects on the resulting budgets. The California Governor can veto one part of a budget (an item veto), whereas the President can only accept or reject the entire budget. The federal budget is divided into 12 separate budgets each

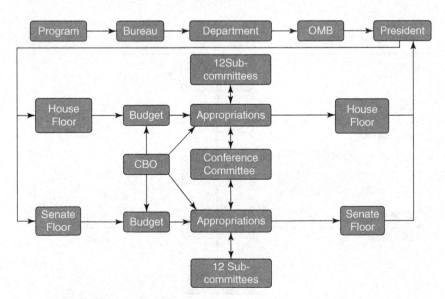

**Figure 11.3**   Federal Budget Process

passed separately, while the California budget is just one budget. The federal budget has a more complex obstacle course in the legislature than the California budget. The overall size of the 12 budgets is set in the House and the Senate by their budget committees before going on to their tax committees which look at tax changes and their Appropriations Committees and 12 subcommittees that set the detailed spending estimates. California has a simpler process with Assembly (six subcommittees) and Senate Budget Committees (five subcommittees) making the budgetary decisions.

Finally, it is worth noting that outside constraints affect the two budget systems differently. The California budget is constrained by the California Constitution to be legally in balance, while the federal budget is not. The federal budget includes both capital and current spending, whereas California separates capital spending from current spending. Finally the California budget is sometimes limited by propositions passed by California voters. Two important examples were the requirement that budgets must be passed by a two-third vote (now repealed) and the still existing requirements that any new tax must be passed by a two-third vote and any large bonds must be approved by a vote of the people after a two-third vote in the legislature.

# The Functions of Government Economic Policy

Those who study public finance see government as having four primary functions. One is the provision of public goods, such as defense or justice, which cannot be supplied in sufficient quantity by the private capitalist market. A second is redistributing income to support the poor and helpless. A third is managing the economy to keep unemployment low, incomes high and inflation low and steady. Finally government regulates private business to make sure that it does not harm citizens. We generally refer to these four aims as allocation, redistribution, stabilization, and regulation.

Because the United States has a federal system, some of these functions are performed by the federal government, some are performed by California state government, and some are performed by local governments. Section 1 of the Constitution of the United States gives primary responsibility over a few areas especially defense, foreign affairs, monetary policy, and foreign and interstate commerce, to the Federal government, with all other areas "reserved to the States respectively or to the people" (10th Amendment).

In practice, however, a series of Supreme Court decisions, based on the concept of implied powers, have considerably widened the powers of the Federal government, with the result that the federal government makes policies in a wider range of areas than those explicitly laid down in Section 1 of the Constitution. There is nonetheless considerable specialization in what each government does.

## Stabilization

Managing the health of the economy is primarily the responsibility of the federal government. Governments primarily rely on monetary and fiscal policy to manage the economy. Monetary policy consists primarily of changing the amount of money supplied by government, in order to raise or lower interest rates. When interest rates increase it slows down the economy and when interest rates decrease it speeds the economy up.

The creation of money is a federal responsibility, and hence this tool is not available to states and local governments.

Fiscal policy involves changing the balance between spending and taxation. When the gap between spending and taxation widens, it creates jobs and stimulates the economy. When the gap between spending and taxation narrows or when taxes exceed spending, it slows the economy down. For this policy to work, it is necessary that government be free to run surpluses and deficits when it considers it to be necessary. The federal government has this freedom. All state and local governments (except Vermont) have constitutional provisions aimed at preventing them from running deficits even in bad times. Because of this, states and localities cannot easily use fiscal policy to stimulate the economy.

## Distribution

In the early days of the Republic, little redistribution took place. Most Americans lived in farming communities and most support of the indigent was undertaken within extended families or through the local government entities' charities and churches. Government redistribution (with the exception of pensions for revolutionary war and civil war veterans and their dependents) was primarily confined to local government support for widows and children. The Great Depression marked a turning point for redistribution. By the 1930s a largely urban population was at the mercy of changes in the economy. Under Roosevelt the first national programs, Social Security and Aid to Dependent Children (now TANF), were put in place to help the poor, elderly, and disabled. In the 1960s the War on Poverty gave rise to a considerable extension in federal and state help to the needy most of which was aimed at payments in kind rather than cash payments. In 1965 Medicare was instituted to provide medical care to the elderly and Medicaid was instituted to provide medical aid to the poor. There had been small federal and state programs to provide help to the poor in housing, food, and child care areas in the 1930s, 1940s, and 1950s. But, in the 1960s and after, help in these areas was expanded and many new programs were added. Programs to provide rental subsidies (Section 8 1974) subsidized food (Food Stamps now SNAP 1964), school lunches (1946), prenatal aid (WIC 1972), and child care (CCDF 1990) were instituted. In 1975 a negative income tax called the Earned Income Tax Credit was enacted to help the working poor. Although a lot of these programs were managed at the County level and many of them involved the State contributing some matching funds toward the programs, these were basically federal programs. By 2014 around half of the federal budget was spent on redistributive programs.

## Allocation

Some goods are not easily supplied by the market. Such goods generally have two characteristics. One is that people who did not pay for the goods can get all or some of the benefits from the goods, as when people watch public television without contributing to it. The other is that the enjoyment of the person using it is not reduced if someone else uses it, as with clean air. Goods that have one or both of these two characteristics will be undersupplied by the private market.

The provision of public goods and quasi-public goods is something that is done at all levels of government. Each level of government tends to specialize in particular public goods with the general rule being that the larger the number of people benefiting from the good, and the greater the economies of scale in paying for the good, the more likely that the good will be provided at the federal or state level. Thus the armed forces are provided at the federal level, education primarily at the state and local level, and sewage and fire service mainly at the local level.

# Government Spending

## Federal Expenditures

Figure 11.4 shows at which level some of most important public goods and redistributive goods are provided. Defense expenditures are provided almost exclusively by the federal government, with the only exception being a tiny amount of spending by states on the National Guard. Pensions are also primarily provided by the by the federal government. While the figure seems to show considerable spending by state and local governments on pensions, both this spending and some of the federal spending is primarily pensions for its own employees. Social security, the main government pension program,

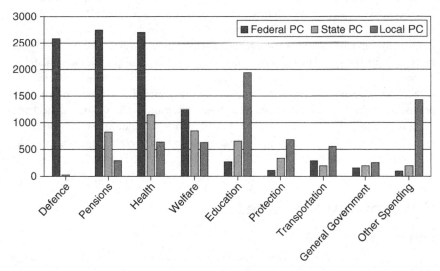

**Figure 11.4**

*The data for Figures 11.4,11. 6, and 11.7 can be found at http://www.usgovernmentspending .com/, which compiled it from federal, state, and local government sources. The federal figures are total amounts for the United States divided by the number of people in the United States. The state and local figures in Figure 11.4 are spending in California divided by the number of people in California. The assumption behind this, is that everyone in the United States benefits equally from government spending. The reader should note that while this is generally true, redistributive expenditures may vary from one state to another.

is provided exclusively by the federal government. Health and welfare expenditures are made by all three levels of government but the federal share is again larger than the chart would lead one to believe, because much of the state and local expenditures are financed by transfers from the federal government. For example, the largest federal program in California, Medicare, is exclusively provided by the federal government and the second biggest Medi-Cal gets around half its funding from the federal government, but is provided by the state and counties.

## California State Expenditures

At the state level the largest areas of expenditure are health, welfare, education, and justice. Most of the health expenditure is California's share of Medi-Cal expenditure. Most of the welfare expenditure is the state's share of temporary aid to needy families, and the State's share of various payments in kind, of which the largest is CalFresh, delivering food subsidies to around 4 million Californians. Most of the education expenditures goes to support the campuses of the University of California, the California State University, and the Community Colleges. Most of the spending on protection supports the State prison system, the courts, and the highway patrol.

## Local Government

Figure 11.4 shows the two largest areas of spending being education and other spending. Both of these are not quite what they appear. The education spending is for primary and secondary education in California. At one time this was supported by local property taxes raised by School Boards. The money is still spent by School Boards but the decisions on how much to spend are now made largely by the State of California. This is even more true for the spending on welfare and health where local counties administer the offices that distribute money largely provided by the state and the federal governments. Finally, the large amount Figure 11.4 shows as other expenditures largely measures the provision of utilities by local entities. Garbage collection, water provision, electricity, gas, and public transit provision are often provided by what amount to local government owned businesses. Most of the other spending at the local level is the cost of providing these services (Figure 11.4).

# Government Revenues

## Federal Revenues

Figure 11.5 shows revenue sources at the federal, state and local levels. The major source of federal revenues is the income tax. This is a highly progressive tax with the top 5% of income earning families paying 59% of the tax and the bottom 50% paying less than 3% of the tax. The federal social insurance tax is a mildly regressive tax with the main burden falling on the middle and upper middle income earners and the rich and the very poor bearing less of a burden. The corporate income tax falls initially on those who own firms but most economists think it is partly shifted onto wages or prices in the longer term, making it only mildly progressive.

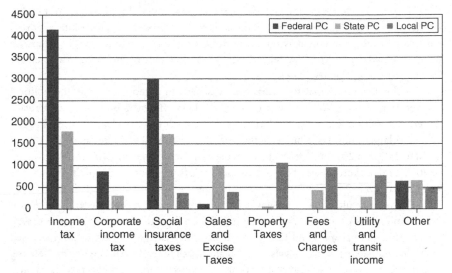

**Figure 11.5**

*The data can be found at http://www.usgovernmentrevenue.com/, which compiled it from federal, state, and local government sources. The federal revenues are total amounts for the United States divided by the number of people in the United States. The state and local figures are revenues in California divided by the number of people in California. The reader should note that these taxes are not paid equally by everyone. For example most income tax is paid by the richest 10% of the population and fees charges and utility bills are paid only by those using those services.

## State Revenues

The state income tax is the biggest source of California state revenues. While it is much less progressive than the federal income tax, it is one of the most progressive of the state income taxes and may be mildly progressive on balance. The sales tax falls disproportionately on the poor. Although it appears that social insurance is a big revenue source, three-quarters of this are state employee's contributions to their retirement fund and the rest is unemployment insurance for all workers.

## Local Revenues

All revenues at the local level are regressive. The least regressive is the property tax, which, thanks to Proposition 13, contributes less to local coffers than in almost any other state. Fees and charges are primarily public hospital fees, university student fees, and airport and port fees. Utility fees are the bills for sewage and garbage, water, electricity, and gas paid to public businesses. Sales taxes have become a more important source of local revenue since Proposition 13 was passed in 1975, and are regressive, though less so than fees and utilities.

## The Politics of Budgeting—Long-Term Changes

Over the period since World War II, a number of changes in American society have altered the content of budgets and the way that they are decided, at both the federal and the California levels. Over time globalization and technological change have resulted in a devaluing of low skilled workers as their skills were mechanized or their jobs exported overseas. At the same time new opportunities for capital in underdeveloped countries have increased the return to capital and managerial skill. One result has been an increase in inequality in the United States.

At the same time that the workplace was becoming more unequal, the political market increased the voting power of the poor. Less affluent groups such as African-Americans, Hispanics, and the elderly grew as a percent of the population and began voting in larger numbers. The percentage of African-American increased from 10% in 1950 to 14.2% in 2014, the percentage of Hispanic increased from 2.1% in 1950 to 17% in 2014, and the percentage of the elderly increased from around 8.5% of the population in 1954 to 14% in 2014.

The main result of these changes is that budgets became more redistributive. As we can see in Figures 11.6 and 11.7 the amount spent on the redistributive categories of welfare, health, and pensions and the quasi-redistributive category of education increased at the federal, state and local levels. In 1950 almost all federal spending was on defense, public goods, and the overhead costs of running a government. Looking at federal spending, we can see that by 2013 the real amount spent on public goods such as defense, transportation, and crime protection per person had only barely increased, while spending on pensions, welfare, and health was almost two-thirds of federal spending. Social Security was continuously expanded after 1950, and new programs such as Medicare, Medicaid, Food Stamps (SNAP), and the Earned income Tax Credit led to the expansion in health and welfare.

California health and welfare expenditures were largely driven by their share of the new federal programs. California also expanded spending for college and university education while increasing primary and secondary education less than most other states.

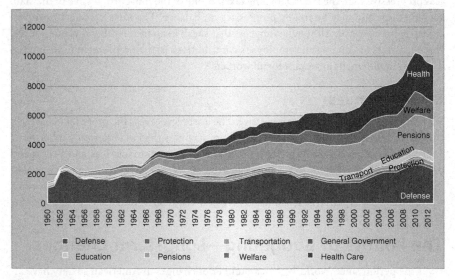

Figure 11.6

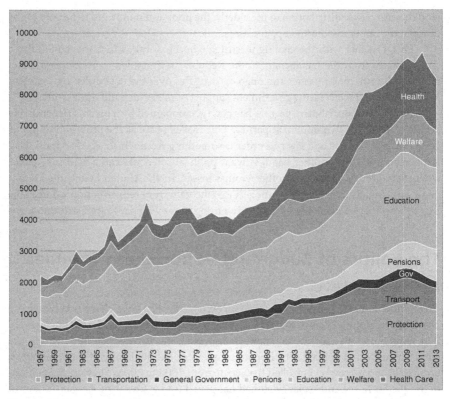

**Figure 11.7**

The other two sectors with big increases, state pensions to their employees and spending on law and order, are generally seen as due to mistakes in policy. While part of the pension increase is indirect compensation for higher housing costs, part is due to overly generous pension increases at both the state and local level, especially in the public safely area. The increase in criminal justice spending followed public panic after crime rates doubled in the 1980s. As a result, as crime rates dropped after 1993 California imprisoned more and more people at around $40,000 per inmate.

The money for these new redistributive programs initially came primarily from the middle classes. Social Security and Medicare were paid for by a mildly regressive Social Security tax while California's limited spending in these areas came from social insurance and sales taxes. But by 2014 federal spending was increasingly paid for by income taxes largely paid by the top 10% of income earners and California was increasingly reliant on a mildly progressive income tax. Between 1979 and 2005 the percent of all federal taxes paid by the top 10% of income earners rose from 41% to 55% (Tim Curry NBC News How the Tax burden has changed since 1960).[1] Thus there was an increasing

---

[1]This might at first seem surprising given the increasing importance of the regressive social security tax and the drop in the highest rate of the income tax. It is largely an artifact of the steady increase in the percent of all income earned by the wealthy, especially the top 1% of income earners.

tendency for new redistribution to the elderly, the poor and minorities to be paid for by those in the upper middle and upper classes.

This, together with the civil rights struggle in the South, which moved Southern conservatives from the Democratic to the Republican Party, led to an increasing gulf between the two major parties and ongoing struggles over the tax burden on wealthier Americans and the increasing government support of minorities and the less affluent.

This more redistributive process has been accompanied by a much sharper divide between America's two dominant parties. This makes sense as the provision of public goods such as defense and law and order is something from which all Americans gain. Redistribution, on the other hand, is what political scientists call a zero-sum game, where one group's gains are another group's losses. In the United States, the Democrats are generally seen as representing those who gain from redistribution whereas the Republican Party is generally seen as representing those who pay for redistribution.

# The Politics of Budgeting—Short-Term Changes

## The Federal Level

The period since 2000 ushered in the 21st century has seen large changes in budgeting outcomes in both the United States as a whole and in California. At the federal level the first seven years saw a turn to the right. George Bush was narrowly elected in 2000 and narrowly re-elected in 2004. The Republicans controlled the House of Representatives until 2008 and narrowly controlled the Senate from 2002 to 2006. They used their new-found power to try and replay what had happened under President Reagan. They cut taxes, especially on the rich, they started an unnecessary war, they failed to cut domestic spending and relaxed regulation. Taken together this converted budget surpluses to budget deficits and provided some of the prerequisites for the financial crisis of 2007–2008.

The attempt to prevent this crisis from turning into a Great Depression has dominated federal policy in the period since then. The main reactions have been increases in taxes on the rich, loosening of monetary policy, increased federal spending including support for states and localities, and reregulation in the banking area. In addition the Obama Administration managed to push through the national health care proposal which the Clinton Administration had tried and failed to pass. This was a significant expansion of redistributive policy and appears to have provided health care to significant numbers of the uninsured.

## California

Until 2010 the California Constitution severely limited the ability of the majority party to determine budgetary outcomes. A two-third majority in both the Assembly and the Senate was required for large bonds, new taxes, and spending changes, a balanced budget requirement limited deficits and most bonds must be confirmed by at least a majority vote of the people. In good years these provisions resulted in compromise and logrolling. But as the two parties widened their differences in the 1990s, it increasingly led to gridlock, late budgets, and poor policy choices.

Given this, budgetary outcomes in California are largely determined by federal initiatives and the strength of the economy. When the economy was strong in the 2000 to 2001 period, Gray Davis was able to expand spending on primary education and reduce class sizes. When the economy soured in 2002 the class sizes increased again. During the Great Recession two moderate Governors, Arnold Schwarzenegger and Jerry Brown cut spending they supported, to maintain budgetary balance, with the most notable example being Brown's large reductions in state welfare spending. While the repeal of the two-thirds voting requirement for the budget in 2010 and the huge Democratic majority after 2011 eased the constraints somewhat, it remains true that California state and local spending rises and falls with California Income tax revenue.

## Summary

The budgetary system which delivers government goods and redistributes income is complex and intertwined. It is not possible to summarize all the different strands and show each interaction is a short piece like this. But it seems to this author that there is one change which dominates much of the budgetary action over the last 60 years or so. Over this period economic inequality has worsened in the United States because of globalization, technological change, and changes in family structure. Over the same period many of the groups most harmed by these changes have gained more political power than they used to have as they have come to use their voting power. The result has been a huge increase in redistribution as federal and state governments attempt to compensate for the changes in inequality.

## Reference

Harris, Benjamin. 2009. *Corporate Tax Incidence and its Implications for Progressivity*. http://www .urban.org/uploadedpdf/1001349_corporate_tax_incidence.pdf .

**Places to look for data and generally unbiased analysis**
The following are useful websites with generally up to date and reliable data and analysis of United States and California budgetary concerns.

**Websites for the data used in this article**
Government spending at all levels http://www.usgovernmentspending.com/total_chart_gallery
Government revenues at all levels http://www.usgovernmentrevenue.com/revenue_history

**Websites for Current California Information**
California Department of Finance http://www.dof.ca.gov
The Legislative Analyst's Office http://www.lao.ca.gov/Publications
The California Budget Project http://www.cbp.org
Public Policy Institute of California http://www.ppic.org/main/pubs.asp

**Websites for National Data**
The Office of Management and Budget http://www.whitehouse.gov/omb
The Congressional Budget Office http://www.cbo.gov/
Economic Report of the President http://www.gpoaccess.gov/eop/tables08.html
Current Economic Indicators http://www.whitehouse.gov/fsbr/esbr.html
Statistical Abstract of the United States http://www.census.gov/compendia/statab

# CHAPTER 12

# California Education Policy

*Shelly Arsneault & Sarah A. Hill*

## Introduction

California's approach to education, both K-12 and higher education, is a history of attempts at equity and access, with often uneven results. Significant political events in the 1970s greatly affected the funding available for education, and ever since the state has been working to play "catch-up" to bring funding back to previous levels. Beginning in 2008 with the Great Recession, the education system faced another round of significant budget cuts. How has the largest education system in the country managed these and other challenges? We explore California's history and current education policy below.

## K-12 Education

As in most states, California's K-12 education system evolved from primarily a local responsibility into a system in which local school districts have authority to make some decisions under regulations and supervision by the state. During the 20th century the state government slowly gave more and more funding to K-12 schools, and with that came the strings of regulation for local school districts.

Public education in the state is a complex hierarchy overseen by the California Department of Education (CDE) which serves as a resource and provides accountability for schools, particularly in keeping track of funding and test scores. CDE is led by the Superintendent of Public Instruction who is directly elected by the state's voters on a nonpartisan ballot every 4 years (rather than being appointed by the governor as is the case in many other states). The Superintendent is also the executive officer of the State Board of Education (SBE) which governs the education system and sets policy, especially in regard to academic standards and curriculum. The Governor appoints the other 11 members of the SBE to 4-year terms. Each county then has a County Office of Education (COE) to provide services to local school districts, in particular financial and academic accountability. A major function of the COEs is to provide education to special needs students, such as those with significant learning disabilities or juvenile offenders who cannot attend their regular public schools (California Department of Education, 2014).

There are then over 1,000 school districts in California with over 10,000 schools and about 6,200,000 students; this means that one in eight children in the United States is educated through California's public schools. Districts are elementary, high school, or unified (with both elementary and high schools), and vary tremendously in size. Los Angeles Unified School District serves over 660,000 students, while Blake Elementary School District had five students enrolled during the 2011–2012 school year. These districts can coincide with city boundaries or not, and a few even cross county borders. Even with these great differences, the school districts have similar governing systems. Each school district's charter specifies how a school board is elected to serve as the governing body for that district. Members of a school board can be elected at large or by districts, and the number of school board members can vary (five or more), but all school board elections are nonpartisan. The school board has the task of setting policy for the district within state regulations; their budget decisions are generally considered the most important policy that they set. The other key function of the school board is to hire the district's superintendent, a professional education administrator who is directly answerable to the board and makes key decisions, especially when it comes to the hiring of school principals and other top administrators.

Historically K-12 education was primarily financed by property taxes raised locally with some money from the state for specific items, such as textbooks. In 1947 California started to use a foundation program which guarantees a minimum amount of support to all schools from the state with local funds still making up half of school spending in 1970 (Picus, 1991). The concern about this method of support for schools is that the value of the property in their districts varies widely; therefore, school districts have very different abilities to raise funds. While California public schools were highly regarded during the 1960s and spending on public education was fairly high compared to other states, the disparities in wealth between school districts in the state had become quite noticeable and troubled some parents and observers (Silva & Sonstelie, 1995). As a result parents brought a lawsuit over these disparities, and in 1971 the California Supreme Court ruled in the *Serrano v. Priest* decision that these inequalities were a violation of the state constitution. The decision notes, for example, that in the 1968–1969 school year, Baldwin Park School District spent about $577 per pupil while Beverly Hills School District spent about $1,232 per pupil. Through this and later decisions, the California Supreme Court ordered the legislature to make per pupil spending between districts more equitable. The state responded by centralizing its education finance system at the state government level to provide more equitable funding across school districts (Picus, 1991).

The next big change to California's public schools came with Proposition 13 of 1978. Upset over increasing property taxes, California voters passed this initiative to significantly cut property taxes and protect them from future rapid inflation. While Proposition 13 was popular with voters, it had several unintended consequences, including a decrease in funding for public schools. The state responded by increasing the money that it allocated to public schools, but not to pre-Proposition 13 levels. The effect of *Serrano* and Proposition 13 has been to make education funding primarily the responsibility of the state rather than local governments, and most observers believe the result has been less funding for public education, especially compared to other states (Picus, 1991).

The statistics for public education in California today are not impressive. In 2013 California had the highest student teacher ratio in the country with almost 25 students per teacher (the national average is 16). California ranked 38th in its per pupil spending for K-12 education, spending $9,060 per pupil against the national average of $10,938 (National Education Association, 2014). When the cost of living is factored in, California drops to 49th in per pupil spending (EdSource, 2013a). Test scores are similarly disappointing. On the 2013 National Assessment of Educational Progress, eighth graders in the state ranked 43rd on the math exam and 42nd on the reading exam (EdSource, 2013b).

What can be done? How can education be fixed in the Golden State? Unfortunately there are no easy answers, but many parents and reformers have been working to create alternative solutions. One trend in the United States that has also been popular in California is the growth of charter schools. Charter schools are public schools created by parents and community organizers; what makes them different is that they are exempt from many of the normal regulations on public schools. For example, teachers may not be granted tenure or be subject to the same hiring restrictions as in regular school districts. Attendance is still free of charge, but students do have to apply to attend charter schools; when there are more applications than spots available, students are selected for a charter school by a lottery. Many charters schools have an emphasis such as a focus on math and science or environmentalism. The idea of charter schools is popular because many reformers believe that giving administrators and teachers freedom from regulations enables them to provide a better education to students, and there are now over 1,000 charter schools in California (California Department of Education, 2014). The question is how well the charter schools are doing in comparison to traditional public schools; overall the results have been mixed. For example, one recent report on charter schools in California indicated that, "Data for six years of students in grades 2 to 11 in nearly 1,000 charter schools showed that overall they performed better in reading but did worse in math" (EdSource, 2014). Studies show that some charter schools perform much better than traditional schools, but others clearly lag behind. Thus if charter schools are to be considered as a way to improve California's public schools, there needs to be careful consideration of what makes them successful, understanding that having a charter school is not an automatic solution in and of itself.

While *Serrano* sought to equalize school spending and Proposition 13 means that school districts cannot raise their property taxes to increase revenue for their own schools, in some districts parents who are concerned about the lack of funding for schools have found other ways of raising needed dollars. Since Proposition 13, there has been an increase in nonprofits created specifically to raise money for school districts or even individual schools. These nonprofits vary widely in how much revenue they raise, but many of them argue that since the state does not provide enough funding for a quality education, they are trying to fill in the gap with additional money. These nonprofits (sometimes called local education foundations or LEFs) can have large fundraisers to provide students with art, music, and other extracurricular opportunities that would not be possible with state funding alone. While on the one hand, it is important to have parent involvement in the schools, these nonprofits raise a question of who receives these kinds of benefits. Are they equally available to all children? Current research indicates that it is school districts in wealthier areas that have the nonprofits which are able to raise the most revenue per pupil (Hill, Kiewiet, & Arsneault, 2014). Another way around *Serrano* and Proposition 13 is for districts to pass a parcel tax, a tax in which each parcel of land in the district pays the same tax regardless of the value of the property. The revenue from these parcel taxes is kept entirely for local use, and as with the nonprofits, research is showing that wealthier districts are passing and making use of parcel taxes.

Thus after years of effort and reforms making an effort for equality in public education in California, those districts with more resources have been able to find ways to provide more educational opportunities to their students. More changes are coming, though. Like many states California has moved away from the federal government's No Child Left Behind program, instead adopting and working toward implementation of Common Core Standards. These set guidelines of what students should know in every grade in math and language arts with a goal of college and career readiness when students graduate from high school. In addition many believe that having common standards will make transitions easier for any students who change schools, which happens more frequently in California than in other states (Rumberger, Larson, Ream, & Palardy, 1999). The new standards focus particularly on critical thinking and problem solving skills rather than just knowing how to pass a standardized test. Common Core has been controversial in its adoption, in many cases because it has been misunderstood (e.g., many thought it was a mandate from the federal government when it actually has been a state-led policy), but also because it will be expensive to implement. California has had to invest a great deal of money into computers for the program (students will take their tests on computers) and to train teachers on the standards. It is not yet known how successful Common Core will be, but many hope it will help students develop important skills to prepare them for their future careers. Whether Common Core improves education or another policy does, California will have to consider very carefully whether it has a priority of ensuring all children receive a quality education and if it is willing to commit the resources to make that possible.

# Higher Education

Similar to K-12 education, California has a long tradition of seeking equity and universal access to higher education for its residents. In 1910 California was the first state to create a system of public junior (community) colleges. During this time Californians went to college in high numbers. In 1930 the percentage of college-age Californians attending college was double the national average, and in 1960 45% of college-age adults in California attended college compared to 25% nationally (Douglass, 2010). The higher education system, however, was an organizational mess. As early as 1932 California commissioned a study to examine its system of higher education from community colleges through graduate degree granting universities. Finding a lack of coordination, the legislature commissioned a State Council for Educational Planning and Coordination; however, the State Council had only advisory power and the system grew increasingly disorganized. By the 1950s the pressures of increased student enrollment and political fighting over where to build new universities left the state without a coherent policy to address its growing higher education needs (Callan, 2009; Douglass, 2010). In 1959, to address these problems, Assemblywoman Dorothy Donohue introduced a resolution to the State Assembly calling for the preparation of a Master Plan for Higher Education;

her resolution was adopted by both the Assembly and Senate and in 1960 the Master Plan became law.

The Master Plan resolved many problems and created the first organized system of higher education in California and the nation. The provisions of the Plan designated the junior/community colleges (CC) as "open to all Californians who were capable of benefiting from attendance" (Callan, 2009, p. 8). In addition to providing instruction through grade 14, they would include courses that allowed students to transfer to the two state university systems. The state colleges were transformed into the California State University (CSU) system which would offer undergraduate and graduate degrees through the master's level. More selective than the community college system, the CSUs would admit students from the top third of their high school classes. The University of California (UC) system was to offer undergraduate degrees to the top 12.5% of high school graduates. The UCs would be the only institutions to grant doctoral degrees (Ph.D.), or degrees in law, medicine, dentistry, or veterinary medicine.

The Master Plan allowed for open access to all at the community college level, therefore, this was the level at which most growth in the higher education system was allowed. Explicit in the Master Plan was the idea that students enrolled in a community college who were academically qualified could transfer to one of the university systems after 2 years. Further, the Master Plan expected public higher education in California to be affordable, recommending continuation of "the long established principle that state colleges and the University of California shall be tuition free to all residents of the state" (A Master Plan, 1960, p. 14). While fees for labs, equipment, and services would be collected, the Master Plan reflected the state's commitment to accessibility by renewing the promise that Californians would not pay tuition (Callan, 2009).

California's innovative higher education policy quickly gained national attention, making the cover of *Time* magazine; the state was described as "the leader in American higher education policymaking" by *Science* and the *Reader's Digest* (Douglass, 2010, p. 2). As most students reading this chapter know, the California Master Plan for Higher Education has fallen far from this lofty acclaim. Although the Master Plan authors optimistically suggested that the state's government and residents would continue to support the higher education system at adequate levels, including financially (A Master Plan, 1960), this support has severely eroded in the intervening 60 years.

Until the early 1990s California's universities remained among the most affordable in the nation, but a severe recession in California caused the CSUs and UCs to raise tuition and fees, which doubled between the late 1980s and mid-1990s. By 2011, the UC system was 33% more expensive than similar large, public, research universities around the country (Johnson, 2012). At the same time, state funding for higher education declined. In 2014, California spent nearly 40% *less* per university student than it had in 2004 (Murphy, 2014). Although the state's budget improvements in 2013 and 2014 led to increases in spending on higher education, the share of university budgets from state funds has declined by approximately 25% since 2000 (California Budget Project, 2014).

In addition to raising fees to deal with budget cuts and increased demand, access to public higher education has also been limited in California. Although high school graduates are increasingly taking the courses needed for admission to the UC and CSU systems, fewer students are being admitted, particularly to their first choice schools

(Johnson, 2012). Instead, the UC has used a "referral pool" system in which eligible students not accepted to their first choice are referred to another UC. In the CSU, high demand campuses such as Northridge and Fullerton have been designated "impacted," making it more difficult for students outside of their admission areas to be admitted. In fall 2011 alone, 12,000 eligible students were denied admission to a CSU campus. Even in the CC system, which must accept all California residents with a high school or equivalent degree, policies such as limiting course offerings and shortening registration windows have reduced student enrollment (Johnson, 2012). A far cry from its earlier status as having one of the most well-educated populations in the nation, today California is in the bottom 10 states in number of young people holding a 2- or 4-year degree. John Aubrey Douglass of UC Berkeley notes that "For the first time in the state's history, the older generation has a higher educational attainment level then the younger generation" (Douglass, 2010, p. 12).

There are a number of factors that have led to the changes we see in California's higher education system including greater than expected population growth, a decline in public spending on education, the lack of long-term planning of the type characterized by the Master Plan, and an overall increase in pessimism about the ability and *desirability* for government to "plan for a future that would be better than the past" (Douglass, 2010, p. 14; Finney, Riso, Orosz and Boland 2014). Add to these the increase in college costs across the country and the Great Recession years that hit California's economy particularly hard, and the Master Plan goals of accessible, affordable college education for all seem unattainable and even naïve.

All of this bad news for California higher education comes at a crucial point in time. The Obama administration has made increased levels of educational attainment by 2020 a national goal, which would require 8 million more degree holders nationally, including 1 million more in California (Douglass, 2010). However, given the state's public higher education woes university enrollments have declined in recent years, with only 55% of the most qualified high school graduates enrolled in a CSU or UC. The largest declines in college attendance have been among African American students (Johnson, 2012). Some of these qualified students have settled for the already-overcrowded CCs, others have chosen to attend California's private universities or to attend college out-of-state, and a small percentage have foregone college altogether (Johnson, 2012). Finally, while degree completion rates are above the national average in the UC, at the CSU they are 10% below the national average. Perhaps more troubling is that for students beginning their college careers at the CC level (nearly half of California students), the 4-year degree completion rate is only half of the national average (Finney et al., 2014). Again, these statistics are particularly problematic at a time when all projections indicate that the state and the nation need a more highly trained and educated workforce.

# Conclusion

While the picture of education in California that has been presented above might not be encouraging, it is important to remember what a significant task the state has to accomplish. The large number of students, over 6 million in K-12 and nearly 3 million in college each year, makes education policy complicated, as does the state's amazing diversity; the Los Angeles Unified School District, for example, has to serve students speaking over 92 languages. Under the best of circumstances the state would be facing an overwhelming task, and the politics surrounding education and state recessions have certainly not helped. But if California is to remain the Golden State, it seems to be time for its residents to seriously consider what they want the state's education system to be and whether they are willing to make a quality education the reality for every student.

# References

*A Master Plan for Higher Education in California.* 1960–1975. Sacramento, CA: California State Department of Education.

California Budget Project. 2014. *From state to student. How state disinvestment has shifted higher education costs to students and families.* Retrieved May 30, 2014, from http://www.cbp.org/pdfs/2014/140506_From_State_to_Student_BB.pdf.

California Department of Education. 2014. Retrieved July 31, 2014, from http://www.cde.ca.gov/.

Callan, P. M. (2009). California higher education, the Master Plan and the erosion of college opportunity. San Jose, CA: The National Center for Public Policy and Higher Education.

Douglass, J. A. 2010. *From chaos to order and back? A revisionist reflection on the California Master Plan for Higher Education at 50 and thoughts about its future.* Berkeley, CA: Center for Studies in Higher Education. Retrieved August 11, 2014, from http://escholarship.org/uc/item/6q49t0hj.

EdSource. 2014. *Mixed results for charter schools statewide in new study.* Retrieved August 1, 2014, from http://edsource.org/2014/mixed-results-for-charter-schools-statewide-in-new-study/63486#.U9vzY6OZjTF.

EdSource. 2013a. *California drops to 49th in school spending in annual ed week report.* Retrieved July 31, 2014, from http://edsource.org/2013/california-drops-to-49th in school-spending in-annual ed week-report-2/63654#.U9rpcaO7jU0.

EdSource. 2013b. *California students among worst performers on national assessment of reading and math.* Retrieved July 21, 2014, from http://edsource.org/2013/california-students-among-worst-performers-on-national-assessment-of-reading-and-math/41329#.U9rtKaOZjU0.

Finney, J. E., Riso, C, Orosz, K, and Boland, W. C. (2014). *From Master Plan to mediocrity: Higher education performance and policy in California.* University of Pennsylvania: Institute for Research on Higher Education. Retrieved August 11, 2014, from http://www.gse.upenn.edu/pdf/irhe/California_Report.pdf.

Hill, S. A., Kiewiet, D. R., and Arsneault, S. 2014. *Filling the gap: The role of voluntary contributions and parcel taxes in supplementing k-12 spending in California.* Presented at the Annual Meeting of the Western Political Science Association, April 2014.

Johnson, H. 2012. *Defunding higher education.* Public Policy Institute of California. Retrieved August 11, 2014, from http://www.ppic.org/content/pubs/report/R_512HJR.pdf.

Murphy, K. 2014. *Higher education: Brown's budget proposal calls for funding increase, tuition freeze.* San Jose Mercury News. Retrieved May 30, 2014, from http://www.mercurynews.com/education/ci_25753843/higher-education-browns-budget-proposal-calls-funding-increase.

National Education Association. 2014. *Rankings & estimates: rankings of the states 2013 and estimates of school statistics 2014.* Retrieved July 31, 2014, from http://www.nea.org/home/rankings-and-estimates-2013-2014.html.

Picus, L. O. 1991. Cadillacs or Chevrolets? The evolution of state control over school finance in California. *Journal of Education Finance, 17*, 33–59.

Rumberger, R. W., Larson, K. A., Ream, R. K., and Palardy, G. J. 1999. *The educational consequences of mobility for California students and schools.* Policy Analysis for California Education, University of California, Berkeley & Stanford University.

Silva, F. and Sonstelie, J. 1995. Did *Serrano* cause a decline in school spending? *National Tax Journal, 48*(2), 199–215.

# CHAPTER 13

# California Criminal Justice Policy

*Kevin Meehan*

## Introduction

The first section of this chapter will use a historical method to analyze the development of criminal justice policy. The next section will analyze how criminal justice policies in California are affected by direct democracy, with a particular focus on the three strikes law. In the final section, the increasing role of the courts in criminal justice policy will be examined.

> "Criminal justice (policy) decision making is implemented through a hierarchical and bureaucratic system in which political realities and opportunities govern final decision making and implementation of policy. Criminal justice policy making is incremental, it's a process." (Garrison, 2009, p. 21)

## The Legislative Model

A historical method utilized to understand criminal justice policy was the development of a "model" as exemplified by the work of Levine, Musheno, and Palumbo (1986, pp. 8–9, quoted in Mays & Ruddell, 2015, p. 9).

1. The first stage is *agenda setting*.
   This is where the problem becomes apparent enough that some governmental action seems warranted.
2. The second stage is *policy formulation*.
   Alternatives are developed for dealing with the problem, and compromises are often worked out.
3. The third stage involves *policy* implementation.
   Administrative agencies formulate a specific program or plan of action to tackle the problem.
4. *Policy impact* is the fourth stage. Impact is concerned with the extent to which the policy that has been implemented addresses the initial problem.

5. *Policy evaluation* is the fifth stage. Here there is an analysis of whether or the extent to which the policy has achieved its goals.
6. The sixth and final stage is **termination**. A policy will be ended if it has not achieved the intended goals and objectives.

The final step may seem to be anachronistic as various well-known programs such as the Drug Abuse Resistant and Education (DARE) and Scared Straight programs continue, likely due to their public relations and political popularity, despite scientific evidence of their virtual ineffectiveness as documented in Table 13.1 provided by "the *Office of Justice Programs*" CrimeSolutions.gov (2014a, p. 1), uses rigorous research to inform practitioners and policy makers about **what works** in criminal justice, juvenile justice, and crime victim services".

Almost 30 years later the policy model has evolved to include more contemporary realities as portrayed by Welsh and Harris (2012, pp. 10–14) in their "Seven Stage Model for Planned Change." (Table 13.2)(Below as submitted).

1. *Analyzing the problem(s)* to be addressed by the new or evolving policy.
2. Establishing realistically achievable and quantifiable *goals and objectives*.
3. Designing the policy.
4. Planning the intervention or action.
5. Implementing the policy.
6. Evaluating the outcomes using "evidence-based practices" (Gardiner, 2014, pp. 32–33).
7. Reassessing, reviewing, and recommending changes.

**Table 13.1**   CrimeSolutions.gov Program Profiles

| Title | Evidence Rating | Topics | Summary |
|---|---|---|---|
| Drug Abuse Resistant and Education (DARE) | No effects | Crime & Crime Prevention Drugs & Substance Abuse Juveniles | A school-based drug use prevention program taught by police officers, starting in the sixth grade and extending through the senior year of high school. |
| Juvenile Awareness Programs (SCARED STRAIGHT) | No effects | Crime & Delinquency— Multiple crime/ offense types | Deterrence-oriented programs that involve organized visits to adult prison facilities for juvenile delinquents and youth at-risk of becoming delinquent. Two meta-analyses found that participation in these types of programs increases the odds that youth will commit offenses in the future. |

Source: CrimeSolutions.gov, 2014b, 2014c.

Table 13.2   Existing Interventions: A Systematic Approach to Program and Policy Analysis

| Stage 1 Analyzing the Problem | Stage 2 Goals and Objectives | Stage 3 Program or Policy Design | Stage 4 Action Planning | Stage 5 Program or Policy Implementation | Stage 6 Evaluating Outcomes | Stage 7 Reassessment and Review |
| --- | --- | --- | --- | --- | --- | --- |
| Document the need for change | Describe goals of the program or policy. | How was the intervention approach chosen? | Identify resources needed. | Design instruments to collect monitoring data. | Develop outcome measures based on objectives. | Planning for failure: avoid exaggerated claims. |
| Describe the history of the problem | Describe the outcome objectives for each goal. | Program design: Define the target. | Plan to acquire or reallocate resources. | Designate responsibility to collet, store, and analyze data. | Specify the research design to be used. | Planning for success: ongoing reassessment, learning, and revision are crucial. |
| Which potential causes were examined? | Who participated in goal setting? | Define target selection procedures. | Specify dates to complete implementation tasks. | Develop information system capacities. | Identify potential confounding factors. | Learning and Adapting: Successful interventions must adapt to change. |
| Were previous interventions examined? How? | Specify assumptions about the impact model. | Define program components and activities. | Develop mechanisms of self-regulation. | Develop mechanisms to provide feedback to stakeholders. | Reassess the entire program's policy plan. | Initiate the program or policy design from Stage 3. |

(continued)

**Table 13.2**  Existing Interventions: A Systematic Approach to Program and Policy Analysis (*Continued*)

| Stage 1 Analyzing the Problem | Stage 2 Goals and Objectives | Stage 3 Program or Policy Design | Stage 4 Action Planning | Stage 5 Program or Policy Implementation | Stage 6 Evaluating Outcomes | Stage 7 Reassessment and Review |
|---|---|---|---|---|---|---|
| Were relevant stakeholders identified? If so, how? | How were compatible and incompatible goals in the larger system addressed? | | Specify a plan to build support | | | Initiate the action plan from Stage 4 Initiate monitoring of program & policy from Stage 5. |
| Was a systems analysis conducted? If so, how? | How were needs for interagency collaboration identified and addressed? | | | | | Collect and analyze evaluation data: provide feedback to stakeholders from Stage 6. |
| How were barriers and supports for change identified and addressed? | | | | | | Reassess the entire program & policy plan and make necessary modifications. |

Source: Welsh and Harris (2013, p. 14).

# Direct Democracy

According to Gianos and Stambough (2014, p. 73), "Direct democracy comes in three primary forms: *initiative, referendum and recall.*

1. A *recall* is when voters decide to remove an elected before their normal term expires.
2. A *referendum* is a proposal for the voters to directly ratify or overturn a law passed by the legislature and signed by the governor.
3. *Initiatives* are proposals for new laws or amendments to the state's constitution that are placed on the ballot by citizens or groups to direct approval/rejection by the voters. *Both the state legislature and the governor are bypassed in this process* (p. 75).

California criminal justice policies are most impacted by the initiative process.

## Three Strikes Law

"In 1992, eighteen-year old Kimber Reynolds was murdered during an attempted purse snatching by a paroled felon, Joe Davis, whose criminal history included auto theft, gun, and drug charges" (Grosskreutz, 2004, cited in Goodno, 2010, p. 464).

Outraged by this horrible tragedy, Mike Reynold's, Kimber's father, worked with Fresno legislator Bill Jones and Judge James A. Ardaiz to craft a bill for a three strikes law that would sentence certain serious or violent felons to a mandatory 25 years to life upon their conviction of a third felony (Meehan, 2000). When the bill stalled in the legislature Reynolds decided to file for an initiative to place the bill directly to the voters on the November, 1994 ballot.

The original bill and initiative gathered unstoppable momentum though with the death of Polly Klaas in 1993 at the hands of Richard Alan Davis, a parolee with a history of violent offenses who had recently been released from prison. An alliance of the "California Correctional Peace Officers Association (CCPOA) . . . and the National Rifle Association" provided financial support for the resuscitated bill, which with the political guidance of Governor Pete Wilson, who was seeking re-election, was easily passed by the legislature and signed by Wilson in March, 1994 (Zimring, Hawkins and Kamin, 2001, p. 5).

At that point the law went into effect essentially through the legislative process. However, Mike "Reynolds, pressed on with the initiative version due to his distrust of politicians and the fact that laws created via initiative can only be changed by a vote of the citizens or a two-thirds majority vote of the state legislature" (Meehan, 2014, p. 183).

> The law stipulated that any convicted felon whose commitment offense was a *serious or violent felony* (California Penal Code, section 667) would accrue his or her first strike but no enhanced punishment. Then, upon the conviction of any second felony, the *striker* would receive a punishment that was double the normal sentence for the offense. In addition, if the felon was charged and convicted of another serious or violent

felony, he or she would now be eligible for a third strike upon the commission of any subsequent felony. It was this provision, which was essentially unique to California's version of the law that explains the anomaly that 3,675, or over 40%, of the total 8,813 third strikers (all crimes against persons plus 1st degree burglaries) are essentially non-serious or non-violent crimes. (Meehan, 2014, pp. 183–184)

This process was formally tested with the Three Strikes Reform Act of 2004, which was defeated by a margin of 53% to 47% (Families to Amend California's Three Strikes Law, 2014) largely due to the unscrupulous campaigning of Governor Arnold Schwarzenegger, who's deceitful claims that over "26,000 dangerous criminals" would be unleashed upon the unsuspecting public, likely changed the predicted outcome of the initiative (Schwarzenegger, 2006, p. 1).

By 2011 there were over 41,000 strikers, of which approximately 32,300 were second strikers and 8,700 third strikers in the California Department of Corrections and Rehabilitation institutions (CDCR, 2011, p. 4) at an annual cost of roughly $50,000 per inmate (Legislative Analyst's Office [LAO], 2013).

At that point "the National Association for the Advancement of Colored People's (NAACP) and Legal Defense Fund (LDF) launched the ballot campaign for Proposition 66." With the "Stanford University Three Strikes Project" (SUTSP) providing legal representation the Three Strikes Reform Act of 2012 was approved by the voters (2014a, p. 1).

By August 2013, over 1,000 former three strikers had been resentenced and released (SUTSP, 2014b, 1). With over 2,000 additional inmates potentially eligible for release, taxpayers will realize over $1 billion in savings over the next decade if the majority of these inmates are released (2014b, p. 2).

In summary, California's Three Strikes Law, perhaps the most influential and expensive law in the state's criminal justice history, was a hybrid creation as it was approved both through the traditional legislative process and direct democracy, then later amended through the initiative process.

# The Increasing Role of the Courts in Criminal Justice Policy

On October 1, 2011, California's "Public Safety Realignment Act" (LAO, 2012) plan was enacted in order to reduce the population in the overcrowded CDCR. While on the surface this new law appeared to be a traditional legislative action, in fact, it was only reluctantly designed and implemented due to a federal court order that was eventually upheld by the United States Supreme Court (*Brown v. Plata*, 2011).

A brief chronological review of the highlights of the case will provide the perspective of the influence of the courts on this shift in California Criminal Justice Policy.

## Coleman v. Wilson, 1990

In 1991 Ralph Coleman, who would later be joined by other inmates in a class action lawsuit, decried the lack of adequate mental health care throughout the CDC institutions.

"Plaintiffs raised claims under 42 U.S.C., Section 1983 based on alleged violations of the Eight and Fourteenth Amendments to the United States Constitution and under the Rehabilitation Act, 29 U.S.C., Section 794" (*Coleman v. Wilson*, 1994, p. 1).

The court ruled that Coleman et al. (1994) "presented significant evidence that there are many inmates throughout the California prison system who are both on psychotropic medications and in prisons which are subject to extreme heat conditions" (p. 3).

Unfortunately, over the next 20 years as documented by the U.S. Supreme Court "the state of mental health care was deteriorating due to increased overcrowding" (*Brown v. Plata*, 2011, p. 1; Schlanger, 2013). In fact from 1996 until "The Three Judge Court Tentative Ruling" "a least 77 substantive orders [were issued] to the defendants" (*Plata & Coleman v. Schwarzenegger*, 2009a, p. 4).

## Plata v. Davis, 2001

In 2001, Marciano Plata, along with "ten male California inmates filed a complaint . . . alleging that the CDC's inadequate medical care system violated the Cruel and Unusual Punishment Clause of the Eighth Amendment, as well as the Americans with Disabilities Act ("ADA"), 42 U.S.C. § 12101 et seq., and section 504 of the Rehabilitation Act, 29 U.S.C. § 794" (*Plata v. Davis*, 2001a, p. 1).

A primary example of the "class action allegations" was:

> Thousands of prisoners in CDC custody suffer from serious medical conditions. All prisoners are at risk of developing a serious medical condition while in prison and thousands need care and treatment to prevent serious medical conditions. All prisoners are entirely dependent on defendants for the provision of medical treatment (*Plata v. Davis*, 2001b, p. 1).

Like Coleman, Plata languished for a decade before the United States Supreme Court despite the fact "the State conceded that deficiencies in prison medical care violated prisoners' Eighth Amendment rights and stipulated to a remedial injunction" (*Brown v. Plata*, 2011, p. 1; Schlanger, 2013).

## Plata & Coleman v. Schwarzenegger, 2009

In 2007 the "The United States District Court for the Northern District of California" issued an "Order Granting Plaintiffs' Motion to Convene [a] Three Judge Court" as authorized by the "Prison Litigation Reform Act" (PLRA) of 1995 (*Plata v. Schwarzenegger*, 2007, p. 1). The primary reason for this action was to consider an order to reduce the CDCR prison population to resolve the constitutional deficiencies relative to the inadequate provision of mental and medical health services to inmates.

Next, the "Three Judge Court Tentative Ruling" to enact the prisoner reduction order specifically to reduce the severe overcrowding in the CDCR prisons was issued in February 2009. The Court "decided to make the tentative ruling in order to give the parties likely notice of the likely nature of the opinion, and allow them to plan accordingly" (*Plata v. Schwarzenegger*, 2009a, p. 1).

The Court, which noted that in 2008 "California's prisons were operating at close to 200% of capacity (over 160,000 inmates in space designed for approximately 80,000), anticipated a cap in the range of 120% to 145% of design capacity" (p. 7).

Then, in August 2009, citing "crowding as the primary cause (p. 55) of repeated and continuous constitutional violations the Court issued its formal Opinion and Order" (*Plata v. Schwarzenegger*, 2009b, p. 11) directing "Within 45 days, defendants shall provide the court with a population reduction plan that will in no more than two years reduce the population of the CDCR's adult institutions to 137.5% of their combined design capacity" (p. 183).

### Brown v. Plata, 2010–2011—The Appeal and Ruling

In November 2010 Attorney General Jerry Brown appealed the Three Judge Court Prisoner Reduction Order to the United States Supreme Court (*Schwarzenegger v. Plata*, 2010).

According to Myers and Sun (2014, p. 1) the primary issues were:

1. Did the three-judge district court have jurisdiction to issue an order releasing inmates from California prisons?
2. If the district court did have jurisdiction, was the prison release order the only option capable of providing adequate physical and mental health services to California inmates while still preserving public safety?

Finally, in May 2011, the U.S. Supreme Court by a 5–4 vote rejected the appeal by the State of California and affirmed the orders of the Three Judge Court (*Brown v. Plata*, 2011, p. 1). Justice Kennedy, writing the majority opinion concluded:

> The medical and mental health care provided by California's prisons falls below the standard of decency that inheres in the Eighth Amendment. This extensive and ongoing constitutional violation requires a remedy, and a remedy will not be achieved without a reduction in overcrowding. The relief ordered by the three-judge court is required by the Constitution and was authorized by Congress in the PLRA. The State shall implement the order without further delay (p. 48).

Since the end of the "hands off" policy (Clear, Cole, Petrosino and Reisig, 2015, p. 281), the federal courts have become increasingly involved in adjudicating prisoners' rights issues, especially pertaining to Eighth Amendment concerns regarding violations of the "cruel and unusual punishment" protections with significant policy ramifications. It is highly probable this trend will increase in a litigious environment like California.

## Conclusion

While the legislative model continues to be the primary method used to create laws, the increasing popularity of direct democracy, and the undeniable power of the courts must be appreciated in understanding criminal justice policy in California.

In fact, within a month California voters will have the opportunity to decide whether proposition 47, which proposes the reduction from felony to misdemeanor status and corresponding sentences for "certain drug and property offenses" with the dual goals of accruing "state and county criminal justice savings potentially in the high hundreds of millions of dollars annually" while reinvesting those funds on school truancy and dropout prevention, mental health and substance abuse treatment, and victim services" (Bowen, 2014, p. 1).

# References

Bowen, Debra. 2014. "Proposition 47. Criminal Sentences. Misdemeanor Penalties. Initiative Statute." California Secretary of State. Retrieved from http://www.voterguide.sos.ca.gov/en/propositions/47/.

Brown v. Plata. 2011. "Syllabus." Retrieved from http://www.supremecourt.gov/opinions/10pdf/09-1233.pdf.

California Department of Corrections and Rehabilitation. 2011. "Second and Third Striker Felons in the Adult Institution Population." Retrieved from http://www.cdcr.ca.gov/reports_research/offender_information_services_branch/Quarterly/Strike1/STRIKE1d1103.pdf.

Clear, Todd R, Cole, George F, Resiwsg, Michael D. and Carolyn Petrosino. 2015. *American Corrections in Brief.* Stamford, CT. Cengage Learning.

Coleman v. Wilson. 1994. "Findings and Recommendations." Retrieved from http://www.clearinghouse.net/chDocs/public/PC-CA-0002-0035.pdf.

CrimeSolutions.gov. 2014a. "About CrimeSolutions.gov." Retrieved from https://www.crimesolutions.gov/about.aspx.

CrimeSolutions.gov. 2014b. "Program Profile: Drug Abuse Resistance Education (DARE)." Retrieved from https://www.crimesolutions.gov/ProgramDetails.aspx?ID=99.

CrimeSolutions.gov. 2014c. "Program Profile: Juvenile Awareness Programs (Scared Straight)." Retrieved from https://www.crimesolutions.gov/PracticeDetails.aspx?ID=4.

Families to Amend California's Three Strikes Law. 2014. "Proposition 66: The Three Strikes Reform Act of 2004." Retrieved from http://facts1.live.radicaldesigns.org/section.php?id=9.

Gardiner, Christine L. 2014. "The Influence of Research and Evidence Based Practices on Criminal justice Policy." In Mallicoat, Stacy & Christine Gardiner (eds.), *Criminal Justice Policy.* 1st Edition, Durham, NC. Carolina Academic Press.

Garrison, Arthur H. 2009. "The Influence of Research on Criminal Justice Policy Making." *Professional Issues in Criminal Justice*, 4(1), 21. Retrieved from https://kucampus.kaplan.edu/documentstore/docs09/pdf/picj/vol4/issue1/PICJ_V4N1_Garrison_9_22.pdf.

Gianos, Philip P. and Stephen J. Stambough. 2014. "California's Constitution, Direct Democracy, and the California Criminal Justice System." In Christine L. Gardiner and Pamela Fiber-Ostrow (eds.), *California's Criminal Justice System* (2nd Edition). Durham, NC. Carolina Academic Press.

Goodno, Naomi Harlin. 2010. "Career Criminals Targeted: The Verdict is in, California's Three Strikes Law Proves Effective, 37 *Golden Gate University Law Review* (2007/2010)." Retrieved from http://digitalcommons.law.ggu.edu/ggulrev/vol37/iss2/3.

Grosskreutz, Scott A. 2004. "Comment, Strike Three: Even Though California's Three Strikes Law Strikes Out Andrade, There Are No Winners in This Game, 43. *Washburn Law Journal*, 429, 433–434.

Kennedy, Anthony. 2011. *Brown v. Plata.* 2011. Syllabus. Retrieved from http://www.supremecourt.gov/opinions/10pdf/09-1233.pdf.

Legislative Analyst's Office. 2005. *2006 Initiative Analysis: Three Strikes Reform Act of 2006*. Retrieved from http://www.lao.ca.gov/ballot/2006/060098.htm.

Legislative Analyst's Office. 2012. The 2012-2013 Budget: *The 2011 Realignment of Adult Offenders.-An Update*. Retrieved from http://www.lao.ca.gov/analysis/2012/crim_justice/2011-realignment-of-adult-offenders-022212.pdf

Legislative Analyst's Office. 2013. *California's Criminal Justice System: A Primer*. Retrieved from http://lao.ca.gov/reports/2013/crim/criminal-justice-primer/criminal-justice-primer-011713.aspx#Introduction.

Levine, James P., Musheno, Michael C., and Dennis J. Palumbo. 1986. *Criminal Justice in America: Law in Action*. New York, NY: Wiley.

Mays, Larry G. and Rick Ruddell. 2015. *Making Sense of Criminal justice: Policies and Practices* (2nd Edition). New York, NY. Oxford University Press.

Meehan, Kevin E. 2000. California's Three Strikes Law. *Corrections Management Quarterly*, 4(4), pp. 22–33.

Meehan, Kevin E. 2014. California Corrections. In Christine L. Gardiner and Pamela Fiber-Ostrow (eds.), *California's Criminal Justice System* (2nd Edition). Durham, NC. Carolina Academic Press.

Myers, Sara and John Sun. 2011. *Schwarzenegger v. Plata* (09-1233). Legal Information Institute (LII). Cornell University. Retrieved from http://www.law.cornell.edu/supct/cert/09-1233.

Plata v. Davis. 2001a. "MTA. United States Court of Appeals, Ninth Circuit." Retrieved from http://caselaw.findlaw.com/us-9th-circuit/1047153.html.

Plata v. Davis. 2001b. "Complaint Class Action." Retrieved from http://www.clearinghouse.net/chDocs/public/PC-CA-0018-0088.pdf.

Plata v. Arnold Schwarzenegger. 2007, July 23. "Order Granting Plaintiffs' Motion to Convene Three-Judge Court." Retrieved from http://prisonlaw.com/pdfs/Plata3JudgeOrder.pdf.

Plata v. Arnold Schwarzenegger. 2009a, February 9. "Three Judge Court Tentative Ruling." Retrieved from http://www.cdcr.ca.gov/News/Press_Release_Archive/2009_Press_Releases/docs/tentative_ruling.pdf

Plata v. Arnold Schwarzenegger. 2009b, August 4. "Three Judge Court Opinion and Order." Retrieved from http://cdn.ca9.uscourts.gov/datastore/general/2009/08/04/Opinion%20&%20Order%20FINAL.pdf.

Plata & Coleman v. Brown. 2014. "Three-Judge Court Opinion Re-Order Granting in Part Defendants' Request for Extension of December 31, 2013, Deadline." Retrieved from http://www.cdcr.ca.gov/News/docs/3jp-Feb-2014/Three-Judge-Court-opinion-2-20-2014.pdf.

Schwarzenegger, Arnold. 2006. "Arnold Schwarzenegger Lies about Proposition 66. YouTube." Retrieved from http://www.youtube.com/watch?v=7F6PBldQxZc.

Plata v. Arnold Schwarzenegger v. Marciano Plata. 2010, June 14. Appeal from the UnitedStates District Courts for the Eastern District and the Northern District of California. Retrieved from http://scholar.google.com/scholar_case?case=17822044773800823033&q=schwarzenegger+v.+plata+2010&hl=en&as_sdt=2006&as_vis=1Schlanger, Margo. 2013. "Plata v. Brown and Realignment: Jails, Prisons, Courts, and Politics." *Harvard Civil Rights-Civil Liberties Law Review (CR-CL)*, 48(1). Retrieved from http://papers.ssrn.com/sol3/papers.cfm?abstract_id=2133511

Schlanger, Margo. 2013. "Plata v. Brown and Realignment: Jails, Prisons, Courts, and Politics." *Harvard Civil Rights-Civil Liberties Law Review (CR-CL)*, 48(1). Retrieved from http://papers.ssrn.com/sol3/papers.cfm?abstract_id=2133511.

Stanford University. 2014a. "Stanford University Three Strikes Project." Retrieved from http://www.law.stanford.edu/organizations/programs-and-centers/stanford-three-strikes-project.

Stanford University. 2014b. "Stanford University Three Strikes Project Progress Report: Three Strikes Reform (Proposition 36) 1,000 Prisoners Released." Retrieved from http://www.law .stanford.edu/sites/default/files/child-page/441702/doc/slspublic/Three%20Strikes%20 Reform%20Report.pdf.

Welsh, Wayne and Philip Harris. 2012. *Criminal Justice Policy and Planning* (4th Edition). Anderson Publishing. New York, NY. Routledge.

Zimring, Franklin E.,  Hawkins, Gordon and Sam Kamin. 2001. *Punishment and Democracy: Three Strikes and You're Out in California.* New York, NY. Oxford.

# CHAPTER 14

# California
# Environmental Policy

*Justin Tucker*

## California in Context

California is many things to many people. With a population equal to Poland and a gross domestic product equivalent to that of Italy (Economist, 2011), California is not just any state, but a mega-state. Equally impressive is California's diverse set natural resources and ecosystems. From the top of Mt. Whitney at 14,505' to Death Valley at −282' elevation, California's ecosystems vary greatly. These include the forests of the Sierra Nevada, the agricultural lands of the Central Valley, the Mojave Desert, the coastal shores, and the man-made landscapes of urban cities. The environmental concerns for each ecosystem are unique and multifaceted. Adding to this environmental complexity are the incentives and agendas of a variety of stakeholders throughout the state. For example, water from the San Joaquin River and its tributaries naturally flows north into the San Francisco Bay to refresh fisheries maintain the bay, but it could easily be diverted to agricultural lands for increased crop production, or pumped south over the mountains to Southern California where it could be used in manufacturing or for housing. Each choice is laden with competing values that could stimulate the economy in a variety of ways, protect wildlife and natural resources, or preserve the character of the state. Often there is no single clear "best" environmental policy choice.

In order to understand the state and its policies, it is important to look at its history. When thinking about California's environmental history, most people look to the 1849 Gold Rush and the changes it brought to California. Landscapes were altered both by the people who came seeking their fortunes but also by the technology they used. Lumber was needed to build mining towns and gold sorting technology, which depleted ancient forest resources. The mining and lumber industries continued to grow and develop, as was typical of the United States at that time. Business owners sought their fortunes and in order to accelerate growth in these industries, they sought new technologies that would be more efficient and effective. Less invasive methods like panning gave way to long-toms, sluicing, and finally hydraulic mining in which powerful water cannons scoured the hillsides in order to extract the gold more quickly. This dramatically changed the landscape and caused immediate impacts on rivers, streams, and forests. Later, dredging and hard rock mining continued mining's environmental impact on the state through the use of chemicals that helped separate gold from the rest of the material extracted. The pattern identified in this California example is typical of the colonization of the West, except that many states have had fewer resources to develop than California. So while the California's Gold Rush is a great example, it is only one example among many of how California has been impacted by colonization, development, and technological advances.

Historically, California has been on the forefront of technology and been a major leader in a number of industries. As technology increases the human impact on our natural environment, it most often creates new or unanticipated problems. The state saw an oil boom in the late 1800s, first in the north and then in the south part of the state. At multiple periods in time, California produced more oil than Oklahoma. The expansion of oil extraction built cities throughout the state and brought new wealth to the population. It also left a wake of oil production wastes and environmental damage that is still being remediated to this day.

Because of the vastness of California's resources, it has always drawn people seeking new opportunities. In part due to an excellent climate, California was well positioned to develop a significant aviation manufacturing industry. World War II accelerated this industry and brought over 100 military installations to the state (California currently has around 40 active military installations and numerous converted or abandoned facilities). These defense facilities processed or stored corrosive chemicals, oil products, weapons ordinance, and other hazardous materials, most often in an expeditious but not necessarily environmentally safe manner. For example, portions of the former El Toro Marine base (now inside the city limits of Irvine) have been declared Superfund sites that require long-term monitoring and remediation.

Historically, Californians have been some of the most forward-thinking people, and the resources of the state allow many to pursue their dreams. As citizens observe or are impacted by these environmental problems caused by new technologies, they have sought recourse through government protection.

In the 1950s, geologists made a significant discovery of oil in the shallow waters off the coast of Santa Barbara, California. For decades, the oil industry had seen major growth in the southern-central valley and along the coast of Southern California. After some legal fights, a compromise was struck between the state and the City of Santa Barbara that prevented drilling within three miles of the coast nearest to the city. Shortly thereafter the state began issuing permits outside of this zone to businesses who would extract these reserves. While offshore drilling had been technologically possible since the first rig was installed in 1896, it was always publicly controversial because it threatened the aesthetics of the beach as well as created the possibility that a leak would wash oil to the shore. The first rig built to extract this new find began operation near Santa Barbara in 1957 with installations continuing through the subsequent decade. On January 28, 1969, a catastrophic oil spill occurred, eventually washing over 2 million gallons of oil onto the beaches. Citizen reaction was immediate and forceful. Within days, citizen attitude toward offshore drilling could be heard throughout from Santa Barbara to Sacramento and eventually Washington DC. While oil production still off the coast in some areas, citizens and lawmakers successfully passed numerous laws that changed the way offshore drilling is regulated.

Because California exists inside of a federal system, its laws and policies must also conform to federal laws as well. As CA implements federal law, as well as its own, some confusion and redundancy occurs as state agencies with overlapping jurisdictions attempt to coordinate their environmental work. Federal agencies with offices inside the state coordinate with leaders of state agencies in Sacramento, regional state offices, regional oversight boards, and local governments in order to implement both federal and state environmental policies. In some instances a state environmental agency must implement both a federal law and a state law simultaneously, even when the laws are different. Other times multiple agencies attempt to coordinate their behavior to implement a single law or rule. As a report on environmental legislation to the state legislature put it: "To say the majority of environmental laws and regulations are long and complex is an understatement. The complex web created by agency interaction, federal and state parallel structures, and state and local overlap adds to the intricacies of the California environmental regulatory system" (Seiver, 1995, p. iv).

# Environmental Policy

If we are to look at environmental policy in CA, it is important to note what makes the study of environmental policy different than other approaches to studying politics. As a subdiscipline, public policy is a different approach to studying political science. While some scholars study institutions (i.e., congress, presidency, courts, bureaucracy) or behavior (voting, social mobilization, interest groups), scholars of public policy most often follow a specific topic or interest through all of the institutions and behavioral models in order to understand policy changes and outcomes. A scholar of environmental policy would follow a specific topic (e.g., hazardous waste, water quality, federal parks, and lands) as it works its way through the entire system, from citizen demand, to institutional action, to a policy outcome.

Environmental policy is a very broad category within public policy because as a subject it has the possibility to include anything that contains any naturally occurring substance as well as anything manufactured, created, or disposed of in the environment. It could include anything pertaining to how these affect human health, plants, animals, or other natural resources. For example, scholars of environmental policy have studied group decision making in watersheds, protection of endangered species, indoor air quality rules, brownfields redevelopment, and production management systems in business operations.

In addition to the actions governments take to protect the environment, studies of environmental policy can include our inaction, because when it pertains to humans and ecosystems, both action and inaction create outcomes in a natural world. In short, environmental policy could have an enormous scope, even if we limit our analysis to what efforts the government of California has taken on these issues.

Just as in environmental policy throughout the United States, environmental advocates in California pursue policy change at all levels and through all structures of government. California has many more opportunities and institutional access points for policy changes than other states or the federal government. Rather than undertake a comprehensive analysis of all possible environmental policies, a better approach is to understand how the relevant institutions and actors function in the system while providing a number of salient examples in order to demonstrate the range of environmental policies in California.

# Institutional Framework for CA

California and the U.S. federal government have similar or parallel agencies and statues for most of the typical "environmental issues" such as air and water quality, hazardous materials, and parks. Even though the governments appear similar, some attention should be paid to how California is different than the federal government.

## Bureaucracy

The work of implementing environmental policy occurs inside the agencies of the state. The vast majority of these agencies exist within two mega agencies; the California Environmental Protection Agency (Cal EPA) and the California Natural Resources Agency. Just like at the federal level, other functions of what we might call "environmental protection" occur in the Department of Food and Agriculture, the Transportation Agency, the State Water Board, or various agencies throughout the state. Each has some unique responsibility to implement a state or federal law.

Cal EPA was created in 1991 to consolidate much of the environmental work of government into a single, cabinet level agency. Most of the issues that Cal EPA regulates are regulated at the federal level by the US EPA. The departments in Cal EPA include the Air Resources Board (ARB), the State Water Resources Control Board, the Office of Environmental Health Hazard Assessment, the Department of Toxic Substances Control, Department of Pesticide Regulation, and the Department of Resources Recycling and Recovery.

The California Natural Resources Agency is an overarching Agency that leads a variety of departments that are similar in composition to the US Department of the Interior. These include the Department of Fish and Wildlife, Department of Water Resources, Department of Conservation, Department of Forestry and Fire Protection, and the Department of Parks and Recreation.

The directors of Cal EPA and Natural Resources are appointed by the governor, just like many of the other administrative leaders in the state. They must be responsive to current events, the state of scientific knowledge, general political pressures, and the direction of the governor as they manage of all of the departments under their stewardship.

One of the major principles upon which the state operates is regionalism. The work of environmental protection is delegated to regional bodies tasked with implementing federal and state statues. For example, the responsibility of meeting ambient air quality standards under both the state and federal Clean Air Acts throughout the state belongs to the ARB. In order to address the diversity in the state, the ARB delegates authority to regional air quality management districts. These air quality boards are tasked with creating and implementing regional air quality plans, which can be tailored to the specific needs of their region. For example, in the development of their implementation plan, the South Coast Air Quality Management District (SCAQMD) must consider the impact of vehicle travel from commuters, emissions from diesel engines at the ports of Long Beach and Los Angeles, industrial manufacturing, and even fire rings at the beaches along the coast. Each air quality management district then submits their plan to ARB, which uses them to produce a statewide plan that addresses the regional differences that exist in the state.

Regional administrative bodies are led by a combination of appointed and elected members. People who sit on these governing bodies come from a variety of backgrounds and represent both citizen and executive preferences throughout all the regions of the state. The board members can respond to local political pressures as well as the environmental concerns of their region (geography, weather patterns, natural and man-made hazards). One of the most important functions of these boards is to coordinate the efforts of all of the relevant environmental agencies to address regional issues.

In order for the state environmental policies to be implemented, coordination between the state, regional, county, and municipal levels of governments also must occur. While the majority of broad rules come from the state, regional and local governments have significant discretion in how they implement or expand these directives. For example, in water pollution control under the federal Clean Water Act, jurisdictions need to have National Pollutant Discharge Elimination System permits for point source pollution (i.e., pollution that can be traced to a single point of origin, like a factory drain pipe). In many other states, each city is responsible for issuing these permits within their state guidelines. However, in southern California, and in other parts of the state, these permits are issued at a regional level and may require coordination between multiple cities in order to meet federal standards. In this way, the region becomes more important than each individual jurisdiction and requires a significant amount of coordination between levels of government. In fact, most environmental policies in California involve coordinating the behavior of multiple diverse agencies, jurisdictions, and citizen stakeholders in implementing environmental policy.

## Governor

As was noted in previous chapters, the governor of California has a variety of roles in directing and managing the state. When it comes to environmental protection, the governor has often taken the lead in coordinating various efforts throughout the state and proposing a broad vision for the expectation for Californians. In the most recent past, Governor Brown has used his role as governor to negotiate a deal with the legislature and citizens on groundwater regulation, high-speed rail, and a water project. Previously Governor Schwarzenegger made environmental protection a priority and a number of statewide and national efforts to combat climate change. Thus, the governor can use his position to leverage public support against and overcome some of those structural problems in the legislature.

Much like the president of the United States, the governor has a very large number of positions where he can appoint individuals of his same opinion to manage agencies or sit on oversight boards. These appointees exert their influence from the highest levels of the state to the very lowest and can extend the preferences of the governor deep into the affairs of environmental protection.

Because the governor appoints the head of Cal EPA and natural resources, he and his staff are able to write many of the regulations used to implement state law. While this might seem like a menial task to many people, this detailed level of direction greatly impacts individuals' everyday lives. Take, for example, Proposition 65, the Safe Drinking Water and Toxic Enforcement Act of 1986, which requires that the governor annually compile a list of chemicals and substances that are known to the state of CA to cause cancer, birth defects, and reproductive harm. Any facility, including restaurants, theme parks, or public locations, where these chemicals may be found are required to display a Proposition 65 warning. It's not uncommon to walk into a restaurant or what we might think of as a "safe" place and see a Proposition 65 warning on the outside of the building. Because the governor, in consultation with scientists, can determine which chemicals are placed on the list, he also has a very powerful ability to change the way that individuals perceive the places that they frequent.

## Legislature

As noted in other chapters, the legislature in CA has a major role in crafting the framework for the state. In environmental policy, its most important role is that of crafting legislation. Arguably the most important environmental legislation in California was passed in 1970. The California Environmental Quality Act (CEQA) was in many ways a state level corollary to the National Environmental Policy Act (NEPA). While there was little disagreement about the law when it passed in 1970, the use and expansion of its protections has generated a significant amount of contention since its passage.

Just as NEPA requires that the federal government consider environmental values in its decision making via the issuance of an Environmental Impact Statement (EIS), CEQA requires that a similar Environmental Impact Report (EIR) be made for all state and local government decisions that could have an impact on the environment. One major component of an EIR is the proposal of alternatives and anticipated effects of action. In this regard an EIS and an EIR serve as a mechanism to make government transparent and allow the public to access the information used in decision making. Both statutes require a public comment period where interested parties can lodge complaints, propose alternatives, and challenge the analysis. CEQA is such a major part of life in California that an entire industry has developed in response to the needs of state, local, and private organizations seeking help with CEQA compliance for their projects.

While CEQA lays out the general framework for protection, the legislature has addressed many environmental issues far quicker and more comprehensively than the federal government. For example, the state passed the Surface Mining and Reclamation Act (1975) 2 years prior to a similar law at the federal level. The state's leadership in water waste water recycling and water conservation are still unmatched at the federal level. When the legislature is unable to act on an environmental issue, laws and policies are often addressed through the courts and citizen propositions.

## Courts

The CA court system, as noted in other chapters, plays a vital role in understanding and interpreting major legislation, as well as citizen complaints. The courts in CA have tended to clarify as well as expand the limits to which the environment is protected in the state. While many court cases deserve attention, or could explain this point, the most obvious example is the way in which CA courts have expanded the protections provided under CEQA to private development and land use.

Originally CEQA was intended to only apply to actions of state and local governments, but in 1972, a set of cases in the court system (*Environmental Defense Fund, Inc. vs Coastside County Water District*, 27 Cal.App.3d 695; *Friends of Mammoth vs Board of Supervisors*, 8 Cal.3d. 247) broadened the application of CEQA to include any private action that required discretionary governmental approval. That is to say that if a government agency issues a permit to a residential real estate development project, then that action is a government choice that is subject to the provisions of CEQA. Within the year of the rulings, the legislature responded with an amendment to CEQA that, among other things, allowed state and local governments to require those seeking approval for projects to conduct the required research necessary to produce an EIR for their project. This shifted the financial burden of the research outside of the government, even though approval of the EIR and the project was retained within government authority. These simple court cases expanded the scope of CEQA in ways that the initial legislation could have never envisioned. Now most private development actions that could possibly have an impact on the environmental must be addressed in an EIR that is approved by a government agency.

In addition to these major cases expanding the power of CEQA, there are other instances in which the CA court system have provided new opportunities for environmental activism through the courts. Because of citizen attitudes toward environmental protection, many CA courts have increased access in environmental claims by granting standing more liberally than other states. The issue of standing is important because it is the first hurdle to overcome in order to pursue a case.

# Citizens, Groups, and the Initiative

Californians' forward thinking has pushed the state's laws and policies toward being a national leader among states in environmental protection. Because the state constitution allows for citizen initiative through direct democracy, and because of the weak party system and legislative difficulties inside the state, a significant amount of environmental policies have been adopted through citizen initiative. While California is not unique among states in having a constitutional provision for direct democracy, there is no such provision in the federal constitution.

Citizens retain all of the power in deciding which propositions they will support via their vote, but interest groups are the most likely to craft, propose, and fund the ballot initiatives. Additionally, as proactive members of the legislature fail to find adequate support inside the legislature, they have turned to supporting ballot initiatives in concert with these groups. The legislature is not the only institution that uses the initiative process for its own benefit. In the past 25 years, a number of environmental propositions (e.g., water bonds, high-speed rail bonds) have been supported or proposed by the Governor.

Given the choice between lobbying legislatures, the governor, or the courts, or turning it over to the general public for a vote, environmental interest groups may opt to write environmental legislation themselves, pay for it to be on the ballot, and take their fight to the court of public opinion. Evidence of the amount of effort spent on environmental-themed propositions is in the sheer number that appear on statewide ballots: 46 between the years of 1990 and 2014 (7 between 2010 and 2014, 12 between 2000 and 2009, 27 between 1990 and 1999). While many are not successful, the rapid swings in public opinion combined with the ease of placing propositions on the ballot have changed the dynamic of environmental policy in the state.

One example of the power of citizen propositions is that of Proposition 65 discussed earlier. Passed via citizen initiative, this law gives both the governor and the average individual a significant amount of power. For the governor, it provides a mechanism to understand and interpret scientific evidence either to expand or limit which chemicals are placed on the list. For the average individual, it forces the facilities to disclose something that would otherwise be opaque, what chemicals may be present in their vicinity. For the average restaurant patron, it can be disconcerting to pass a Proposition 65 on the way to be seated. While Proposition 65 requires disclosure of the presence of the substance, one never knows if the chemical is in the food, in the cleaning supplies, or in the construction materials used to build the restaurant.

In the same way that pro-environmental activists use the initiative process to support environmental protection, anti-environmental groups use the same process in an attempt to overturn major statutes or environmental policies. Such is the case with Proposition 23, where economic and business interests funded a proposition to repeal AB 32, the State's signature greenhouse gas legislation. AB 32 requires California to inventory its greenhouse gas emissions and craft a plan for their reduction to 1990 levels by 2020. When it was passed in 2006, the economic outlook for the state appeared bright. By 2009 it was clear that the state and the economy were both in significant long-term trouble. Opponents of AB 32 who had lost in the legislative battle and pro-business interests in the state joined forces to support Proposition 23, which would have suspended the implementation of AB 32 until the state unemployment rate fell below 5.5% for four consecutive quarters. Ultimately the proposition was rejected by the voters in 2010, but it demonstrated that an environmental win in one arena (the legislature) could have been quickly overturned by another (direct democracy).

Even outside of the context of lawmaking, interest groups often perform an oversight and coordinating role in their respective areas. When different interest groups have overlapping interests in an issue, coalitions of similarly minded groups can ally themselves to magnify their power over an issue area. As opposing interested groups join forces with each other, an entrenched system of competing interest groups can dominate an issue area or environmental policy for long periods. As they battle over the policies, they exploit as many institutional opportunities as possible to achieve their policy goals. For example, members of the competing groups make comments at multiple public regulatory meetings, lobby legislators in the Sacramento, craft and disseminate information for the public, seek access to the courts, and petition for regulatory changes in agencies. Because of California's complex multilayered system of oversight boards (both by region and topic) and coordinating agencies, these battles rage across space and authority.

One of the best examples of long-term struggle between environmental interests in California is that of the water in the Sacramento and San Joaquin River watersheds. Water that flows into the San Francisco Bay from the San Joaquin and Sacramento rivers is a precious commodity. It recharges the marine ecosystem of the bay and provides a multitude of benefits to plants and wildlife in its tributaries and surrounding riparian zones. Salmon use these rivers to access spawning grounds, which later benefit humans through replenished fisheries. Dams along these river systems have provided irrigation infrastructure that has allowed the central valley to become one of the most diverse and productive agricultural areas in the world. Agricultural products grown in the central valley include nearly every nontropical crop including peaches, melons, tomatoes, strawberries, and cotton. Nearly 90% of the world's almonds are harvested from crops in the central valley. Water from this watershed is also pumped south out of the valley and over the hills to southern California via the California Aqueduct. Water from this project has facilitated population growth in the Los Angeles area, which has brought tax revenues to the state from a robust economic center. Without this supplemental water from the central valley, the cities of southern California would collapse.

These three competing interests (ecosystem health, agriculture, and human consumption) have staked out positions on how the water from this watershed should be distributed. There is no single group of citizens who advocates exclusively for one of these issues such as agricultural interests, rather multiple interest groups scattered throughout the area align themselves with each other to pursue common goals where overlapping interests exist. Whenever a government decision making body is set to review, revise, or craft a policy that deals with water from this watershed, the groups mobilize so that their position may be heard. Because the watershed is a vast and complex issue, multiple agencies at varying levels of authority have jurisdiction over portions of the system. The coalitions of interest groups on all sides interact regularly at local, regional, and statewide meetings. While the composition of the coalitions and groups may change slightly over time, these three interests have dominated water policy in that watershed for decades.

Interest groups and advocacy coalitions need not be extremely large to be effective. For instance, residents in the unincorporated portion of Riverside County called the Temescal Valley formed a small interest group (WeAreTV.org) in order to prevent being annexed by a nearby city. The group's mission is to "preserve, promote, and protect" the valley. After the annexation battle was won, members of that organization continued their efforts by organizing into small subcommittees that were tasked with being involved in a specific issue area such as transportation issues, development issues, or oversight of the El Sobrante landfill. These committee members attend all of the relevant oversight hearings, municipal advisory council meetings, county board of supervisors meetings, as well as lobby for their interests with local, regional, and state political leaders. In doing so, they have used all of the venues that California has created for citizens to exert their collective influence.

When beachside residents in Newport Beach community complained about the smoke from beach fire rings at public beaches near their houses, they approached the California Coastal Commission and SCAQMD in an effort to ban their use, citing air quality concerns. The SCAQMD has responsibility for air quality in the region but the Coastal Commission regulates all of the beaches in the state. Scientists from the SCAQMD detailed the negative health and air quality effects of the fire rings but the coastal commission leaned in favored of retaining them as part of a long-standing traditional use of coastal resources. While retention of the public fire rings eventually prevailed, it was not without a fight that lasted months under the scrutiny of public opinion battles and scientific expertise. The new rules allow the city some discretion in the fuel used and the location of the rings, but disallow their complete removal from state beaches.

The preceding two examples demonstrate that the complex web of related agencies and oversight boards dispersed throughout the state creates many opportunities for citizen interests to be reflected in the environmental outputs of the state.

## Local and State Relations

In the same way that the US federal government "learns" from the experiences of individual states, the state of California has adopted and adapted local policies to create statewide policies. As cities have met with successes and failures as they attempt to adopt municipal provisions to deal with local environmental problems, like single use plastic grocery bags being discarded as litter and eventually ending up on beaches. When pro-environmental rules prevail in single cities, they can create "micro-protection-zones" within a larger urban area. This disharmony of rules between cities can lead to confusion as contractors and businesses attempt to reconcile practices while operating in multiple jurisdictions in the area. In the case of single use plastic grocery bags, city-wide bans have prompted state lawmakers to introduce to a statewide ban on single use plastic bags. Publicly lawmakers indicated that this bill was crafted to reduce confusion where cities had different rules and that a statewide ban would harmonize the rules throughout the state and reduce confusion. There is no doubt that it was also an opportune time for pro-environmental groups to promote a local cause to a bigger and more impactful arena. At time of press, the bill passed the legislature but has yet to be signed by the governor.

## California as a Leader in Environmental Issues

California has been at the forefront of many policies. In fact the state's leadership in environmental protection has filtered horizontally to other states and vertically to the federal level. While many examples of this leadership exist, the most prominent have occurred in air pollution and climate change.

From the 1960s to the 1980s, air quality in portions of California was the worst in the nation. In part this is simply a problem of geography. As the fresh offshore breezes blow into the San Francisco metropolitan area, it picked up industrial air pollution and brought it inland. There it met diesel exhaust and dust from agricultural production in the Central Valley and pushed the combined air pollution up against the Sierra Nevada, sometimes filling the entire Central Valley with poor quality air. In the south, ocean breezes would pick up industrial manufacturing air pollution and exhaust fumes from commuter traffic and the ports and blow them inland towards southwestern Riverside and San Bernardino counties. In both of these examples, the air pollution would be trapped against the mountains and backfill the basin until rain removed the pollutants or weather patterns moved the polluted air out of the state. Recognizing this problem, the state implemented an air quality program that included a more rigorous vehicle emissions policy for new vehicles than every other state. Additionally, it was one of the first states to require a regular "smog check" as part of the vehicle registration process.

For many years, cars throughout the United States were sold with California emissions equipment or as 49-state compliant. Even now, some motor vehicles cannot be registered in California because they were not in compliance with state emission standards at the time of production. Over time, the federal government learned from the experiences of California's effort to reduce smog and air pollution and increased the federal air quality standards to match California's. Thus California's leadership on air pollution translated to policy changes throughout the entire United States and the automotive industry.

California has also been a leader on efforts to address climate change, including the passage of AB 32. As discussed earlier AB 32 is the state's signature policy to reduce greenhouse gas emissions. The historical context behind passage of the bill was that climate change policy was making no progress at the federal level, so state legislators, the governor, and pro-environmental interests took action at the state level to address issue. When passed in 2006, the bill started the process of cataloging $CO_2$ emissions with the intent to return these emission levels to 1990 levels by 2020. AB 32 gave power to the Air Resources Board to lead a number of state agencies to regulate and reduce at least seven of the most prominent greenhouse gasses. In the scoping process, cities in each of the Air Quality Management Districts had to submit an inventory of emission sources as well as a reduction plan. These were forwarded to the Air Resources Board for the construction of a comprehensive, state-wide strategy. While cost estimates vary to how much this policy will impact the state, it will not be an insignificant amount of money. No similar policy at the federal level was in place until 2012, when an appeals court upheld the right of the US EPA to regulate greenhouse gasses under the Clean Air Act.

California has not only used typical command and control regulation to change behavior, but it also implemented a variety of market-based policies. One example of California's leadership in environmental policy and the use of economic incentives is the beverage container recycling program. In short, an individual pays a deposit when they purchase a beverage in a can or bottle. The deposit on the empty container can be redeemed at a recycling facility. While this deposit (CRV) is nearly imperceptible for most individuals, it embeds value into an otherwise disposable piece of plastic, glass, or metal that would have taken space in a landfill. This simple monetization of plastic and metal recyclables was estimated in 1995 to have led to a 89% recycling rate (Seiver, 1995).

Various levels of government in California have taken a similar approach for energy issues in California. These initiatives include incentives for rooftop solar panel installation, rebates for energy efficient home appliances, cost offsets for shade producing landscape, and free CFL light bulbs. While these policies may have been passed as single proposals, their combined efforts constitute policy bundles that have a large cumulative effect on the environment of California.

# California's Environmental Policies in the Future

As we look to the future of California, environmental issues and policies will continue to be of significant importance. As has been the case historically, water issues are still unresolved as we enter another year of projected drought conditions. The battle over water quality, allocation rights, distribution, storage, and recycling has yet to be won by any single group. Agricultural interests continue to be pitted against urban developments, and ecosystem health. Any policy choice will have environmental and economic effects. At the time of publication, the governor, the legislature, citizen initiatives, and numerous state, regional, and local agencies are working to solve this problem. If they are to be successful, they will need to craft policies that acknowledge and satisfy the disparate needs of population of this diverse state.

If the past is any predictor of future performance, California and Californians will continue to react to perceived environmental problems long before they appear on the national stage or in the agendas of other state lawmakers. Policy changes in California take place at many levels, in many venues, through a variety of mechanisms. Environmental advocates understand this and will continue to make efforts to advance in the ways they have done in the past.

# References

The Economist online. 2011. *Comparing US states with countries: Stateside substitutes.* January 13, 2011. http://www.economist.com/blogs/dailychart/2011/01/comparing_us_states_countries.

Seiver, Owen H. 1995. *California Environmental Goals and Policy, Part II: Inventory of Major California Environmental Legislation and Accomplishment since 1970.* Faculty Fellows Program, Center for California Studies, California State University, Sacramento.

# Index

CPSIA information can be obtained
at www.ICGtesting.com
Printed in the USA
FSOW04n1550180816
23941FS

9 781465 267122